Anthony Leakey.

COME TO THE OPERA!

STEPHEN WILLIAMS

has also written

WOMAN: AN ANTHOLOGY FOR MEN

THE FLOWING BOWL

COME TO
THE OPERA!

by

STEPHEN WILLIAMS

WITH A FOREWORD

by

SIR THOMAS BEECHAM, BART.

HUTCHINSON & CO. (Publishers) LTD
London   New York   Melbourne   Sydney   Cape Town

First Published February 1948
Reprinted ...... *March 1948*

Printed in Great Britain
by The Anchor Press, Ltd.,
Tiptree, Essex

ACKNOWLEDGMENTS

The author wishes to thank the following copyright-holders for kindly allowing him to quote musical passages from the operas named:

Messrs. Ascherberg, Hopwood & Crew, Ltd.: *Pagliacci* and *Cavalleria Rusticana.*

Messrs. W. Bessel & Co., Ltd.: *Boris Godounov* and *The Snow Maiden.*

Messrs. Boosey & Hawkes, Ltd.: *Prince Igor, The Bartered Bride* and *Der Rosenkavalier.*

Messrs. J. B. Cramer & Co., Ltd.: *Carmen* and *The Tales of Hoffmann.*

Messrs. A. Durand et Fils: *Pelléas and Mélisande* and *Samson and Delilah.*

Miss Ada Gow: *Manon.*

Messrs. Heugel et Cie: *Louise.*

Messrs. Novello & Co., Ltd.: *The Perfect Fool.*

Messrs. Ricordi & Co.: *Andrea Chénier,* Puccini's operas and the later Verdi operas.

Messrs. Schott & Co., Ltd.: *Hänsel and Gretel* and the Wagner operas.

To
DIANE

CONTENTS

FOREWORD

by

SIR THOMAS BEECHAM, BART.

Any literary work that may have the effect of arousing public interest in the subject of Opera is to be commended and recommended. For probably at no time during the last seventy years has this branch of the musical art declined to so low a level in England as today.

There was a time when London was able to maintain three great Opera Houses running simultaneously: and all stocked with star vocalists of the first rank. Before the First World War, Covent Garden maintained a proud position as one of the three or four leading Opera Houses of the world. The Summer, or Grand, Season was never less than thirteen weeks, and there were regular Autumn or Winter Seasons of hardly less importance.

After the war there was a lamentable disintegration of all serious cultural endeavour followed by a national descent into a bubbling pit of frivolity. Things did right themselves after a while, although we never returned to those glories which passed away in 1914. In spite of an energetic drive on the part of some of us, we never succeeded in accomplishing more than a partial restoration of what had been, and the prestige of London, as an operatic metropolis, left us to take up its abode in such centres of the New World as New York and Buenos Aires. Today, after seven years of operatic deprivation, we are in a pitiable plight.

The newer public in this country, mysteriously and miraculously expanded to unprecedented dimensions, has little knowledge of the lyric works of the great Masters, and none at all of a high standard or even correct method of performance. We have touched rock bottom, and if we are to have opera again of any consequence we shall have to rebuild from a crude beginning.

One of the unfortunate features of this gradual decline has been the continual contraction of repertoire given to the public. Probably the average citizen is unacquainted with the names of more than a dozen operas. If we are to bring about a revival there will have to go along with it a steady measure of education, or at least information. This can be contributed only by those who both love opera and can write about it intelligently as well as attractively.

The author of this work is excellently fitted for a task which is both timely and essential.

Summer 1946.   THOMAS BEECHAM.

PROLOGUE

Spoken by the Author

Dear Reader: I imagine you as one
Who, loving opera, has of late begun
To puzzle out the reasons of his love;
Why some works fall below, some rise above
The common level; why some pilgrims flee
From Verdi, who to Wagner bend the knee.
Perchance in opera houses you have sat,
And wondered what the devil they were at;
Perchance your records are in foreign tongues—
So baffling when exhaled from foreign lungs.
You listen to my broadcast talks and doubt 'em—
I know, because you write to me about 'em,
Demanding, in a general opera 'quiz',
A guide book on the subject. Here it is.

Here I submit to your judicial gaze
Some sixty operas. In these barren days
One's choice in this direction must be tentative,
And only light on operas representative
Of public favour. Tush, we are not here
To suckle fools and chronicle Meyerbeer—
Except *The Huguenots*—*that* may 'scape the sorties
Made by the purists of the nineteen-forties.
So Robert, that dour offspring of the Devil,
Makes way for barber-surgery from Seville.
Gluck is not here, nor very early Verdi,
Which some have likened to the hurdy-gurdy;
Nor have I dabbled in the later Strauss,
In which the mountain oft brings forth the mauss.
Chide not that I am generous with Puccini,
But terse with Donizetti and Bellini;
And give full licence to the noble frenzy
Of Wagner's works—except the dull *Rienzi*:
For surely ne'er has fate's relentless hammer rung
More fatally than in the *Götterdämmerung*.

Oft 'my chaste muse a liberty must take—
Start not, still chaster reader'—I but make

The dialogue in the stories sound less petty
Than it appears in those archaic *libretti*.
The English to the musical quotations
Is copied from the orthodox translations—
Though I confess to an occasional blush
At 'Malapropisms', false quantities or slush;
And where no English version fills the bill
I've made my own—with deeper blushes still.
But Russian vanquished me: the *mortis rigor*
Set in full soon with operas like *Prince Igor*.
So my defects compelled me to confine
Such illustrations to the vocal line.

Soft—one word more: I first conceived the notion
To write on opera without emotion,
And, striving to appease pedantic souls,
To be as practical as Grove or Scholes;
But, as Johnson's friend admitted with a grin,
Why, cheerfulness would still keep breaking in.
Well, 'tis all one; whoe'er makes special pleading
Without enthusiasm is not worth reading.
And many books on operatic scores
Are written by unoperatic bores.
So if these rhapsodies encourage you
To hire a camp-stool and to join the queue,
I shall rejoice my words had power to move.
For even opera lives—if you approve.

LUDWIG VAN BEETHOVEN

(1770–1827)

Fidelio

Libretto by Sonnleithner.
Time: Eighteenth Century.

First Production,
Vienna, 1805

> 'You are my true and honourable wife,
> As dear to me as are the ruddy drops
> That visit my sad heart.'
>   SHAKESPEARE: *Julius Caesar.*

Fidelio, Beethoven's only opera, was founded on a drama by Bouilly
Léonore, ou L'amour Conjugale, of which Sonnleithner's *libretto* was a
free translation. The drama had already been used by three composers, the third being Ferdinando Paër; and there is a story (probably
untrue but undoubtedly amusing) of Beethoven meeting Paër after
his first night and remarking: "I like your opera; I think I'll set it to
music." And he did.

Before examining *Fidelio*, let us, in Dr. Samuel Johnson's phrase,
'clear our minds of cant'. After Shakespeare, no creative artist has
suffered more than Beethoven from the kind of idolatry that is blind
but unfortunately not dumb. To say that Beethoven was a great
composer is, of course, a truism; to say that in the greater symphonies,
the late quartets and other works he said things which will probably
never be said in any art with more profound or heart-searching truth
is only to echo established opinion. But to imply that in every phrase
Beethoven wrote his hand was guided by the hand of God is the kind
of nonsense that gets us nowhere. It certainly gets us no nearer a sane
understanding of Beethoven's art. Whereas to hint that 'the Divine
Beethoven' is occasionally dull, prosaic and infuriatingly repetitive,
saying the same thing over and over again until one is tempted to
shout out, "Yes, yes, get on with it; we know that bit now!"—merely
to hint this is to send apoplectic old gentlemen all over the country
leaping out of their clubroom chairs to write to *The Times* about it.
And in saying that *Fidelio*, despite sublime periods, can become tedious
in action, I know I am thrusting my head simultaneously into innumerable lions' jaws—if such a feat were possible to anyone but
Hydra. I am quite impenitent about it. In this book I am going to
air quite a lot of my own opinions. I am going to write passionately on
subjects I feel passionately about—in the unshakable belief that anyone

15

who writes without passion on music—especially such a passionate form of music as opera—is merely wasting paper.

Beethoven, then, in my opinion, was not at his happiest as an opera composer, and *Fidelio* is a piece of great music rather than a great opera. I say 'in my opinion'. You may have an exactly contrary opinion; and, if so, you will be in good company, for an eminent critic once wrote: "As a drama and as an opera, *Fidelio* stands almost alone in its perfect purity, in the moral grandeur of its subject, and in the resplendent ideality of its music." After hearing it you may go even further and decide that, besides having these qualities, *Fidelio* is as effective, *as* opera, as anything written by Mozart, Wagner, Verdi or Puccini. Good luck to you: you will be in a state of mental health. For the great thing in music is to voyage forth oneself and not merely to echo ready-made opinions. It is this unthinking reliance on ready-made opinions that has made so many people assume that anything Beethoven did he did, as a matter of course, better than anyone else. The title of this book is *Come to the Opera!*: if what I say goads you into coming to the opera the book will have been worth writing; if what you see and hear moves you into violently disagreeing with me afterwards, it will have been worth reading.

Let us see what *Fidelio* is about. Perhaps some of you know it only by its overtures. Beethoven is said to have taken tremendous pains with *Fidelio*, and one piece of evidence is that he wrote no fewer than four overtures to it: the *Leonora*, Nos. 1, 2 and 3, and the *Fidelio* Overture. There has been 'great argument about them and about'—the order in which they were written and their comparative musical value; and to discuss these matters fully would require another chapter—perhaps another book. They are well known in the concert-hall, and all we need remember now is that it is the custom to play the Fourth in E major, the *Fidelio* Overture, before the opera begins, and the *Leonora* No. 3 in C between the first and second acts.

ACT I

It is the courtyard of a prison in Spain. Giacchino (tenor), an assistant gaoler, is in love with Marcellina (soprano), daughter of the head gaoler, but we gather from the dainty little duet with which they open the opera that her heart has changed and 'metal more attractive' has come her way; and we guess the truth when Rocco (bass), her father, greets Fidelio (soprano), a youth who has recently entered his service. The four express their feelings in a quartet:

Mir ist so wun - der - bar,
I hope, yet hope and fear,

during which Fidelio drops a broad hint (to the audience) that Marcellina is 'doomed to pine in vain'. Fidelio is sorry for her, but nothing can be done about it. Rocco openly confesses that he prefers Fidelio as a son-in-law to Giacchino, but —the young couple have no money; and he gives them a bit of worldly advice, in an air which has always been popular with basses, but which may now strike us as rather pedestrian:

Hat man nicht auch Gold bein-e - ben
They who boast not cash in plen-ty

Pizarro (bass), Governor of the prison, presently comes in. He orders a trumpeter to ascend the tower and give a signal when he sees a nobleman's coach nearing the prison. And when he reads his despatches we learn that in his power is Don Florestano, a long-hated enemy of his, whom he has imprisoned on some political pretext but really to gratify his hatred. He has announced that Florestano is dead, but his despatches tell him that a Minister of State is to visit the prison. If he finds out that Pizarro has abused his official power for private purposes, all is lost. There is only one remedy: the Governor must make true the false report he has published of Florestano's death. He must kill him. And he gloats over his purpose in a fine declamatory *aria* rather Mozartian in form; in fact, it might be sung by a very angry Don Giovanni:

Ha! Ha! Ha! Welch' ein Aug-en-blick!
Ah! Ah! Ah! what a glow-ing thought!

I am sorry and angry to say that those who possess the 'Royal' edition of *Fidelio* will be able to have a good laugh here: sorry that the (unnamed) translator should have done his utmost to make fine music

B

sound ridiculous, and angry that Sir Arthur Sullivan, who edited this
version, should have allowed him. Pizarro sings:

> *And while his blood is welling*
> *My shriek of triumph yelling*
> *Shall mock his dying whine.*

Later the prisoners put in a few remarks. One would think that they
knew the ways of their Governor by now, poor fellows; yet it is only
after Pizarro has been bawling away in this strain for four and a half
pages that a light of intelligence dawns on them and they sing:

> *Some deed of death foretelling*
> *His venom'd breast is swelling.*
> *He plans some dark design!*

Opera will never succeed in English until we drastically revise most
of our standard English translations and get rid of such injurious
absurdities. And that is a comparatively mild example of them!

Pizarro now summons Rocco and tries to persuade him to kill
Florestano. Rocco refuses to commit murder, but when Pizarro says
he will do the deed himself he agrees to dig a grave in an old cistern
in the vaults. But Fidelio has overheard; and we realise now that
Fidelio is really Leonora, the wife of Florestano, and that she has
taken service in the gaol in order to help him to escape. Now she
wavers between hope and fear in the most famous *aria* in the opera:

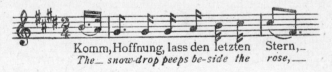

> Komm, Hoffnung, lass den letzten   Stern,
> *The snow-drop peeps be-side the   rose,*

Rocco tells her she is to help him to dig the grave, and Leonora vows
to save her husband or die with him.

ACT II

In the deepest dungeon of the prison lies Florestano in chains.
After an expressive orchestral introduction in the grim key of F minor
he gives voice to his wretchedness. Is it God's will that he should
linger on in this living grave? And he sings of the vanished days of

youth and hope, to an air that has the shadowed beauty of a Beethoven slow movement:

In   des   Le-bens Früh-lings ta-gen
In   my   spring of life,   its beau-ty

Soon the key lightens to F major, and in the dimness of his cell Florestano seems to see a vision of his wife. In some strange way he senses that she is near him and working for his deliverance. His vision is true, for at that moment Rocco and his assistant descend into the dungeon; ironically enough, the first step Leonora has to take towards her husband's rescue is to dig his grave! Pizarro presently joins them. All is ready: it is time for the prisoner to die. The quartet that follows is the most truly dramatic item in the score. Pizarro raises his dagger to stab Florestano, but Leonora flings herself in his way: "First kill his wife!" His wife! All are astounded. Pizarro swiftly recovers, however, and turns on her furiously. "Very well: you have shared his life, you shall share his death!" On his last word a trumpet call rings out from the battlements: it signals the arrival of the Minister of State. Florestano is saved and Pizarro caught in his own trap. The Minister (bass) gives Leonora the joyful task of unlocking her husband's fetters, and the opera ends with a chorus in praise of conjugal love.

Very few operas are made on happy marriages, and Beethoven was certainly bold in flouting the convention that all romantic interest ceases at the altar-rails. It is said that he wrote *Fidelio* as a counterblast to 'the ignoble attitude towards women' exemplified in *Don Giovanni*; and, whatever one thinks about *Fidelio's* essentially *operatic* qualities, there can be no doubt at all, to return to our earlier quotation, that Beethoven clothed 'the moral grandeur of its subject' with music of a 'resplendent ideality'.

VINCENZO BELLINI

(1801–1835)

Norma

Libretto by Felice Romani.
Time: 50 B.C.

First production,
Milan, 1831.

> 'Begin, then, Sisters of the sacred well
> That from beneath the seat of Jove doth spring;
> Begin, and somewhat loudly sweep the string.'
>
> MILTON: *Lycidas.*

Norma, regarded by many people as Bellini's masterpiece, is a perfect example of the *bel canto* opera. Now there is no mystery about the term *bel canto:* it simply means 'beautiful singing', and it represents an art that has fallen into mild decay in the last half century. You will often hear it said that there are no great voices or great teachers today, and that singers no longer learn their jobs properly; and it would undoubtedly be difficult to assemble at short notice a cast to sing such an opera as *Norma* with the sheer physical perfection that the composer demanded. The chief reason, however, is not that singers no longer learn their jobs properly but that they learn them differently. Fashions in opera have almost diametrically changed since Bellini's time (some say it was Wagner who 'killed' operatic singing), and modern works require not physical perfection, but a balance of power between the physical and the intellectual; in other words, intelligent interpretation rather than beautiful sound for its own sake. We are asked to think as well as listen. Now Bellini did not ask either his singers or his audiences to think; he gave them shapely and beautiful melody which required the utmost technical skill and which enchanted the ear without engaging the mind. This melody is said to have powerfully influenced his friend Chopin, and there is certainly an affinity between Bellini's stately, long-breathed *arias* and the romantic languor of Chopin's Nocturnes and slow movements. Bellini was only thirty-three when he died. One does not speculate, as with Schubert or Keats, on how his art might have developed if he had lived longer; the probability is that it would not have developed at all. Bellini did one thing supremely well, and he did it almost as well at the beginning as at the end. In his voice-line lay his genius, and, like Chopin again, he paid little attention to orchestration. He was, first and last, a *singers'* composer.

ACT I: *Scene* 1

We are in Gaul during the Roman occupation. The curtain rises on the sacred grove of the druids. It is night. Under an oak is the stone altar of the deity, Irminsul, and watch-fires are burning here and there among the trees. Oroveso (bass), the High Priest, and the druids pray to the gods to rouse the people so that they may throw off the oppression of the Romans. When they have passed out of sight, Pollio (tenor), the Roman pro-consul in Gaul, and Flavio (tenor), his centurion, approach, talking earnestly. From them we learn that Pollio has been the secret lover of Norma, the High Priestess and daughter of Oroveso. For him she has broken her vow of chastity and borne two sons. But Pollio is now devoured with remorse: he has become infatuated with Adalgisa, a virgin of the temple. It is one of those irresistible onslaughts of fate. Norma means nothing to him now, though he is moved by pity for her and also fears her vengeance. While he is pouring out his heart to Flavio the sacred shield of bronze is struck: it is the hour of sacrifice, and the Romans retreat as druids, priestesses, warriors and bards assemble. Norma (soprano) appears with a golden sickle in her hand. Impatiently her people demand to know the will of the gods. Is it the hour for them to strike the blow for freedom? But Norma is not thinking of her people; she is thinking of one who has forsaken her but whom she still loves. If the Gauls revolt he will be among the first to die. She breaks faith with them still more deeply: the hour is not yet, she says. The gods, speaking through her, declare that Rome will destroy herself; and Gaul would only rush upon her own destruction by attacking her. The moon shines out in full splendour; and Norma invokes the 'chaste goddess' in an air tremulous with loveliness, an air that makes us understand at once why Chopin so revered Bellini's genius:

The Gauls march solemnly away; and to the sacred altar comes Adalgisa (mezzo-soprano), her heart heavy with guilt and grief: guilt because she loves Pollio and grief because she knows that only tragedy can come of such love. She prays for strength to crush her impulses, and as if in ironical answer to her prayer Pollio himself appears. In a passionate scene he breaks down her resistance and forces a promise from her to meet him again before dawn:

Sol pro - mes - sa al Dio tu   fo - sti
Though to heav'n thy vows were pligh-ted

ACT I: *Scene* 2

Norma knows that Pollio is to be recalled to Rome and plans to take his new love with him. Who is this new love? She does not know; and when Adalgisa comes to her in her dwelling to unburden her mind, Norma sympathises with her. It is her own story told again: thus was she herself seduced into a guilty love. For which of the chieftains has Adalgisa conceived this fatal passion? At that moment Pollio appears and Adalgisa betrays herself. It is he! Norma overwhelms him with reproaches, and Adalgisa learns for the first time that Pollio is the father of Norma's children. Their emotions break forth in a dramatic trio:

Oh! di qual sei__ tu vit - ti - ma,
Oh   now   the trai - tor   thou   dost know,

ACT II: *Scene* 1

The two children are sleeping on a bearskin in Norma's dwelling. Norma steals in with a lamp and a dagger. Better that they were dead . . . but she cannot do it. And when Adalgisa comes in she urges her to become Pollio's bride and a mother to the children. Adalgisa, however, cannot consent. She loves Pollio; but he belongs to Norma: he is the father of her children. She will not come between them:

Mi - ra, o Nor - ma,   a tuoi gi - noc - chi
See,   oh   Nor - ma,   be-fore thee knee - ling,

ACT II: *Scene* 2

The Gauls are eagerly awaiting the signal to attack. In the temple of Irminsul Norma learns that Adalgisa's efforts are in vain. Pollio rejects her sacrifice and has resolved to drag her away by force. Demented with rage and jealousy, Norma strides to the altar and strikes the sacred shield three times. The gods have summoned the Gauls to battle. Warriors and druids come thronging in. "What bodes this?" they ask. "Warfare or counsel?" And Norma replies: "Warfare! Carnage! Destruction! Slay every hated Roman!" Then comes a fresh alarm: a Roman has broken into the sanctuary of the priestesses. It is Pollio, and in a few moments he is brought in by the guards. "Mine be the task to slay him!" cries Norma. But her heart fails her, and the dagger drops from her hand. She commands the others to leave her with the captive, and when they are alone she offers him his life if he will renounce Adalgisa. Proudly and scornfully Pollio refuses. Norma blazes out at him: "So be it! I shall strike at thee through Adalgisa. She hath broken her vows and betrayed her gods in loving thee. She shall die." She summons the Gauls again. "A priestess hath dishonoured her sacred calling," she tells them; "let the pile be lighted!" The druids are horrified. "Her name?" they demand. And Norma turns to them with the light of sacrifice shining in her eyes. "It is I—Norma!" She claims her father's forgiveness. The druids cover her with a black veil; and as she is led away to perish in the flames, Pollio, inspired by her heroism, resolves to die with the woman he has loved and betrayed.

GEORGES BIZET

(1838–1875)

Carmen

Libretto by Henri Meilhae and Ludovic Halevy,
after Prosper Mérimée's short novel.
Time: about 1820.

First Production,
Paris, 1875.

> 'And is become the bellows, and the fan,
> To cool a gipsy's lust.'
>
> SHAKESPEARE: *Antony and Cleopatra.*

Carmen is often called the Perfect Opera. The reasons are an intensely moving and dramatic story, admirably constructed and admirably told, and a score which unerringly reflects the passion and humour of the action, and which would still charm us if there were no action at all. On its first production, *Carmen* was not a success, and Bizet died in comparative obscurity a month or two later, without knowing that publishers, impresarios, singers and gramophone companies would make fortunes out of him.

ACT I

The orchestra sets the scene at once with the brazen, brilliant march of the Toreadors, followed later by the anguished phrases that tell of Don José's infatuation for Carmen. Then the curtain is up and we are in a square in Seville, the gay dresses of the women and the scarlet coats of the dragoons flashing in the bright Spanish sunshine. Presently the midday bell sounds and the girls enter from the cigarette factory, singing a chorus in which they liken lovers' vows and sighs to the swiftly dissolving smoke:

Dans l'air___ nous sui - vons des yeux
See, white___ cloud-lets ri - sing,

As the cigarettes burn out and the voices fade into silence Carmen (mezzo-soprano) appears. The orchestra repeats the phrases of José's infatuation, but now they are quick, agile, impudent. It is at once obvious that Carmen is the dominating personality of the opera: a gipsy, handsome, shameless, irresistible, created to make men mad. "She wore a red skirt, very short," says Mérimée, "which exposed to view her white silk stockings, with many a hole in them, and tiny shoes of morocco leather tied with scarlet ribbons. She had thrown back her mantilla so as to display her shoulders and an immense bunch of acacia blossom which was stuck in her chemise. She also carried a flower in her mouth, and she walked with the movement of a thoroughbred filly from the Cordova stud. In my country a woman in such a costume would have made people cross themselves." The dragoons eagerly cluster round her and she taunts them with her arrogant song in praise of love:

L'amour est un ois-eau re - belle _
Love will like a wild bird-ling fly ___

Don José (tenor), a corporal of dragoons, sits by, mending the chain of his sword. Carmen accosts him, but he will have nothing to do with her. She flings him a blood-red flower and runs away. He looks after her, and then commits his first act of folly: slowly he picks up the flower and puts it in his tunic. He has signed his death-warrant. Now enters Micaela (soprano), his betrothed, who has been seeking him all the morning. She comes from his mother, bringing him a letter, a purse and a kiss; and they sing a tender little duet which perfectly expresses the innocent freshness of their love:

Ma mè - re je la vois __
My mo - ther I be - hold __

After Micaela has gone there is an uproar from the cigarette factory. It is a fight, they say. And Carmen is dragged into the square, panting and dishevelled. She has stabbed another girl in a quarrel. She is arrested, and José is told off to escort her to the prison. When they are left alone, she coolly and deliberately begins to seduce him:

Près des rem-parts de Sé - vil - - le
Close by the ram-parts of Se - - ville

Blinded by sudden infatuation, he allows her to escape (he will meet
her later at Lillas Pastia's tavern) and is arrested in her place.

Act II

A short orchestral intermezzo, and we are at Lillas Pastia's tavern.
Carmen is dancing and singing amid a crowd of gipsies, smugglers and
officers:

Les trin-gles des sis-tres tin - taient
'The zi - thers tink-led mus-ic sweet

Escamillo (baritone) swaggers in on his way to a bull-fight, calls for a
cup of wine and pledges the company in the magnificent Toreador's
Song.

Vo-tre toast, je peux vous le ren - dre
Sirs! Your toast, a courteous an-swer claim - ing

Like every other man who meets her eye, he is dazzled by Carmen's
sex-appeal, and a spark falls which is to kindle to a tragic blaze later
in the story. The smugglers, Dancairo (high baritone) and Remendado
(tenor), want Carmen to help them in their latest enterprise. But no;
Carmen has 'fallen in love again': she is waiting for José, who has just
been released from prison. Together with her friends, Mercedes and
Frasquita (sopranos), the smugglers try to persuade her—in one of the
deftest and most bewitching numbers in the whole opera:

Nous a-vons en tête une af-fai - re
All's pre-par'd, our plans are quite clear

But at that moment Carmen hears José singing merrily as he nears the tavern, and she bustles them out. José bursts into the room and passionately declares his love. Carmen proceeds to fascinate him with her dancing. He hears the retreat sounding and knows he should return to barracks, but, stung by Carmen's sadistic mockery, he shuts his ears to it, and falling on his knees, he pours out his heart in one of the most poignant love songs ever written:

La fleur que tu m'a-vais je - té - e
See here, thy flow-ret trea-sur'd well

José is lost. Zuniga (bass), his captain (who also is in love with Carmen), returns and orders him off. He refuses to go, and they fight, but are eventually torn apart by the smugglers. Disgraced and ruined, José throws in his lot with them. Henceforth he has no other thought but Carmen. Her people shall be his people and her gods his gods.

ACT III

Again a charming intermezzo, and the curtain rises on the smugglers' camp in a rocky mountain gorge. Mercedes and Frasquita begin to tell their fortunes by cards:

Et main-te-nant par-lez mes bel - les
Now pret-ty cards, we've plac'd you du - ly

Carmen takes a hand and turns up the Ace of Spades. It is death—first for her, then for her lover. But she is a gipsy—and a fatalist. She merely shrugs her shoulders and leaps gaily to her feet to join the smugglers, who are making for the frontier, leaving José on guard on a nearby rock. When the stage is empty, Micaela appears. She is seeking José with a message from his dying mother. The desolate scene fills her with fear and she prays for courage:

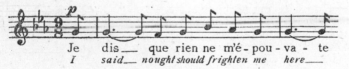

Je dis— que rien ne m'é-pou-va - te
I said— nought should frighten me here—

She catches sight of José on the rock. He suddenly takes aim and fires; she is overcome with panic and hides in a cave. It is Escamillo José has fired at, thinking him a spy. He now comes forward to greet him. Escamillo laughingly confesses that he has fallen in love with Carmen and has come to seek her. Maddened by jealousy, José challenges him and they begin to fight with daggers. The crowd returns just in time to separate them, and with an ironical speech of thanks the Toreador departs, having invited them to his next bull-fight at Seville. Micaela persuades José to go with her to his dying mother. "Yes, go back to your mother, baby," sneers Carmen, now thoroughly weary of her remorseful lover; "you'll never have the pluck to make a smuggler." José turns to go, but he swears that they will meet again. She is his, and she shall never escape him.

ACT IV

He keeps his word. In Mérimée's story José kills Carmen on a lonely mountain road; but Bizet's *librettists* were men of the theatre and evolved a far more spectacular climax. We are at the gate of the Plaza de Toros. The warriors march in to the ringing of bells and the frenzied acclamations of the people, who swarm in after them. Escamillo pauses to take a tender leave of Carmen. "If you love me, Carmen, you will be proud of me today":

Si   tu   m'ai - mes, Car - men,—
If   thou lov'st   me,   Car - men,—

Carmen is about to follow the crowd, but a hand is laid on her arm, and beside her, like a figure of doom, stands José—white-faced, motionless, terrible. We know why he has come. We know it is to be their last meeting. Carmen knows it too. She looks at him, and knows she is looking into the face of death. But she does not shrink. He makes one last despairing appeal: will she go with him and begin life afresh? For answer she hurls his ring at him and makes a blind rush for the gateway—a rush that ends on the point of his dagger, as a wild shout from within proclaims the victory of her new lover. The crowd pours out of the gates where José stands staring in horror at his deed. "I am your prisoner," he cries; "'twas I who killed her. Ah, Carmen, my beloved!"

ALEXANDER BORODIN

(1833–1887)

Prince Igor

Libretto by the composer.
Time: Twelfth Century.

First Production,
St. Petersburg, 1890.

'Pride, pomp and circumstance of glorious war.'
SHAKESPEARE: *Othello.*

Prince Igor is a great historical pageant, a stretch of brightly-coloured heroic tapestry. It is more spectacular than emotional; there is power and nobility here, but nothing that grips us by the throat, as does the Macbeth-like agony of *Boris Godounov*, for example. And its characters have everything *but* character; just legendary figures marching across some vast fresco—but marching to magnificent melodies that stir the blood with their atmosphere of pomp and chivalry. Borodin was a chemist by design and a composer by accident, who wrote his music when he was not well enough to work in his laboratory. That was why his musical friends, instead of saying, "I hope you are well," used to say, "I hope you are ill!" He worked on *Prince Igor* intermittently for eighteen years—presumably in bouts of indisposition—and after his death it was finished by Rimsky-Korsakov and Glazounov. One interesting point about the opera is that, contrary to operatic tradition, the leading characters—Igor, Galitsky and Kontchak—are basses.[1]

THE OVERTURE

is built on themes from the opera and gives us the whole drama in miniature. It is in the nature of a conflict between the martial strains associated with Igor and the sinuous oriental themes belonging to the Polovtsy tribe—music of a pungent, almost acrid flavour.

PROLOGUE

Prince Igor (bass-baritone) and his army are about to march against the Polovtsy in battle. But as he steps out of the cathedral in

[1] Kontchak is a pure bass, but Igor and Galitsky, though they demand the darkness and gravity of a bass voice, are really baritone in compass. I have therefore labelled them bass-baritone.

Poutivle the sky suddenly darkens with an eclipse of the sun. It is an omen of disaster, and those who have come to bid him God-speed are overawed with superstitious fear. His wife, Jaroslavna (soprano), implores him to abandon the expedition; but Igor is what romantics call steadfast and realists stubborn, and he refuses to turn back. He commits her to the care of her brother Prince Galitsky (bass-baritone), and leads away the army with his son Vladimir (tenor).

Act I

As soon as Igor has gone, Galitsky blazes forth in his true colours as a dissolute scamp; and here we find him amid raffish drinking-companions, among whom are Skula and Eroshka (bass and tenor), a comic pair of wandering minstrels. In a fiery, barbaric song Galitsky tells them all what a riotous time they will have if they will elect him Prince of Poutivle in Igor's place:

Presently the scene changes to Jaroslavna's apartment. She is dreaming of her warrior husband and counting the hours till his return . . .

—the warmest approach in the score to genuine pathos. The door opens to admit a crowd of distracted girls who crave her protection: Prince Galitsky has carried off one of their number. At that moment Galitsky himself blusters in. Jaroslavna denounces him as a villain, but he answers her with brutal laughter. He at any rate, he says, is frank in his debaucheries. What of her? How does he know that, beneath that virtuous mask, she herself is unspotted? She indignantly orders him off, and he bids her a mocking farewell—and us; for from that moment Borodin unaccountably forgets about him. Still, he was lively company while he lasted. The second scene ends in calamity: the boyards bring news that Igor and his son have been defeated and captured and that the terrible Khan Gzak has attacked Poutivle.

Act II

Night is slowly descending on the Tartar camp where Igor and his son are captives. Young maidens intone a wailful oriental melody—the colours of which seem to burn 'like a witch's oils'. They dance, and a few moments later the Khan's daughter Kontchakovna (contralto), who has fallen in love with Igor's son, sings a voluptuous song to the night—the night that is to bring her beloved to her arms:

The women gradually disappear. Vladimir comes in and reveals his passionate love for Kontchakovna. This love is only of minor interest, but it produces, in Vladimir's *cavatina*, one of the major masterpieces of the score—a thing of unforgettable beauty:

Kontchakovna appears and they sing a rapturous duet, finally stealing away into the gathering darkness as they hear someone approaching. It is Igor. He is a broken man; his cause lost, his brave warriors slain and he himself languishing like a caged lion. Ah! If only he could regain his freedom and march to battle once again!:

And at home his faithful wife perhaps believes him dead:

But Khan Kontchak is a generous victor and treats him with that courtesy which once made war a gentleman's game. What would he have—treasures, houses, wines, young maidens?:

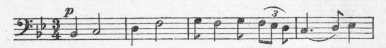

In fact, why not form an alliance with him? Just imagine: together they could conquer the earth! Igor shakes his head sadly; he desires only his freedom. But it is time for the festivities: dancers and singers crowd into the arena of the camp—

—and perform the famous Polovtsian dances before the Khan and his captives. The scene ends with a chorus in praise of the Khan, which rises to a terrifying exuberance.

ACT III

begins with the well-known Polovtsian March. Khan Gzak's army has returned laden with immense spoils, and Kontchak and his followers greet the marauders in savage joy. Igor and Vladimir watch them angrily and in silence. There is feasting and revelry in the camp, and when the prisoners' guards eventually collapse in a drunken sleep Igor and his son make a dash for freedom. But Kontchakovna is mad with grief at losing her love and she arouses the camp. Igor escapes, but Vladimir, torn by conflicting passions, misses his chance. Very well, says the Khan: he shall remain as hostage and marry his daughter.

ACT IV

There is not much more to tell. Back in Poutivle, Jaroslavna laments the tragedy that has fallen on their household. Presently she gazes out of the window, and there in the distance are two horsemen galloping over the plain. As they ride into the town she recognises Igor. His companion is Ovlour, a Polovtsian, who has helped him to escape. To a noble, spacious melody which we heard in the first act, they sing of the joy of their reunion:

The crowd gradually fills the stage, and the opera ends with a majestic chorus of thanksgiving.

BENJAMIN BRITTEN

(1913 –   )

Peter Grimes

Libretto by Montagu Slater, after Crabbe.
Time: Late Eighteenth Century.

First Production,
London, 1945.

'It's no fish ye're buying; it's men's lives.'
Sir Walter Scott: *The Antiquary.*

Peter Grimes is perhaps too near our own time for anyone to pass a perfectly cool and balanced judgment on it. There is about it not only the heat of composition but the heat of controversy. The musical merits of the opera are undeniable, yet its appeal as a complete work of art is uncertain.

It has been said that it was born, like fortune's favourites, with a silver spoon in its mouth; it would be nearer the truth to say that it was born with a whole canteen of cutlery in its mouth. Certainly few operas in history can have arrived at a more opportune time. The war was just over and, however unpalatable the fruits of victory have proved, England had won. There was a tremendous 'boom' in music throughout the country and a new public for opera, some members of which had had their first taste of it from some of the best companies abroad. Here was a new opera on an English subject and by an English composer. It took the stage amid a deafening roar of applause that has hardly died away even now. There never was such a roar of applause. Musical England went completely off its head: *Peter Grimes* was likened to *Boris Godounov* and pronounced equal to representative masterpieces of Mozart, Verdi and Puccini. Whether time will verify these pronouncements is a thing that only time can tell. To this paean of praise there was, nevertheless, a distinctly audible bass: there were those who, while not denying the work's uncanny technical skill, were repelled by the harshness of the subject and the uncompromising 'modernity' of the music. They recall the man who, after a performance of Strauss's *Elektra*, announced that he was going home to play the chord of C major 'to see if it still exists' (an unnecessary experiment, since *Elektra* actually ends on the chord of C major; but perhaps he couldn't wait for the last bar!).

My own reaction at the time can best be expressed by the following extract from a criticism of *Peter Grimes* I wrote for *The Stage* after the

34

first performance: "It is probably the best thing Britten has done: a score uncompromisingly 'modern', as harsh and rough as the homespun jerseys and homespun manners of the fisherfolk; but with moments of a queer, rather pained beauty, which falls all the more poignantly on the ear—and sometimes on the heart—because of the dissonance that has gone before."

The composer is a native of Suffolk, where the scene of Crabbe's poem is laid, and he has told us that he first read *The Borough* in California in 1941 and was at once struck with the operatic possibilities of the *Peter Grimes* story. Montagu Slater's *libretto* was ready in January 1944, and the score was finished thirteen months later.

"One of my chief aims," Britten has said, "is to try and restore to the musical setting of the English language a brilliance, freedom, and vitality that have been curiously rare since the death of Purcell. . . . Good recitative should transform the natural intonations and rhythms of everyday speech into memorable musical phrases (as with Purcell), but in more stylized music the composer should not deliberately avoid unnatural stresses if the prosody of the poem and the emotional situation demand them. . . ."

The musical structure of *Peter Grimes* is too complex and interesting to be analysed in a short space, and fragmentary quotations would hardly give an adequate idea of it. I shall therefore limit myself to a brief summary of the action so that you may be free to concentrate on the music without puzzling out who's who and what's what. If, after hearing it, you wish to study Britten's method in detail, there is an informative booklet published by the Sadlers Wells Opera Company.

PROLOGUE

In the Coroner's Court at Aldeborough they are inquiring into the death of a boy who was apprenticed to the fisherman Peter Grimes (tenor). It is suspected that Grimes's cruelty has caused the boy's death, and, although no definite charge is brought, he realises that the stigma will remain.

> *The case goes on in people's minds (he says)*
> *And charges that no court has made*
> *Will be shouted at my head.*

After the inquest, Ellen Orford (soprano), the widowed schoolmistress, stays behind to try to comfort Grimes and encourage him to face the future.

ACT I: *Scene* 1

Morning in the Borough High Street. Fishermen, fishermen's wives, children and local gossips join in the opening chorus. For the first time since the inquest Grimes has been out fishing with the others, but their attitude towards him is aloof and unfriendly. Soon Ned Keene (baritone), the Borough quack, announces that he has got Grimes a new apprentice from the workhouse. There are murmurs of disapproval, but Ellen Orford undertakes to accompany the boy back in the carrier's cart and take care of him. A storm rises and Balstrode (baritone), a retired captain, remonstrates with Grimes. Is he going to start another scandal? Wouldn't it be wiser to leave the Borough? But Grimes is stubborn: here are his roots. He will stay and defy them; and when he has made his pile he will marry Ellen.

ACT I: *Scene* 2

Those drinking in the 'Boar', a disreputable public-house, hear news of storm damage. Roads are flooded and part of the cliff has fallen in behind Grimes's hut. Later in the scene Ellen arrives with the boy and Grimes takes him home.

ACT II: *Scene* 1

On a Sunday morning Ellen and the boy are sitting outside the church, in which a service is going on. Suddenly she discovers that the neck of his shirt is torn and his neck bruised. He will not tell her how it happened. When Grimes comes along Ellen asks him about the bruise, and a ferocious quarrel takes place, at the climax of which he strikes her. The boy runs away in terror and Grimes follows him. Neighbours have seen this incident through their windows. They crowd into the street, shouting indignantly, and at the end of the scene some of the men go in search of Grimes.

This scene and the next are linked by an impressive orchestral *passacaglia* which may be said to summarise the nature of Peter Grimes himself—his pride, loneliness, hunger for affection, and the wild beast that sometimes leaps within him.

Grimes and the boy are alone in his hut, made from an upturned boat. He orders the boy to put on his sea-boots: they will make a record catch. Then he falls into a long reverie, the apprentice watching him, half fascinated, half terrified. Presently Grimes hears the men coming up the hill. What can they want? He throws his nets through the door and tells the boy to follow them. The boy goes out, but a moment later we hear his scream and realize that he has fallen over the cliff. Grimes rushes after him, and when the champions of social justice arrive they find an empty hut.

ACT III: *Scene* 1

A summer evening. No one has seen Grimes or his apprentice for three days, and the Borough simply seethes with gossip. At a quiet moment, however, Balstrode tells Ellen that he has seen Grimes's boat pulled up on the beach. And we learn also that the sea has washed up the boy's jersey.

ACT III: *Scene* 2

Balstrode and Ellen find Grimes. He has been wandering in a demented state for three days. There is no hope; life has defeated him. There is only one solution, Balstrode says: he must go out in his boat and scuttle it. He obeys.

Dawn breaks, shutters are opened, cleaners brush the doorsteps. Life begins again with a bustle and clatter. Someone brings rumour of a boat sinking far out to sea; someone else looks through the spyglass, but he can see nothing. The day's work goes on.

GUSTAVE CHARPENTIER

(1860-)

Louise

Libretto by the Composer.
Time: 1900.

First Production,
Paris, 1900.

> 'My Paris is a land where twilight days
> Merge into violent nights of black and gold;
> Where, it may be, the flower of dawn is cold:
> Ah, but the gold nights and the scented ways!'
>
> ARTHUR SYMONS.

Louise is a song of Paris. It was written and composed by a man who loved Paris, and the authentic aroma of its music will endear it to the hearts of her lovers for many generations. It is Charpentier's finest work—indeed, for ordinary practical purposes, his only work. Eight years before, he had written the attractive *Vie du Poète*, and thirteen years after he produced *Julien*, a sequel to *Louise*; but neither of these captured a wide public. Charpentier thus joins the small but entertaining company of one-opera composers.

Louise is said to be founded on incidents of his own youth, when he was an arch-bohemian and revolutionary, with the traditional Montmartre hat and flowing tie; and, rightly to assimilate its flavour, we must imagine ourselves back in 1900, before women were what is called 'free', when young girls, especially working-class girls, were tyrannically 'protected' by their parents, and young men who studied or practised the arts were automatically classed as immoral undesirables. The drama is a battle between opposing forces for the possession of Louise's soul: on the one side her rigidly respectable parents; on the other side the eternal glamour of Paris, now expressed in its own multitudinous voice, now through the lips of Julian, her poet lover.

ACT I

Julian's studio is just opposite the tenement of Louise's parents in a working-class quarter of Paris. When the curtain rises we hear Julian (tenor) singing to her across the narrow street—

38

O cœur a - mi! O cœur pro-mis!
O lov- ing heart! O pro-mised heart!

—a figure which is very prominent in the score and seems to symbolise
the irresistible call of Paris, with its gaiety and freedom. Louise
(soprano) responds, and we learn that Julian wishes to marry her and
has again written to her father. If the old man refuses she will run
away with Julian; but she half regrets this promise: she hates the
thought of distressing her parents—particularly her father. Her
mother (mezzo-soprano) comes in to lay the supper. She is a typical
product of years of scrape-and-save respectability: a dour, discontented
woman, no doubt subconsciously jealous of Louise's beauty and youth.
Julian laughs at her and she angrily shuts the window in his face. Her
opinion of him is exactly what one would expect. After some bickering
between mother and daughter, the father (bass) comes home from
work. We see at once the honest, kindly fellow he is and why Louise
loves him. After supper he reads Julian's letter. He is gentle and patient
about it, but he distrusts what he does not understand, and thinks
they ought to find out more about this eccentric young man. Also, of
course, he cannot realise that his daughter is now a grown woman:
"Choosing a husband," he says, "is not like choosing your dollies."
The mother is neither gentle nor patient, and when Louise answers her
back she smacks her face. The father restores peace, and Louise begins
to read him the evening paper. Her voice trembles over the words:
"'Spring has come and the season promises to be most brilliant. Paris
... is very gay ...'" Paris!

ACT II: *Scene* 1

There is a short orchestral prelude, 'Paris Awakes', and then we
watch the awakening from a crossroads at the foot of Montmartre.
It is a characteristic early-morning street scene; and we make acquaintance with a milkwoman, a girl rag-picker, a junkman, a coal-gatherer
and other types including a noctambulist (tenor)—a rakish young
man in evening dress on his way home, who calls himself '*Plaisir de
Paris*' and is evidently a symbolical figure. An old ragman (bass)
joins them, bewailing the seduction of his daughter—also darkly
symbolical. As the light broadens, more people come on the scene, and
later Julian enters with some bohemian friends. He is waiting to

snatch a word with Louise, who works in the dressmaker's establish-
ment on the right. Soon Louise comes along the street on her way to
work, chaperoned by her mother. The mother leaves her at the door,
and as soon as she is out of sight Julian comes forward, ardently
imploring Louise to throw off the tyranny of home. But Louise says it
will kill her father if she runs away; and eventually she breaks from
him and disappears into the house.

ACT II: *Scene 2*

Inside the workroom. A typical crowd of girls, sewing, chattering,
singing, quarrelling. Louise sits a little apart from the others, silent and
troubled. They rally and tease her, but she will not be drawn. After a
while Julian's voice is heard in the street outside:

Dans la   ci - té loin - tai - ne,
O   in   the dis - tant ci - ty

The girls laugh and throw down pennies and kisses. But when the
song becomes too earnest they begin to jeer and hoot at him. Louise
can bear it no longer. She makes an excuse and runs out of the room.

ACT III

After an orchestral prelude, 'Towards the Distant City', the curtain
rises on the garden of a little house on the side of Montmartre. Paris
spreads itself out below.

Parental 'protection' has had its inevitable result, and Louise is
now living with Julian. She recalls the thrill of their first kiss:

De - puis le jour où je me suis don - né - e,
E'er since   the day when un - to thee I gave me,

They join in a passionate duet in praise of their new-found freedom
and love. The lights twinkle out in the city below as they turn and go
slowly into the house. Then follows the famous Carnival scene, based on
an actual ceremony in Montmartre for which Charpentier wrote the

music three years before the production of *Louise*. Bohemians, *grisettes*, street-arabs and idlers crowd into the garden and decorate the house with streamers, paper lanterns and banners. The central figure of the procession is the noctambulist, now fantastically attired as the King of Fools, who proclaims Louise the Muse of Montmartre. When the merriment is at its height there is a sudden dramatic interruption: there on the edge of the crowd stands the mother, like a mute reproachful ghost from the past. The revellers disperse, and then she tells Julian and Louise that the father is very ill, broken in health and in heart. Will Louise go back to him—only for a while, just a little while? And like a background to her appeal we hear the voice of the old ragman as he passes along the lane: 'a father seeking his daughter'. Louise goes with her mother.

Act IV

They do not keep their promise. When we see her again Louise is sitting at home like a caged bird, her parents watching her jealously, angry at her restlessness and discontent. The father especially has aged with illness and grief and become savagely embittered. And when Louise opens the window and looks longingly into the night he begins a resentful tirade against life: one brings a daughter into the world, one tends her and cares for her. She grows like a beautiful flower—

Tout en el - le est ra-vis-sant;
She is love - ly and full of charm;

—(a charming little lyrical episode that is over all too soon). And then, he says, with rising bitterness, a stranger comes along and lures her away. A curse on him who steals such love! Later his mood changes and he takes Louise on his knee, rocking her like a little child and pleading piteously for her love, over a lullaby theme in the orchestra:

Louise is moved by his distress. But she is young and life is too strong for her; and when she hears distant voices from the town, which is gradually lighting up, her excitement rises to a frenzy and she sings and dances like one possessed. "Paris—Paris is calling! Julian! Take me—now and for ever!" The parents are horror-struck: this is not their child, it is some evil spirit. Then the father breaks out in a fury: "Very well, go! They're waiting for you, the wantons. They dance till they split! They laugh till they cry! Go! Go!" Louise, terrified but exultant, rushes out into the night. The old man's rage suddenly dies. He stumbles after her to the stairs, calling, "Louise! Louise!" in a voice choked with tears. But there is no answer. Paris has won. He staggers to the window and shakes his clenched fists at the town with a terrible heart-rending cry: "Oh, Paris!"

CLAUDE ACHILLE DEBUSSY

(1862-1918)

Pelléas and Mélisande

Libretto from Maeterlinck's drama.
Time: legendary.

First Production,
Paris, 1902.

'But there Love's self doth stand,
And with Life's weary wings far-flown,
And with Death's eyes that make the water moan,
Gathers the water in his hand:
And they that drink know nought of sky or land
But only love alone.'

D. G. ROSSETTI: *The Stream's Secret.*

Pelléas and Mélisande is often called the French *Tristan*. Stylistically, of course, it is not in the least like *Tristan*. The glory of Wagner is in his opulence; the subtlety of Debussy is in his reticence. Wagner leaves nothing unsaid, while Maeterlinck and Debussy say just enough to set our imagination dreaming. Tristan and Isolde are swept onward by the full, racing tide of their blood; Pelléas and Mélisande seem to have no blood in them at all. It is easy to see, nevertheless, how the comparison has arisen, for the two operas are at least parallel if not similar. We might indeed call *Pelléas* the French complement of *Tristan*, since, like *Tristan*, it is a memorial, supreme in its kind, to a fatalistic love. Both works symbolise will overruled by fate; both commemorate star-crossed lovers driven to ecstasy and disaster by forces stronger than themselves: 'rapid falcons in a snare'. And in the dim, twilit world of *Pelléas*, in which remote, shadowy creatures pass through love to death as though walking in their sleep, we are even more conscious of this blind, implacable fate than in *Tristan*. The difference may be more naïvely expressed by saying that *Tristan* is red while *Pelléas* is green (it invariably recalls Henley's line about 'the green sky's minor thirds').

The work represents the perfect marriage of true minds. Debussy could not have found fitter material for what he wanted to express in music, and Maeterlinck's frail phantoms could not have found music more potent to give them, for a brief space, the semblance of life. Debussy's attitude to opera was definite and realistic. The music must be conditioned entirely by the dramatic situation. There must be no 'tunes' for the sake of tunes; the recitative must follow natural

43

speech as faithfully as possible and the score should expand into
lyrical fervour—or from speech into song—only when the emotions of
the characters demand it. The theory has infinite possibilities—and
difficulties; difficulties because, opera being essentially an artificial
form of expression, complete realism is out of the question. One might
as well contend, for example, that since music cannot by its very
nature suggest pure evil, then Mephistopheles should *speak* his lines
while Faust *sang* his. Push Debussy's ideas to their logical end and no
one would sing on the stage at all; push them half-way to their end
and we are back to the opera of Mozart's day, where the mundane
business of the 'plot' was carried on by *recitativo secco*, like the prose
passages in Shakespearean tragedy.

Nevertheless, theorising apart, there is no doubt that Debussy
achieved exactly what he wanted to achieve. You may dislike his
opera, you may be bored by it, and if you are not 'in the mood' or
have an unruly sense of humour you may even find the whole thing
faintly absurd (no dramatist invites parody more irresistibly than
Maeterlinck). But you will not dispute that it is, in its way, a perfect
work of art.

Act I

The very first notes set the prevailing atmosphere of darkness and
mystery:

We are in the heart of a vast forest. Golaud (baritone) comes blundering in. He has lost his way while out hunting and he stares about him
in bewilderment. Suddenly he hears sobbing, and in the dim light he
perceives what looks like a child, sitting by a well. It is Mélisande
(soprano). She is a forlorn, fairy-like little creature who seems deranged
with grief, and to all his questions she replies vaguely, as one in a
trance. Why does she weep? They have done her wrong, she says, but
she cannot tell him how. Whence does she come? From far away; she
is lost. A golden crown has fallen from her head into the water; but

Golaud must not recover it for her: she wants it no longer. He reveals himself as the grandson of King Arkel of Allemonde, and she tells him her name is Mélisande. More than this she cannot tell him. He is touched and slightly awed by her distress; gently, tenderly, he persuades her to go with him. But when she asks him where, he replies: "How can I tell? I too am lost." The music continues while the scene changes to a room in Arkel's castle. Geneviève (contralto), Golaud's mother, is reading to the old king (bass), who is almost blind, a letter from Golaud to his younger brother, Pelléas, saying that he has married a mysterious girl he found in a forest. It is six months since he met her, yet even now he knows nothing of who she is or whence she came. Pelléas must prepare Arkel for their homecoming. If all is well he is to light the lamp in the tower overlooking the sea. Pelléas (tenor) comes in. He has received a letter from a friend who is about to die and wishes to see him; but Arkel persuades him to wait—is not his own father gravely ill? And—he is to light the lamp in the tower. Again the orchestra accompanies us on our journey, this time to the castle garden. Geneviève and Mélisande are talking: how dark the garden is, says Mèlisande, and how thickly the castle is surrounded by forests. But Geneviève is accustomed to the gloom: she has lived here forty years. Pelléas joins them and they watch a ship leaving the harbour below—the same ship that has brought Mélisande. In all these scenes the effects are achieved by the sparsest economy in words and music. Nothing is unduly extended or over-emphasised. Indeed, Debussy here gives us the clue to his whole score: his direction for the last four bars of the scene reads, 'Presque plus rien'.

ACT II

Pelléas and Mélisande are together by a well in the castle park. It is called the 'Blindman's Well', he tells her, because it was said that its water could heal the eyes of the blind; but now that the king is nearly blind they come to it no more. "There is always in this place a wonderful silence," murmurs Pelléas; "one can almost hear the water sleep." Mélisande begins tossing into the air the ring Golaud has given her and catching it again. Suddenly it falls into the well. They cannot find it. "What shall we tell Golaud?" asks Mélisande tremulously. "We must tell him the truth—the truth," answers Pelléas as they move away. Once again the orchestra guides us back to the castle. Golaud is lying on his bed, Mélisande tending him. His horse took fright while he was out hunting and threw him—*at the precise moment that Mélisande dropped the ring in*

the well. "I felt sure that my heart had been torn in two," he says;
"but my heart is not injured." He perceives that Mélisande is not
happy; the gloom of the castle, where everyone seems to have grown
old (even Golaud has grey in his hair), and the sunless forests around
it are oppressing her. He takes her hand in his to comfort her and
notices that the ring is no longer there. Mélisande stammers con-
fusedly: it slipped from her finger that morning in a cave by the
sea. Golaud is terribly agitated. She must find it; if she is afraid to go
alone she must take Pelléas with her. "I shall not sleep till I possess it
again," he says. And Mélisande goes out weeping. Pelléas and
Mélisande go to the cave, though she knows it was not there that she
lost the ring. As they are exploring the cave the moon shines out and
shows them three white-haired beggars sleeping together among the
rocks. Mélisande is frightened and they hurry back to the castle. Just
that and nothing more. Yet with every passing moment we feel the
net of fate closing round these hapless children.

ACT III

The moonlight shows us one of the castle towers and Mélisande
combing her unbound hair at the open window. Pelléas comes by
along a watchman's path. He is going away tomorrow, he says; will
she not give him her hand to kiss? She leans out of the window, and
as she does so her hair falls in a cascade over his face. He breaks out in
rapture:

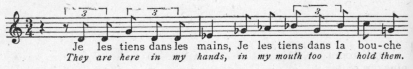

Je   les tiens dans les mains, Je les tiens dans la bou-che
They are here   in   my   hands,   in   my mouth too   I   hold them.

From that moment the music blossoms in passion like a rose as
Pelléas kisses her hair, which blinds him so that he can no longer see
the sky. Suddenly the spell is snapped as some doves dart out of the
tower and fly about them. A footstep is heard: it is Golaud. "What
are you doing here?" he asks harshly, peering at their faces in the
half-light. Then he gives a nervous laugh. "Why, you are children—
children both!" And he repeats, "Children both!", as though to
convince himself. A poignant orchestral interlude eventually leads us
down to the castle vaults. Golaud, with a lantern, is showing Pelléas
the stagnant water whence rises the stench of death. "Stoop down and
look," he says; "don't be afraid. Hold on to me—no, not your hand;

it might slip!—your arm. Do you see the chasm?" His voice and hand are trembling. Pelléas stands up and looks at him. "I am stifling," he says; "let us go out." "Yes," says Golaud, perhaps with a tinge of relief in his voice, "let us go out." They emerge into the sunlight, and at last Golaud speaks of what is torturing his heart. It is not good for Pelléas and Mélisande to be so often together; she is soon to bear a child. Any little shock . . .

The scene changes to a space outside the castle, under Mélisande's window. Golaud takes Yniold (soprano), his little son by a former marriage, on to his knee and questions him about 'his uncle Pelléas and his little mother'.

"Are they often together?"

"Oh yes, whenever you're not there."

"Do they not sometimes send you away?"

"No—they're afraid to have me go away."

"Do they—kiss?"

"Kiss, Father? No—yes, once they did when it rained."

Once! In his agony Golaud tightens his grasp on the child's arm till Yniold cries out in pain; and now and again he breaks forth in a shout of anguish that terrifies him. A light glimmers at Mélisande's window. Golaud lifts the child up so that he can see into the room. Pelléas is there with Mélisande. What are they doing? They are looking at the lamplight. They are still: they do not speak and they never once close their eyes. Suddenly Yniold is overcome with terror. "Father! Father! Put me down! I'm going to scream!" Golaud leads him away, still as far as ever from knowing what he dreads to know.

ACT IV

In a room in the castle Pelléas tells Mélisande that his father is now out of danger. He went to see him, and his father said: "You have the grave and kindly look of those who will not live very long. You must go on a voyage." Pelléas is to obey him, but he must see Mélisande once again before he goes; that night—by the Blindman's Well? She consents. As the youth goes, Arkel comes in. Now that the shadow of death has lifted, he says—

Un peu de joie et un peu de so-leil vont en-fin ren-trer dans la mai-son
Some lit-tle joy and a gleam of the sun may at last find entrance to our house.

—and perhaps Mélisande will be happier. He has pitied her. He is to pity her still more, for in a few moments Golaud strides in. He is distraught, and brutal in his manner. He points at his wife. "Do you see those eyes," he shouts to Arkel, "so proud of their beauty?" "I see a great innocence only," Arkel replies calmly; and Golaud takes up his words in savage irony: "A great innocence—yes! They could give lessons in innocence to God Himself!" His fury rises with every moment, and at last he seizes her by the hair and drags her to and fro on the ground. "Do what you will! Do what you will!" he cries; "I care not; I am too old; and I will not play the spy." Arkel has pressed forward to interfere, but Golaud flings her down and rushes distractedly from the room. And, looking down on the prostrate form shaken with sobs, Arkel murmurs, "If I were God, I should pity the heart of man."

The next scene—the fountain in the park—begins with an appealing little interlude in which Yniold watches some sheep being driven by in the gathering darkness. Suddenly they stop bleating and the shepherd tells Yniold that they are silent because they are not on their way to the fold. The child is puzzled and wanders away. Then comes the great emotional climax of the opera. Pelléas and Mélisande meet by the fountain and declare their love. All the veils are torn down; there is no doubt, no concealment.

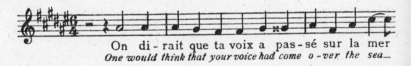

On di-rait que ta voix a pas-sé sur la mer
One would think that your voice had come o-ver the sea

Presently they hear the great doors of the castle shutting. It is too late now: they cannot go back. "Thank God!" cries Mélisande. "Thank God!" When their ecstasy is at its height a dark shadow leaps upon them from the bushes. With one blow of the sword Golaud slays his brother, who falls at the brink of the fountain. Mélisande plunges through the trees, crying out in anguish: "Ah, I am nothing but a coward, nothing but a coward!"

Act V

In the last scene Mélisande lies in bed sleeping, Arkel and a doctor standing by. Golaud wounded her slightly in his jealous madness and she has since given birth to a tiny child—a daughter. But it is not of these things she is dying: one suspects that she has not the will to live. Golaud, a miserable, grief-stricken figure, sits by the bed, bitterly reproaching himself; and when they are left alone he pleads passionately, desperately, for her forgiveness. He too is going to die, he says, and to those about to die people speak the truth. He bends urgently towards her; he *must* be satisfied: did she love Pelléas? Why, of course she loved him, she answers with childlike simplicity. "No, you don't understand," raves Golaud; "Mélisande, for the love of God, tell me the truth: did you love him guiltily?" But as she speaks her voice grows fainter and fainter. Arkel and the doctor hurry back. "I shall never know," Golaud groans out; "I shall go to my grave as one that's blind!" Arkel rebukes him sternly: "Leave her alone, you will kill her." "I have already killed her," says Golaud. They show her the child, but she is too weak to hold her. The serving-women come in, and after a few moments fall on their knees. They know that she has died. Arkel gazes down at her. "There she lies, looking like the sister of her own child. . . . Come, it is the poor little one's turn to suffer now!"

GAETANO DONIZETTI

(1797–1848)

Lucia di Lammermoor

Libretto by Cammarano, after Scott.
Time: Seventeenth Century.

First Production,
Naples, 1835.

'Thought and affliction, passion, hell itself
She turns to favour and to prettiness.'

SHAKESPEARE: *Hamlet.*

Lucia di Lammermoor is generally considered Donizetti's masterpiece. It is also a thoroughly representative example of the golden age of voice-worship, when the forty-horse-power *prima donna* and *primo tenore* were pampered more exotically than royalty, and looked down on composers, conductors, orchestras and impresarios as lackeys whose duty and privilege it was to serve them and exalt their reputations. It is, of course, very easy nowadays to scoff at these 'kings and queens of song' whose voices were usually in inverse proportion to their intellects. They were all airs and no graces; they were troublesome, unmanageable, ridiculous, no doubt. Nevertheless, they had one supreme faculty in common: they could *sing*. And one reason why we so rarely hear operas like *Lucia di Lammermoor* today is that we have no one to sing them—at least, as Donizetti and his contemporaries meant them to be sung. Today our operas demand keen intelligences rather than great voices; consequently nature, ever obedient to art, no longer produces great voices. Aesthetically, no doubt, we are much better off; but— there hath passed away a glory from the earth.

We must keep these things in mind when we listen to operas like *Lucia di Lammermoor*; and we must admire the skill with which the fluent and resourceful Donizetti satisfied both parties—the young men-about-town we meet in Balzac or Thackeray, who slipped into the Duchess of So-and-So's box to hear Malibran's great *aria*, and then went on to the club; and the more enlightened critics, who demanded that opera should have dramatic movement and characterisation as well as odes for nightingales.

PROLOGUE

Lucia di Lammermoor is, of course, a setting of Scott's novel, *The Bride of Lammermoor*, one of the shortest and most harmoniously constructed

50

of his works, and having the inevitable, fatalistic dignity of Greek tragedy. The Prologue prepares us for the tragedy. Sir Henry Ashton (baritone), a Scottish nobleman, is out hunting with his followers when one of them tells him that his sister, Lucy, and his neighbour, Edgar of Ravenswood, have fallen in love and are meeting secretly. There is a centuries-old feud between the two families; also, Sir Henry wants Lucy to retrieve the fallen fortunes of his house by making a more advantageous marriage. He swears that he will rescue her from this entanglement and wreak vengeance on her lover. The scene changes to the entrance of a park with a fountain in the foreground. Lucy Ashton (soprano) tells Alice (mezzo-soprano), her confidante, the legend of the fountain. Alice sees in this a forewarning of tragedy, but Lucy is happily confident in her love:

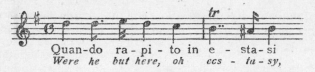

Quan-do ra - pi - to in e - sta - si
Were he but here, oh ecs - ta - sy,

Edgar (tenor) comes in to keep his assignation with Lucy. At dawn, he tells her, he must sail from Scotland for France, where he is to fulfil a diplomatic mission. They sing a long duet of farewell, one theme of which—

Ver - ran - no a te sull' a - u - re
When twi - light sha - dows low - er,

—is recalled with poignant effect later in the drama.

ACT I

Sir Henry is pressing on with his plans. He has intercepted letters between the lovers and has forged a letter in Edgar's handwriting renouncing Lucy. She is to marry Sir Arthur Bucklaw, and today Sir Arthur should arrive to sign the marriage contract. Sir Henry shows his sister the forged letter, which plunges her into a stupor of grief and shame. She hears festive music, and he tells her that it is to welcome her bridegroom. "No!" she exclaims in horror. "My heart is Edgar's. If he is faithless I would rather die!" After an angry scene he leaves her. Bide-the-Bent (bass), Sir Henry's chaplain (sometimes called Raymond), now comes in and gently pleads with Lucy to make this sacrifice for the honour of the family. And, at last, when Sir Arthur (tenor) arrives, she miserably consents and signs the contract. Then occurs the most dramatic scene in the opera. A tragic figure appears at the back of the hall: it is Edgar. In one glance he takes in the scene and denounces them all. Donizetti then builds up a tremendous *finale* beginning with the first notes of what becomes the sextet—

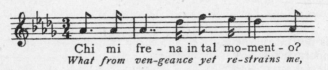

Chi mi fre - na in tal mo-ment - o?
What from ven-geance yet re-strains me,

—which, until Verdi wrote the *Rigoletto* quartet (in the same key and in a rather similar vein), was considered the greatest *ensemble* in Italian opera.

ACT II: *Scene 1*

It is night and a storm is raging. In the gloomy castle of Ravenswood Edgar looks out on the darkness and sees there a reflection of his own fate. He hears the galloping of a horse, and a few moments later Sir Henry Ashton appears. In vindictive triumph he tells Edgar that Lucy has now become the bride of Sir Arthur Bucklaw. Thus half his purpose is accomplished; there remains—Edgar's death. He has sworn to destroy him, and he forthwith challenges him to a duel to be fought at dawn.

ACT II: *Scene 2*

We are back in Sir Henry Ashton's hall, where the wedding festivities are at their height. Suddenly Bide-the-Bent rushes in among the guests. "Silence these sounds of gladness!" he cries, and in tones of horror he tells them of the ghastly discovery he has just made: Lucy has gone mad and murdered her bridegroom. The guests have hardly recovered from the shock of this revelation when Lucy herself totters into the hall, white-faced and distracted; and there follows the celebrated 'Mad Scene'. It is, of course, operatic madness. Shakespeare, with true dramatic insight, makes his mad folk babble nonsensical little songs and nursery rhymes. But it was a strict convention of nineteenth-century opera that when a heroine went mad she sailed

at once into an elaborate *coloratura aria* which could be tackled only by
an accomplished singer with all her wits about her. Nevertheless,
Donizetti has again shown his skill in compromise by sticking to
convention, and yet at the same time writing music that is sometimes
very simple and very moving:

Spar - gi d'a - ma - ro pian - to
Cast on my grave a flow - er,

It is not in any psychological sense the music of madness, and a
contemporary composer in the same situation would no doubt use
the full resources of modern harmony to suggest the character's
disordered brain. But Donizetti lived too early for that.

In the last scene, Edgar, standing desolate near the tombs of his
ancsetors, watches Lucy's funeral procession go by, and maddened
with grief at the loss of all life held for him, stabs himself. He sings a
last heart-broken farewell to her who was his bride in the sight of God:

Tu che a Dio spie-ga - sti l'a - li,
Thou hast spread thy wings to hea - ven,

Don Pasquale

Libretto arranged by the Composer.   First Production,
Time: Eighteenth Century.[1]   Paris, 1843.

'What cloying meat is love—when matrimony's the sauce to it!
Two years' marriage has debauch'd my five senses. Every thing I
see, every thing I hear, every thing I feel, every thing I smell, and
every thing I taste—methinks has wife in't.'

VANBRUGH: *The Provok'd Wife.*

Don Pasquale is the finest of Donizetti's comedy operas, and in these
sour times many people will no doubt find the wit of the pre-Verdi
Italians more palatable than their sentiment. He is said to have
composed it in eleven days, and although the effect of ease is often the
product of the hardest labour, the score of *Don Pasquale* does suggest a

[1] This period is now usually adopted, though at first the opera was produced in
contemporary costume.

man racing merrily along and delighting in his work. The story is
traditional eighteenth-century comedy: we have the penurious lovers
scheming to benefit by other people's money, the wily intriguer, the
fake notary, the mock marriage and, above all, that indispensable
stock figure of fun, the amorous old man. Artificial comedy would be
in a poor way without the infirmities of age to mock at, and it is
automatically taken for granted that an amorous old man is an
optimistic old fool. If he is a husband he is cuckolded to the top of his
rival's bent; if he is a bachelor (like Don Pasquale) he is gulled, cheated,
tormented and beaten until he is cured of his unwarrantable presumption. It all seems rather heartless, but with artificial comedy we
take Charles Lamb's advice and leave our hearts outside the theatre.
The music of *Don Pasquale* is full of wit and vivacity, equal to Rossini
in invention if not in force, and here and there, in some sparkling little
innuendo, faintly anticipating *Falstaff*.

ACT I: *Scene 1*

Don Pasquale (bass) is hobbling up and down his room, glancing
impatiently at his watch. Surely it is time Dr. Malatesta was here?
Yes—here he comes; and the old man runs eagerly to meet him.
What news? The doctor (baritone) is a gay, debonair man of intrigue, a
kind of aristocratic Figaro. He tells Pasquale he has found the ideal
wife for him—the incarnation of beauty and virtue:

Bel - la sic-co-me un an-ge-lo
Fair as   an an-gel   from a-bove,

"And her name?" asks the old man, trembling with eagerness.
"Malatesta," answers the doctor. "Ah! Then she is——?" "My sister."
Don Pasquale is overjoyed; and when Malatesta has left him, promising
to bring his sister in the evening, he capers round the room like a
schoolboy. He will be married! He will have children! And he proceeds, quite literally, to count his chickens long before they are hatched:

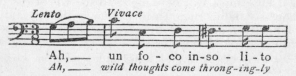

Ah,___ un fo - co in-so - li-to
Ah, ___ wild thoughts come throng-ing-ly

Now for his nephew! Ernesto (tenor) enters, and his uncle reminds him that he has disobeyed his wishes by attaching himself to Norina, the gay young widow, instead of the bride Pasquale intended for him. Very well: he has himself decided to marry, and thereby disinherit him. Ernesto is dumbfounded, and the old man chuckles maliciously at his dismay.

ACT I: *Scene 2*

It is, of course, Norina herself (soprano) who is to be Malatesta's 'sister'. In a vivacious *coloratura aria* she tells us what a merry widow she is, and when the doctor joins her he explains his plot. She will go through a mock wedding ceremony with old Pasquale and afterwards lead him such a dance that he will repent his folly and agree to her marriage with Ernesto. They rehearse the part she is to play in a duet that scintillates with brilliant mischief.

ACT II

Ernesto, realizing that without his uncle's money he cannot marry Norina (no comedy hero worthy of the name was ever capable of earning his own living), sings a wistful farewell to love and happiness:

Cer-che-rò lon-ta-na ter-ra,
Re-fuge in some far land seek-ing,

When Ernesto has disappeared, Malatesta leads in the 'bride' and presents her to Don Pasquale. Norina plays her part well; no little novice from the convent ever simpered so artlessly. Pasquale is enchanted and immediately goes through the mock wedding ceremony. Ernesto comes in and staggers on seeing Norina, but he is quickly 'put wise' by Dr. Malatesta.

The moment the ceremony is over, Norina changes from a saint to a virago, summons the major-domo, doubles his wages and orders him to engage a new staff of servants. She orders new furniture for the whole house and commands the services of a hairdresser, a tailor and a jeweller—all in a few moments. Don Pasquale feebly protests, "Am I not master here?" Then comes Norina's great chance. "You—master? You dolt! You boor! You unmannerly brute!" So the storm breaks;

and by the end of the act she has turned the whole house upside down, driven her pretended husband nearly out of his wits, and openly declared that she will take Ernesto as a lover.

ACT III: *Scene 1*

Don Pasquale now realises that May and December will never agree. His 'wife's' caprices and extravagances have turned his comfortable home into a gilded madhouse; and when he remonstrates with her she smacks his face. After she has gone he finds a letter in which she promises to meet a lover in the garden. It is the last straw, and the old camel feels his back breaking. In a towering rage he sends for Malatesta, and the two of them swear to scotch this intrigue, in a duet which spins along at a speed that makes even the Gilbert-and-Sullivan patter-songs seem leisurely.

ACT III: *Scene 2*

The lover is Ernesto, and in the garden he sings his serenade:

Com' è   gen - til ____   la not-te a mez-zo a - pril,
Soft beams the   light ____   of bal-my sum-mer's   night,

Norina joins him in a charming duet. When Pasquale and Malatesta descend on them like a couple of police officers, Ernesto hides and Norina vows that she is alone. Eventually, however, the three conspirators confess their plot and Don Pasquale is too relieved to be angry with them. The opera ends with a dashing 'Rondo Finale' pointing the moral that crabbed age and youth cannot live together —a truism which has been voiced by poets and philosophers of all time, but which Don Pasquale, presumably not a well-read man, had to find out for himself.

UMBERTO GIORDANO

(1867-   )

Andrea Chénier

Libretto by Luigi Illica.
Time: Late Eighteenth Century.

First Production,
Milan, 1896.

> 'Revolutions have never lightened the burden of tyranny: they
> have only shifted it to another shoulder.'
>
> BERNARD SHAW

Andrea Chénier is thoroughly representative Italian opera of the late
nineteenth century. It is lyrical and sunlit and passionate, splashed
with bright colours, full of strenuous emotional climaxes, and eminently
'singable'—a singers' opera, in fact. Giordano has been described as
'a refined Mascagni', but to me there is also a strong flavour of Puccini
in his music, and he shares the limitations of both these composers.
It is perhaps a paradox that although he gives no key signature from
the first to the last page of *Andrea Chénier*, and so leaves himself free to
wander into any tonality he likes, the ultimate effect is of a score very
much in the one mood. One gets just a slight feeling of monotony;
one suspects also—as sometimes with Puccini, often with Mascagni—
that the emotion is a trifle too easily turned on. The effect is sometimes
grandiose rather than grand, and now and then his melodies seem to
exhaust themselves with their own energy and exuberance. But—they
have energy and exuberance, and where these are disciplined the music
carries one along with a splendid speed and purpose. 'André Chénier'
(to give him his native spelling) was a poet, the only French poet of
real distinction at the time of the French Revolution. It has been said
of the French Revolution that, like Saturn, it devoured its own children;
in other words, the times were not propitious for poetry. Poets may
produce political upheavals, but political upheavals seldom produce
poets.

> *Not that I love thy children, whose dull eyes*
> *See nothing but their own unlovely woe. . . .*

Chénier was not a great poet; but he was a reputable one, and
generally considered the pioneer of French poetry of the last century.
Arsène Houssaye said of him, "All the poets of the nineteenth century,

except Lamartine, set out in the golden argosy of André Chénier to sail across the Ionian Sea and listen to the songs of Homer and Sappho." Chénier's golden argosy had only a short voyage: he was sent to the guillotine at thirty-two—in his own words, 'to die without emptying my quiver'. The opera does not follow the true facts of his career very faithfully, but that probably makes it a better work of art.

Act I

The orchestra strikes at once into a bright, bustling melody that reminds us of the opening of Puccini's *Manon Lescaut*. At the château of the Countess di Coigny (I shall adopt throughout the spelling of the Italian *libretto*) they are preparing for a ball. Gérard (baritone), a lackey and an ardent revolutionary at heart, is haranguing his father, the gardener. "Wretched old man," he says, "for sixty years you have toiled here, a slave to the arrogant aristocracy. Heart and brain cry out against this tyranny; but the time is coming when we shall overthrow it:

Son ses-san-t'an - ni, O vec-chio, che tu ser - vi!__
For six-ty years now, O fa - ther, you have served them!

The Countess (soprano) and her daughter, Maddalena (soprano), with whom Gérard is secretly in love, now enter and, to some courtly and brilliant music, receive their guests. Among the guests is Andrea Chénier (tenor), the poet, who, like Gérard, is dreaming of an age when men will be free. Maddalena asks him to improvise a poem on love. Now the real Chénier, whose idyllic and pastoral poetry Gautier called 'a fresh breath from Greece', would probably have found it hard to resist such a proposal; but the operatic Chénier, to create an operatic situation, accepts it as a political challenge and retorts with an impassioned ode on the wrongs and sufferings of the poor. Above smiles the beautiful azure sky, he says, and below the meadows are full of flowers; nature is bounteous and abundant—and all the while men and women are oppressed, persecuted, dying of hunger:

Un   di   al - l'az-zur-ro   spa - zio guar-dai pro - fon - do
See there, how the sun shines out in the a - zure hea - vens

The guests are scandalised. But not Maddalena: she is caught and held by the poet's fine frenzy. Their eyes meet and they lose their hearts to one another.

ACT II

A café in Paris several years later. The people of France have risen and overthrown their oppressors. Tumbrils rattle along the streets to the guillotine, carrying the poor feckless men and women who were so slow to see the abyss that was opening at their feet. Also, as so often happens, the revolutionaries themselves have become tyrants, and are sharply divided into warring factions. Chénier has offended those in power by denouncing Robespierre and is being spied on. Maddalena, who has written him a letter, now seeks him out, and in a passionate duet they confess their mutual love:

It is at least possible that Puccini had this melody in his subconscious mind when he wrote the lovers' duet in *Gianni Schicchi*. Gérard, now an important political figure, surprises Chénier and Maddalena. The two men draw their swords and fight, and Gérard is wounded. "Fly, Chénier, fly," he gasps out as he falls; "protect Maddalena." The lovers escape.

ACT III

At a revolutionary tribunal the crowd sings the 'Carmagnole'. Chénier has been captured, and it falls to Gérard to sign the warrant condemning his rival to death. "An enemy of his country," he says; but in his heart he knows that Chénier is no enemy of his country. And the conflict of his feelings expands into a declamatory *aria* whose main melody begins:

Maddalena pleads for her lover's life, and, Tosca-like, offers to give herself to Gérard if he will save him. At the trial Gérard protests that the indictment against Chénier is false; but the mob clamours loudly for the poet's death, and Chénier is condemned.

Act IV

At midnight in the prison of St. Lazare, Chénier waits for the final summons. 'The messenger of death will soon makes these long dark corridors echo with my name,' wrote the poet in his last hour. But—he is not to die alone: Maddalena steals in. She has bribed the gaoler to let her take the place of a woman prisoner. She will go to the guillotine with her lover. In a last duet—

La nos-tra   mor-teè il trionfo del - l'a - mor!
Our mor-tal   love will   tri-umph o - ver   death!

—they sing their farewell to the world; but not in grief: "Our death is a triumph of love. It will make our passion immortal!"

CHARLES GOUNOD

(1818–1893)

Faust

Libretto by Jules Barbier and Michel Carré, after Goethe.
Time: Sixteenth Century.

First Production,
Paris, 1859.

> 'We must not so much as taste of the devil's broth, lest at last he
> bring us to eat of his beef.'
>
> THOMAS HALL: *Funebria Florae.*

Faust is the world's most popular opera; consequently it has been
condemned as strongly as it has been admired. Its critics angrily
assert that composer and *librettists* degraded Goethe's tremendous
drama of the soul of man to the level of a penny novelette, turning
the frustrated philosopher into a common seducer who sells his soul
for a pretty face, and the spirit of evil into a combination of pantomime demon and tavern brawler. Its admirers obstinately continue
to fill the theatre whenever it is played, to revel in its swift dramatic
action and to whistle its splendid tunes. They are both right; and the
best course is to forget Goethe's *Faust* for what it was and enjoy
Gounod's *Faust* for what it is: a lurid and exciting musical melodrama.

ACT I

Be punctual: because some of the opera's very finest music is in
the first forty bars of the orchestral introduction. Here is the true
Faust, yearning to break down the barriers of human knowledge and
pierce the secret of the universe. Then the high mood suddenly collapses and we drift into the rather tawdry melody of Valentine's song,
'Even Bravest Heart'. It is just as though the composer, having got so
far, threw down his pen and said: "Oh, come, what's the use of this?
Let's chuck it and make money!" When the curtain rises we see Faust
(tenor) in his study, an old man bowed with weight of knowledge.
What has life brought him? Like Browning's Cleon, he has reached
the age when he knows most and can least enjoy. He hears the voices
of youths and maidens outside. They know nothing, but they have that
for which he would sacrifice all. In his despair he curses God and calls
on the powers of evil. Mephistopheles (bass) appears. "I come to

61

serve you," he says. "What would you have? Riches? Glory? A kingdom?" And Faust replies, "I would have what outbuys them all —youth." The devil states his terms and, when Faust hesitates, shows him a vision of the lovely Marguérite, to a melody we hear later in the love-duet. Faust hesitates no longer. The bargain is sealed. The years fall from him, and he and Mephistopheles sing an exultant duet:

A moi - les plai-sirs— Les jeun - es mai-tress-es
Be mine— the de - light— Of beau - ty's car - es - ses

Act II

Soldiers, students and villagers are drinking and singing outside the village inn. Valentine (baritone) is about to march to the war, and, clasping a medallion given him by his sister, Marguérite, he sings the famous song which Gounod interpolated specially for Santley in the English production:

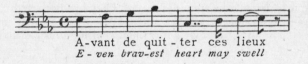

A-vant de quit - ter ces lieux
E - ven brav-est heart may swell

Siebel (mezzo-soprano), a youth humbly in love with Marguérite, promises to protect her while Valentine is away. Mephistopheles joins the drinkers outside the tavern and sings a cynical but splendidly rousing song extolling the power of gold:

Le veau d'or——— est tou-jours de - bout!
Clear the way——— for the Calf of Gold!

He then shows his devilish power by changing the wine and shattering Valentine's sword in a quarrel. The soldiers guess who he is and retreat, each holding up his sword to form a cross. Faust, now a handsome cavalier, joins Mephistopheles, and during a village dance—

—they perceive Marguérite (soprano) on her way home from church. Faust accosts her with the utmost respect, but she timidly refuses his escort and hurries away.

ACT III

The garden of Marguérite's house. Siebel comes in through the gate, and to a dainty little air—

—lays some flowers at her door. Mephistopheles leads in Faust, saying, "This is the place," and later Faust, left alone, contemplates the humble cottage made holy by the presence of maidenhood.

Mephistopheles has quite a different estimate of maidenhood; and beside Siebel's flowers he lays a casket of jewels, confident which gift will prove the more attractive. He is right. When he and Faust have retreated, we see Marguérite at her spinning-wheel, singing the plaintive ballad of the King in Thule and breaking off now and then to wonder who was the stranger who addressed her that day:

Suddenly she notices the casket, opens it and, in a fever of delight, begins to deck herself with the jewels. And here her music changes completely, transforming her from a simple rustic maid into a vain and luxurious woman.

The rest of this act is really a long-drawn-out quartet, Faust and Marguérite swiftly approaching the consummation of love, while Mephistopheles obligingly pairs off with Martha (contralto), Marguérite's old nurse, and keeps her out of the way, commenting humorously on his bad bargain. The music is Gounod at his best, full of tender sentiment, coloured like a lovers' moon and fragrant with the perfumes of the summer night.

Act IV

The dream of love is over, and now the drama begins to move inexorably to its tragic end. The soldiers are returning from the war, and they file down the street singing their marching-song, one of the best-known tunes in the world:

It has often been condemned as vulgar, but it is surely just the kind of swinging, four-square tune that soldiers *would* sing, and is no vulgarer than 'Tipperary', to which millions of soldiers marched in the first world war. When the soldiers have passed, Faust and Mephistopheles enter and linger by Marguérite's house. Faust is remorseful, but Mephistopheles jeers at him and sings a mock serenade, holding his sword like a guitar and strumming on it with his finger-nails:

At the sound of Mephistopheles's voice Valentine rushes out to them. He has learned of his sister's disgrace and he recognises and attacks her seducer. Mephistopheles watches his chance and, suddenly darting in, helps to give Valentine his death-wound. They hurry away, and a moment later the crowd comes in, guided by the noise of the duel. Marguérite bends over her dying brother, but with his last breath he curses her for a harlot. The scene changes to the interior of a church. Marguérite is trying to pray, but all the while the voice of Mephistopheles thunders in her ears, and at last she falls in a faint, the pious worshippers carefully stepping round her body as they leave the church.

ACT V

It is the end. Marguérite has killed her child and Faust finds her in prison, on a miserable bed of straw, awaiting her execution. When she hears his voice she wanders back to the past, singing little snatches of the music that gave magic to their love. Faust desperately tries to rouse her. He can rescue her, he says, and he urges her to break out of the prison with him. Mephistopheles appears at the door. "Hasten," he says, "it is time! The horses pant in the courtyard!" But Marguérite catches sight of him and knows him for the Fiend. She screams, "I will not go with thee!" and bursts into an impassioned prayer for salvation:

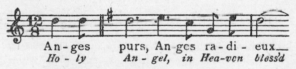

An - ges   purs, An - ges ra - di - eux
Ho - ly   An - gel, in Hea-ven bless'd

"Go," she says; "I am not thy victim!" and falls back lifeless on her straw. And as Mephistopheles drags Faust away to perdition we see the soul of Marguérite borne up to Heaven.

Romeo and Juliet

Libretto by Jules Barbier and Michel Carré, after Shakespeare.   First Production, Time: Fourteenth Century.   Paris, 1867.

'O lyric Love, half angel and half bird
And all a wonder and a wild desire,—'
ROBERT BROWNING: *The Ring and the Book.*

Romeo and Juliet has never been as popular as *Faust*. It lacks *Faust's* dramatic tension and gripping narrative power, and although it has passages more delicate and sensitive than any in the earlier opera, it

E

never hits the target quite so squarely. Perhaps Gounod aimed too high in trying to match the most breathlessly beautiful of Shakespeare's plays, the incomparable rose of all youthful poetry. Gounod's lovers have not quite the fresh, springtime magic of Shakespeare's; they belong more to nineteenth-century Paris than to fourteenth-century Verona. The houses of Montague and Capulet are opera houses. It may be argued, of course, that Gounod aimed almost as high in setting Goethe; but then, he did not set Goethe: what he set was a highly effective melodrama made from Goethe's material. Nevertheless, *Romeo and Juliet* has a distinct poetic charm of its own, and will always hold the affection of those for whom the coarser texture of *Faust* may have worn threadbare.

Prologue

This is sung by the chorus on a darkened stage:

> *Two households, both alike in dignity,*
> *In fair Verona, where we lay our scene,*
> *From ancient grudge break to new mutiny,*
> *Where civil blood makes civil hands unclean.*

The orchestra follows with a tender melody which expresses the love of Romeo and Juliet and which is heard frequently during the opera.

Act I

They are dancing at Capulet's house, and the jewels and brightly coloured dresses gleam in the light of the torches. Romeo (tenor) and his friends approach. It is death for any Montague to be seen there, and Romeo has a premonition of disaster, although he cannot know, of course, that it is love, not hate, that will at last destroy him. He has been troubled by a dream. "O, then," says Mercutio (baritone), "I see Queen Mab hath been with you." And he sings the ballad of Queen Mab, a nimble, flashing *scherzo* for the voice, in which we seem to hear the rustle of fairy wings. In the hall the fourteen-year-old Juliet (soprano) expresses, not her own feelings, but the feelings of any popular *prima donna*, in the intoxicating and highly sophisticated 'Valse Song'. A mistake, if you will, but a mistake that is very agreeable to listen to:

Je   veux   vi - - vre ____
Song,   jest,   per-fume and dan - ces,

Romeo and Juliet meet and exchange gallantries in a courtly and charming little duet:

Ange. a - do - ra - ble,   ma main cou-pa-ble
O   shrine of beau- ty,   If I   pro-fane thee

But Tybalt (tenor), Juliet's cousin, has recognised Romeo and spoken his name—a name that strikes Juliet to the very heart. "My grave is like to be my wedding-bed!"

Act II

Romeo leaps the orchard walls and stands beneath Juliet's windows. "It is the east, and Juliet is the sun. Arise, fair sun, and kill the envious moon!"

Ah! le - ve- toi, soleil!   fais pâ-lir les é - toi - les
Ah! fair- est dawn, a-rise 'Neath thy ray Hes-per fail - eth

Juliet appears at the window and they pledge their love. He will send to her tomorrow, saying where they may meet and marry. And they linger on in the enchanted night because parting is such sweet sorrow.

Act III

The lovers have met in the cell of Friar Laurence (bass). There shall 'holy church incorporate two in one'. And the Friar invokes the blessing of God:

Dieu,_ qui fis l'homme à ton i - ma - ge!
O____ smile, fair Heav'n up- on this mar - riage,

To music of a strength and nobility rare in Gounod, he joins their hands and pronounces them man and wife. Towards the end of the scene, part of the early duet is repeated, but transformed into a majestic, chorale-like theme now the love that began so light-heartedly is solemnised in the sight of heaven.

The scene changes to a street in Verona. Stephano (soprano), Romeo's page, taunts the Capulets in a bantering song:

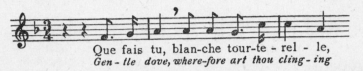

The Capulet servants attack him. Other members of both households come on the scene, and soon a violent street fight is raging. The excitement rises to a feverish pitch. Tybalt slays Mercutio; and Romeo, who has hung back because Tybalt is now his kinsman, bounds forward to avenge his friend, and runs Tybalt through. The Duke of Verona appears and sees a street littered with bloody corpses. Again these brawling Montagues and Capulets! In a towering rage he banishes Romeo. Romeo leans on his sword, stunned by this death-blow. Then he slowly finds his voice—

—a spacious melody, afterwards taken up by the chorus. Coincidence-hunters will notice in it a rising phrase identical in line and key with a phrase in Act III of Verdi's *Othello*—composed twenty years later.

Act IV

Under cover of night Romeo steals back to Verona to be with his bride. The scene is one long love duet, the chief theme beginning:

But Juliet is to be married to Count Paris, and in the next scene Capulet brings in Friar Laurence to instruct her in her duties. When they are alone the Friar gives her a phial. In it is a potion which will cause her to fall into a deathlike slumber. As he tells her this the orchestra plays a slow and beautiful melody whose chords fall as gently as the benediction of sleep:

They will think her dead, and they will lay her in the Capulet sepulchre to await burial. There her husband will waken her and together they will begin a new life far from Verona.

ACT V

Those who know Shakespeare's tragedy will remember how piteously these plans miscarry. Romeo, thinking Juliet dead, breaks into the sepulchre.

> *O my love! my wife!*
> *Death that hath suck'd the honey of thy breath,*
> *Hath had no power yet upon thy beauty.*

He pledges her in a phial of poison. Juliet wakens—just one moment too late. They sing an impassioned duet, recalling in their music the early splendour of their love, and when Romeo sinks down from the effects of the poison, Juliet stabs herself. And so these lovers make a swan-like end, fading in music; not great music, but music full of love and pity. Gounod did not equal Shakespeare, but he did not dishonour him.

GUSTAV HOLST

(1874-1934)

The Perfect Fool

Libretto by the Composer.

Time: legendary.

First Production,
London, 1923.

'Speak but one word to me over the corn.'
WILLIAM MORRIS.

The Perfect Fool is included in this book because I think it one of the funniest of all operas, and because I hope some enterprising management will revive it. It and *Gianni Schicchi* would make an ideal evening of comedy. This short opera is the one work in which Gustav Holst—that gentle creature who strikingly belied his personality by writing such iron-tongued music—put into sound the spirit of sly mischief that lay behind his benign, thickly magnifying spectacles. 'The author asks that the spirit of high comedy shall be maintained throughout,' Holst wrote in a foreword; but people were determined to see more in it than just high comedy. The Princess, they said, was the Muse (or, if you like, the spirit of opera), who was wooed in turn by the Troubadour (Italian opera), the Traveller (German opera), and eventually fell in love with the Fool (British public), who loutishly rejected her. An entertaining allegory; but it is hard to tell which bank of the Nile it favours. Who, for instance, is the Wizard? He does indeed suggest a Klingsor in reduced circumstances; but why have *two* Wagnerian figures—the Wizard and the Traveller? Much better shove these allegories into the river, concentrate on this impish frolicsome music, with its frequent stretches of Holst's characteristic seven-in-a-bar measure, and enjoy *The Perfect Fool* as a charming musical farce. In short, let 'the spirit of high comedy be maintained throughout'.

We can't prevent it. As soon as the curtain rises we see the Wizard (baritone) brewing a love-potion—

Spir-its of the Earth, Come at my call! O-bey my voice!

—and we feel that if Wagner had written a fourth act to *Parsifal*, Klingsor or his successor might have begun it in just those accents. Then the Wizard summons the spirits of water and fire also, and each group gives its ingredients to the magic cauldron. The mother (contralto) comes on, dragging her son, the Fool (speaking part),[1] after her.

He is the most uncouth bumpkin that was ever pulled through a hedge backwards. Every time they stop he collapses in the road and sinks into a stupor. But his mother has high hopes of him, for, Parsifal-like, he is the subject of a prophecy: "He wins a bride with a glance of his eye; with a look he kills a foe; he achieves where others fail—with ONE WORD." The Wizard rehearses to her his love song for the Princess, who is soon to pass that way. She, also, is the subject of a prophecy: 'She shall marry the man who does the deed no other can do.' The Wizard then composes himself to sleep, and the ambitious mother steals his magic potion, pours it down her son's throat and substitutes water for it. The Princess (soprano) arrives with her train and complains, in a melody of austere charm, how tiresome it is to be so beautiful that no man can look on her without loving her. Her first suitor is the Wizard, who sings his own praises, to the main theme of the 'Dance of the Spirits of Earth'. He drinks the potion that is to restore his youth; but as it now consists only of water, no miracle takes place. He storms away, swearing vengeance. Then comes the Troubador (tenor), a kind of deposed Duke of Mantua, who tells his love, to a typical Verdi-gurdy accompaniment:

From far-off land I come, A— land of vine and o-live tree:

But alas! Before long he finds, as so many other confident people have found, that Italian opera is not so easy as it sounds, and towards the end of a pretentious cadenza his voice fails him. The Princess finishes the cadenza for him with a disdainful brilliance and tells him to go home and learn to sing better. But who is this who strides forward with such histrionic solemnity? It is the Traveller (baritone). He wears a voluminous gown, an immense hat and a beard like a doormat, and has altogether the air of Wagner's Wanderer, still fresh and vigorous despite his thousand or so leagues a day. He enters to grandiose chords recalling those of the Wanderer's entrance into Mime's smithy, and declares his love in the most extravagant terms:

[1] As the Fool speaks only one word in the whole opera, this is perhaps an extravagant way of describing him.

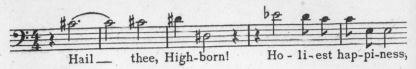

Hail— thee, High-born!   Ho-li-est hap-pi-ness,

"But, sir," says the Princess (to the notes of Siegfried's horn-call), "I think we have heard this before." "Nay, O nay," shouts the Traveller. "Noisiest negative!——" and he trips over the Fool, who wakes and stares straight up at the Princess. 'He wins a bride with a glance of his eye.' He has done so: the Princess suffers a sheer lightning-stroke of infatuation and stands rooted to the spot, gazing at him. Everyone is astounded. "She's fallen in love with a beggar," they cry. "She's bewitched!" And the Troubadour gathers his retainers round him and sings, "She shall be mine! She shall be mine!" in the best early-Verdi manner. Every now and again the Traveller interrupts them with explosions of Wagnerian alliteration: "Vaulting vengeance my bosom burneth!" and similar thunderbolts of invective familiar to all who know their *Ring* in English. But now a sudden silence falls on them: a shepherd has stumbled in, breathless with running. He tells a tale of panic: the countryside is on fire; the fire is sweeping towards them, djinns and demons dancing in the flames. "Our land is doomed," he cries; "hell is here!" The Princess heeds nothing. "What matters hell?" she sings; "I am in heaven"—gazing in ecstasy at the Fool. The excitement rises. Peasants carrying bundles rush across the back of the stage, lurid in the red glare of the approaching fire. They all urge the Princess to save herself; but she is lost to everything but the miracle that has transfigured her.

The incendiary is, as we have guessed, the Wizard, who now appears urging on the spirits of fire. General stampede. The mother alone remains calm. She turns her son's face towards the Wizard: 'With a look he kills a foe!' And he does: the Wizard collapses and is at once swallowed up in the earth. The fire dies down. The Fool has fulfilled two thirds of the prophecy: he has won a bride with a glance of his eye, and with a look he has killed a foe. The third? The Princess asks him if he loves her; and he achieves, where others fail, with one word—"NO!" He then falls asleep, just as the High Priest approaches to crown him.

And so Holst brings down the curtain. What have we learned? Nothing much, perhaps; but we have heard a great deal of very vital and exhilarating music, and we have certainly had a good laugh— chiefly at the expense of Verdi and Wagner. Still, they can afford it.

ENGELBERT HUMPERDINCK

(1854–1921)

Hänsel and Gretel

Libretto by Adelheid Wette.
Time: Fairy Time.

First Production,
Munich, 1893.

> 'Now through the dusk
> With muffled bell
> The Dustman comes
> The world to tell,
> Night's elfin lanterns
> Burn and gleam
> In the twilight, wonderful
> World of Dream.'
>
> WALTER DE LA MARE.

Hänsel and Gretel always sets me off parodying a rhyme that was popular in my childhood:

> *Sugar and spice*
> *And all that's nice,*
> *That's what this opera's made of!*

It is indeed a lovely, luscious, treacly score, in whose richly spiced harmonies one can almost *taste* the succulent cake and candy that plaster the walls of the Witch's little cottage. There is a flavour of Wagner here—the Wagner who created David and made Sachs unbend to his boyish fancies with such gruff kindliness—a faint echo of Weber, perhaps, and a clear note of the horns of elfland that blew through the forests of German folklore. It is, above all, a *children's* opera. When one listens to this music one's vision dwindles until everything else is portentously magnified as it was long ago: when the cot was a plunging galleon and the nightlight was the North Star; when the dark reaches of the nursery stretched to the farthest limits of ocean and the shadows on the ceiling were grotesque, malformed witches riding on broomsticks across a haggard sky. That is the essential magic of *Hänsel and Gretel*: it charms children because they *are* children and grown-ups because they can remember when they were. The Overture is of the *pot-pourri* type, combining the most colourful elements of the score in a neat and gracefully executed patchwork. Then comes

ACT I

and we are in the cottage of Peter, the broom-maker. All is lovingly
true to tradition: it is a poor cottage (it always is) and it stands on the
edge of a vast and mysterious forest (it always does). Hänsel (mezzo-
soprano) is making brooms, and on the other side of the fireplace
Gretel (soprano) is knitting a stocking. They are hungry and discontented; but children's woes are quickly forgotten, and soon they
begin to dance and play together. The mother (mezzo-soprano) bursts
in at the height of their merriment. Like all mothers in fairy-tales, she
is a good-natured soul whom years of worry and poverty have turned
into a scold. She rates the children soundly and sends them into the
forest to gather strawberries. By and by we hear the notes of a rollicking
song, and the broom-maker (baritone), a typical fairy-tale father,
jovial, feckless and improvident, comes into sight:

Well, he may be a little tipsy, but he has had a good day at the
market, sold his brooms at the highest rates and brought home money
and provisions. But—where are the children? The mother tells him
she has sent them into the forest. He stands aghast. Into the forest?
Doesn't she know about the horrible Witch who lures children into
her red-hot oven and roasts them for her dinner? Getting more and
more excited, he enlarges on the blood-curdling details until the
mother is as frightened as he. Together they rush out to seek Hänsel
and Gretel.

ACT II

The orchestra plays the 'Witches' Ride', and then we are in the
heart of the forest with the children. They have filled their baskets
with strawberries, but now they fall to quarrelling and eating them in
turn until—consternation!—they are all gone! It is too late to pick
any more. They must get home; but which way is it? Surely the forest
is growing larger and denser and darker every moment? The shadows
close in and a thick mist fills the spaces between the trees. They begin to
see weird women moving in the mist, goblins capering in the gloom,

ghostly faces grimacing at them through the foliage. But soon the mist lifts in one corner and a little grey man with a sack on his back hops forward. He is the Sandman (soprano), a friendly little being, and from his sack he scatters sand over their eyes:

Der klei-ne Sand-mann bin ich,
I shut the child - ren's peep-ers,

They are sleepy; it is too late and too dark to go home. But first they must sing their evening prayer:

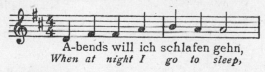

A-bends will ich schlafen gehn,
When at night I go to sleep,

Guardian angels slowly descend on to the stage and form a ring round the sleeping children.

ACT III

It is daybreak. The Dew Fairy (soprano) wakens the children by shaking dewdrops over them from a bluebell. He sings a dainty little song which begins like that of the Sandman, but rises later in ascending phrases, suggesting the rising of the sun, whereas the later phrases of the Sandman's song slanted downwards. The children listen to the birds greeting the morning. Slowly the mists rise and then, to their astonishment, in place of a clump of fir-trees, they see a quaint little house with an oven on one side and a cage on the other. It is a tempting house—built of chocolate cream, cake, candy, Turkish delight and other ingredients of children's dreams! They begin to eat it; but suddenly the Witch appears, casts a spell over them and eventually imprisons them. What a luscious feast they will make! And she seizes a broomstick and begins to ride round the house, laughing and crowing to a fantastic polka:

Hurr hopp hopp hopp, Ga-lopp lopp lopp! Mein Besen-gaul,
So hop, hop, hop, gal-lop, lop, lop! My broomstick nag,

The rest of the story is well known to all who, when they were children, had the sense to read nonsense like this instead of books of the more 'improving' type. The Witch orders Gretel to get into the oven to see if the honey cakes are done. Gretel pretends to be stupid and asks the Witch to show her how; and while she is demonstrating they push her in. The oven collapses and a group of imprisoned children are released. The father and mother join them, the Witch reappears, 'done to a turn' as a gigantic honey cake, and all join in a hymn of thanksgiving, to the melody of the evening prayer. The curtain falls, and, a little regretfully, we resume our proper ages.

RUGGIERO LEONCAVALLO

(1858–1919)

Pagliacci

Libretto by the Composer.
Time: 1865–70.

First Production,
Milan, 1892.

'And let those that play your clowns speak no more than is set down for them.'
SHAKESPEARE: *Hamlet.*

Pagliacci is the second of what are usually called the heavenly twins of opera and affectionately known as *Cav. and Pag.* Both Mascagni and Leoncavallo wrote several other operas (Leoncavallo even set *La Bohème*), but none of these found much favour, and to the general public Mascagni means *Cavalleria Rusticana* and Leoncavallo means *Pagliacci.* The two works are roughly of the same length and have much in common: both are little masterpieces of stagecraft; both tell brutal, hard-hitting stories of love and crime, set to music of a fierce, elemental passion that punches home the dramatic crises with terrific effect. Leoncavallo's score is on the whole the more refined of the two: one is conscious of a more poetic, more discriminating mind behind it, and the music has occasionally a dignity and beauty that are missing from the rather fetid emotionalism of Mascagni.

PROLOGUE

The opera begins with four pompous chords making an abrupt and striking rhythmical figure. All the shabby glamour of the circus is here—the showman's drum, the smell of the sawdust ring. Tonio, the clown (baritone), appears between the curtains. Their play is not a piece of pretty make-believe, he says: the characters are living men and women, and the story we are to hear is true. And it really was: Leoncavallo took his *libretto* from a police-court case.

ACT I

So here is the story. We are at a crossroads near a village. On the right is the stage of a 'fit-up' travelling theatre. The villagers are here, wildly excited, eager to get a glimpse of the strolling players. Canio (tenor) and his troupe march on to the beating of drums and the cheers of the crowd. "At seven o'clock this evening," he sings, "I invite you to our performance." One of the peasants makes a flippant remark about Canio's wife, Nedda. Canio turns on him, and the laughter suddenly dies:

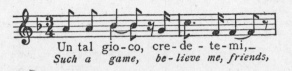

Un tal gio-co, cre-de-te-mi,—
Such a game, be-lieve me, friends,

He goes off for a drink with the villagers. Nedda is alone. But she is not thinking of Canio; she is thinking of Silvio, her lover. She hears the birds singing overhead and her heart sings with them:

Stri-do-no las-sù,——
High a-loft they cry——

Tonio is attracted by her singing. He shambles forward from behind the theatre and clumsily attempts to make love to her. She strikes him in the face with her whip, and he slinks off, swearing revenge. Through the bushes comes Silvio (baritone), a young farmer with whom Nedda has broken her marriage vows. He eventually persuades her to run away with him:

E al-lor per-chè, di— tu m'hai stre-ga-to
Why hast thou taught me— love's mag-ic stor-y

Suddenly there is a noise in the undergrowth. Tonio has brought Canio back to spy on them. Canio bursts in, and Silvio dashes away through the trees. The terrible truth falls on Canio like a thunderbolt, and in one moment he changes from a boisterous boon companion to a wronged husband, demented with rage and grief. His whole world has crashed into ruin. The woman he has loved and trusted is false to him. He stands, a big, stupid figure, stunned by forces of emotion he never thought existed. An hour ago life was rich, life was happy. Wh has God done this to him? But—it is nearly time for the show. And the show must go on. He must play the fool—yes, laugh and sing— even though there is hell in his heart.

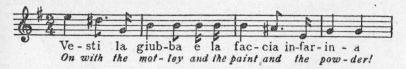

Ve - sti la giub-ba e la fac - cia in-far-in - a
On with the mot - ley and the paint and the pow - der!

ACT II

And the show does go on. But before the curtain rises the orchestra points the tragedy in an intermezzo, recalling themes from the prologue. Then—it is seven o'clock and the villagers are streaming in and taking their seats on the wooden benches. Silvio slips in quietly while Nedda is going round collecting the money, and as he hands her his coin he whispers—reminding her that they are to escape together that night.

THE PLAY

The curtain rises on the mimic stage and the Harlequinade begins. Columbine (Nedda) listens while Harlequin (Peppe—tenor) sings a serenade beneath her window:

O_____ Co-lom -bi - na il te - ne - ro fido Ar - lec - chin
O_____ Co-lum-bine, un - bar to me thy lat-tice high,

The Clown (Tonio) enters, and in a comic scene he contrives to give a ting to some of his words which only Nedda understands. The audience laughs delightedly at his fooling. But presently the door opens and Punchinello (Canio) stands there. At once we have a premonition of tragedy—like a cold wind suddenly blowing. He breathes heavily and staggers like a drunken man. The white powder on his face is blotched with tears. A shout of laughter greets him and he starts in bewilderment. What are they laughing at? Oh yes, of course—he must play his part. And, stumbling at every cue, he begins to blunder miserably through his dialogue. Yesterday it was the breath of life to him. Tonight it means nothing; he can't even remember it. And when

Nedda tries to rally him—"Come, Punchinello, Punchinello!"—he loses all control in a tremendous outburst—

No! Pa-gliac-cio non son;
No Pun-chi-nel-lo no more!

"—I am a man again; the man who loved you and whom you have wronged!" The spectators have never seen such fine acting. "Bravo!" they shout, rising in their seats. But Nedda is now thoroughly frightened. She tries to resume the play.

It is no good. By this time Canio is past all reason; he no longer knows what he is doing. "Tell me thy lover's name!" he yells at her. "His name! His name!" One by one the spectators scramble to their feet. "Stop them! Stop them! He's in earnest!" As Nedda tries to leap down into the audience, Canio stabs her. "Silvio!" she cries with her last breath. "Nedda!" calls Silvio, and fights his way to the front. Canio springs upon him—"Ah, 'tis you, then!"—and drives the dagger into his heart. The people surge round him, clutching at his arm. He turns to them with a ghastly smile. "The comedy is ended!"

PIETRO MASCAGNI

(1863–1945)

Cavalleria Rusticana

Libretto by G. Targioni-Tizetti and G. Menasci,
  after the short story by Giovanni Verga.
Time: Late Nineteenth Century.

First Production,
Rome, 1890.

> 'The ground was level there; the daffodils
> Glimmered and danced beneath their cautious feet,
> Quartering for openings for the blow that kills.
> Beyond the bubbling brook a thrush was sweet.
> Quickly the footsteps slid; with feint and cheat,
> The weapons poised and darted and withdrew.'
>
> JOHN MASEFIELD: The Daffodil Fields.

Cavalleria Rusticana is the first and best of Mascagni's operas and the most successful one-act opera ever written. He followed this meteoric triumph with a number of other works, but though he occasionally wrote better music, he never recaptured that stunning force of attack, that incandescent flair for drama, that perfect timing of the knock-out blow that make *Cavalleria Rusticana* one of music's minor masterpieces. Here is a score every line of which is packed tight with combustible passion, and along which the conductor's hand moves like a match lighting up a train of crackling fireworks. But it is useless to analyse this opera: the sheer punch of the thing knocks you flat—even though, when you get up again, you may be slightly ashamed of having been knocked flat so easily.

The orchestra begins quietly, rising to a passionate climax, and then the music seems to catch its breath, so to speak, as we hear behind the curtain the notes of a harp and the voice of Turiddu singing to Lola—singing of the love that is to ruin four lives:

O Lo - la, ch'ai di lat - ti la cam-mi - sa,—
O Lo - la, pret - ty one, white as the may, love,—

The curtain rises on a village in Sicily. It is Easter morning and the peasants cross the square and pass into the church. Santuzza

F

(soprano) enters and speaks to an elderly woman: "Mother Lucia, where is your son, Turiddu?" As Lucia (contralto) answers her we hear the cracking of a whip and the jingle of bells and in comes Alfio (baritone), the carrier, singing a song of the open road:

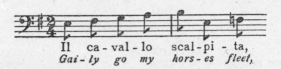

Il ca - val - lo scal - pi - ta,
Gai - ly go my hors - es fleet,

It is time for Mass. The villagers assemble in the square and sing the triumphant Easter hymn:

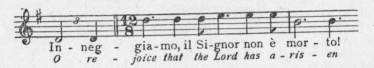

In - neg - gia - mo, il Si - gnor non è mor - to!
O re - joice that the Lord has a - ris - en

Santuzza and Lucia are left alone; and Santuzza pours out her bitter grief:

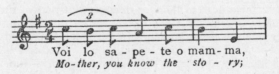

Voi lo sa - pe - te o mam - ma,
Mo - ther, you know the sto - ry;

The gay and handsome Turiddu has returned from the wars, she says, to find Lola, his former love, married to Alfio. He has consoled himself with Santuzza and made her his mistress. But now his fancy turns again to Lola. Santuzza is dishonoured, despised and deserted, but— she still loves him. "O Mother, go into the church and pray for me! I cannot go in; I am accursed!" Turiddu swaggers in. Santuzza bars his way to the church. Is it all over, she asks him piteously; does he love her no more? "Yes, it *is* over," shouts Turiddu. "Get out of my way!" At that moment Lola passes, singing a saucy little *stornello*:

Fior di giag - gio - lo___
O gen - tle flow'r of gold___

Lola disappears into the church and Turiddu starts after her. But
Santuzza clutches him desperately in a last appeal—

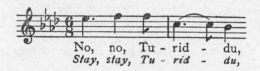

No, no, Tu - rid - du,
Stay, stay, Tu - rid - du,

—a duet that rises to a terrific climax in mounting, throbbing phrases
that seem to spurt out like jets of blood. Turiddu tears at her hands to
free himself—how hateful is the love of one whom we have ceased to
love!—and finally dashes her to the ground and runs into the church,
her curse ringing in his ears. Santuzza struggles to her feet as Alfio
strolls in. Now is her moment! And in a fit of jealous rage she tells
him the whole shameful truth about Turiddu and his wife. He becomes
livid with fury and strides off, swearing to kill Turiddu. Santuzza
follows him, now thoroughly frightened at the storm she has unloosed.
After the familiar intermezzo—

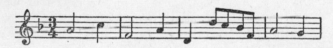

—which is played to an empty stage, the drama sweeps impetuously
to its climax. The villagers stream out of the church and Turiddu
leads them in a vivacious drinking-song:

Vi-va il vi - no spu-meg-gian-te
See the mer-ry wine is wink-ing

Alfio appears, and at the sight of his death-white face the song dies on
the drinkers' lips. Turiddu tries to laugh away the tension and offers
him a drink. "No, thank you," says Alfio, deadly calm. "The drink
you offer is poisoned!" Turiddu, stung by the insult, springs at him
and bites his ear—a challenge to a duel. "Very well, Master Turiddu,"
says Alfio, "we understand each other. I will wait for you in the
garden." Left alone, Turiddu is suddenly seized with panic. What has
he done? It was the wine—the wine made him mad. He calls out for

his mother. "Bless me, Mother, as once you blessed me when I went to battle!":

Ma pri-ma vo-glio che mi be-ne-di-te
But ere I leave thee, bless me O my Mo-ther!

He tears himself from her and rushes to his fate. In a few moments it is all over. The villagers come running back from the garden, and Santuzza falls senseless as a woman's voice shrieks out: "Turiddu is killed! Turiddu is killed!"

JULES MASSENET

(1842–1912)

Manon

Libretto by Henri Meilhac and Philippe Gille after Prévost.
Time: Eighteenth Century.

First Production,
Paris, 1884.

> 'O never give the heart outright,
> For they, for all smooth lips can say,
> Have given their hearts up to the play.
> And who could play it well enough
> If deaf and dumb and blind with love?
> He that made this knows all the cost,
> For he gave all his heart and lost.'
>
> W. B. YEATS.

Manon is the most representative of Massenet's operas, and shows his qualities at their best: his gift of scented, voluptuous melody, his pretty pathos, his feminine grace and sentiment, and that romantic fervour in his music that sometimes rises to real passion. All these are combined in a score that displays tasteful musicianship, characterisation and an astute sense of the theatre.

Prévost's novel, that little sachet of sentiment, was perfect material for Massenet. It is the testament of one who indeed 'gave all his heart and lost'. Like his hero, Des Grieux, Prévost himself had apparently been enriched and degraded by a disastrous love, and here he told of the *splendeurs et misères* of his own youth. He wrote other books, probably with more ambitious care, but they are forgotten—perhaps for that very reason. Only this remains—a simple little tale; in some ways, perhaps, a rather silly little tale, and yet an immortal one. Manon is an eternal type: the embodiment of charm and beauty without moral sense. She is as instinctive as an animal, a beautiful and utterly innocent exponent of what we call 'cupboard love'. She sees no earthly or heavenly reason why she should not leave her bewildered lover when she wants the luxuries he cannot buy, and then return to him and expect their love to begin again exactly where it left off. One cannot hate a creature who is so honestly unconscious of the evil she does; one can only love her and suffer. There will always be men to love and suffer for Manon; and those who elude her emerge richer in well-being but poorer in spirit.

Manon's story is told to a stranger by the Chevalier des Grieux, and it is through his tortured mind that we follow this tragedy of love without esteem. Nothing she does can shake his devotion. He suffers incredible indignities for her sake, and sinks deeper and deeper into dishonour, degradation, self-contempt and despair. When she dies, his last act of love is to dig a grave with his sword and hands and cover the beauty that has inspired and ruined his life. We may think that such fidelity deserved a worthier object; yet if he had found it, we should be poorer by one imperishable love-story and at least four operas. Auber, Halévy, Massenet and Puccini all set *Manon* to music. Massenet's and Puccini's operas are the only ones we hear nowadays, and their popularity is about equal.

Act I

In the courtyard of an inn at Amiens they are waiting for the diligence from Arras. Townsfolk gather in the yard, and the inn-keeper and his scullions serve dinner to a group of travellers who include Guillot de Morfortaine (bass), Minister of France; a noble-man named De Brétigny (baritone); and three high-spirited 'actresses'. Lescaut (baritone), of the Royal Guards, an affable blackguard of a fellow, comes in and tells his friends he is waiting to meet his cousin, Manon Lescaut. The coach arrives, and among the passengers step-ping out of it is a shy young girl (soprano) who seems bewildered by the noise and bustle. Lescaut guesses who she is and greets her with easy *bonhomie*. She explains prettily that she is fresh from home and knows nothing of the world. The first statement is true, but not the second: Manons are *born* with a knowledge of the world. Indeed, hardly has she stepped from the coach than she begins her devastating career: old Guillot catches sight of her, and while Lescaut is away attending to the luggage, offers her his 'protection'. He will order a carriage and postilion to carry her off; she must jump into the carriage and—afterwards she will know more. He slips away when Lescaut returns, but later Manon is left alone again and the youthful Des Grieux (tenor) approaches. He has finished his studies and is returning to his father. "I had fixed the day for my departure from Amiens," he says in the book. "Alas! That I had not fixed it one day sooner! I should then have carried to my father's house my innocence un-tarnished." At the sight of Manon he stands spellbound. It is love at first sight, a sheer convulsion of the heart. And we hear in the orchestra the theme that is to symbolise their passion:

In one moment his honour, his family, his career, all are forgotten. Manon tells him she is on her way to a convent, and he breaks out in anger that one so young and fair should be condemned to a living tomb. Guillot's postilion appears. "Quick!" whispers Manon to Des Grieux, "here is the old fool's carriage; he tried to make love to me just now. Let us take it and be revenged on him!" And away they go towards Paris. Lescaut comes out of the inn the worse for drink and roughly accuses Guillot of abducting Manon. The innkeeper declares that she has gone off with a young fellow in Guillot's carriage, and, true to the stage tradition that an old man in love is always absurd, the crowd roars with laughter at Guillot's frustration.

ACT II

"My mistress was to me so perfectly lovable that I could not doubt her power of captivating my father, if I could only find the means of making him acquainted with her good conduct and merit." So—he has written him a letter; and in their little apartment in Paris Des Grieux and Manon read it over together. "Do you think he will consent to our marriage?" she asks. "Oh, surely he will do as I wish," he reassures her. But as he is going out to post the letter Lescaut, with Brétigny disguised as a fellow-guardsman, is introduced. In a skilfully staged scene Lescaut engages Des Grieux's attention while Brétigny tells Manon that her lover's father is to take his son from Paris by force this evening. Her first impulse is to warn him, but Brétigny plays his cards well. "With him, life will be nothing but pinching poverty," he says; "but *I* will make you rich and splendid!" No Manon was ever able to resist a proposal like that; and when they have gone, and Des Grieux has slipped out to post his letter, she gazes rather remorsefully at their little supper-table:

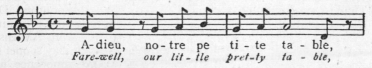

A-dieu,   no-tre pe ti-te ta-ble,
Fare-well,   our lit-tle pret-ty ta-ble,

He returns gaily and, to a strain of melting tenderness, he tells her his dream of their life together: a tiny cottage in a wood, the stream tinkling by and the birds singing overhead:

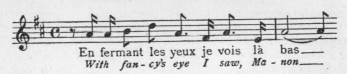

En fermant les yeux je vois là bas____
*With fan-cy's eye I saw, Ma-non*____

The dream is broken by a knock at the door. Manon knows what it means and has a sudden rush of pity for him. He shall not go, she says: let them knock! But he laughs at her and goes out. There is the sound of a struggle, and then carriage wheels rumbling away from the house. She runs to the window, and the curtain falls to a passionate phrase that Brétigny has sung earlier in the scene.

ACT III: *Scene 1*

Brétigny has kept his word and Manon is now queen of fashionable Paris. She has everything that caprice may demand and money can buy, and when she appears here at the Cours-la-Reine the tradespeople think she is a duchess at the very least. It is a lively, festive scene. We meet Guillot again and find that his three mistresses are still leading him a pretty dance, dodging him in the crush and 'getting off' with the younger men. Lescaut is here too, ruffling it in fine feathers and bragging of his luck at the tables, and we may surmise that his scruples about family honour have not deterred him from profiting by the sale of his cousin. But presently a grave elderly man enters, and Brétigny recognises him as an old friend. It is Des Grieux's father, the Count (bass). He tells Brétigny that his son has entered the Seminary of St. Sulpice and is to preach his first sermon this evening. Manon overhears and, getting rid of Brétigny, approaches the Count and asks for news of his son. She—knew him slightly, she says; he was in love—with a friend of hers. The Count assures her—somewhat ironically, for he knows who she is—that the young man has renounced the world and is now thoroughly absorbed in his vocation. "Youth soon learns its lesson and forgets," he says lightly. "And forgets . . ." echoes Manon; and then, when the Count has turned away: "Lescaut! My chair! I am going to St. Sulpice!"

ACT III: *Scene 2*

"I now thought myself entirely safe from the dangers of love. I fancied that I could have preferred a single page of St. Augustine, or a quarter of an hour of Christian meditation, to every sensual gratification, not excepting any that I might have derived even from Manon's society." Thus Prévost's hero. And here in the Seminary we watch the congregation filing past, overawed by the piety and eloquence of the young Abbé. The Count congratulates his son, but hints that the priesthood is no life for a man of spirit; much better go out into the world and marry some maiden worthy of his rank. But the young man protests that he has done with the world, and when he is left alone he breaks out into a desperate invocation to the image of Manon to depart and leave him to God:

Ah! fuyez, douce image, à mon à-me trop chè-re;
Ah! de-part, im-age fair! Leave me now at rest

At that moment she appears. "She had no wish, she repeated with a flood of tears, to attempt to justify her infidelity. What is your wish, then? cried I. I wish to die, she answered, if you will not give me back that heart, without which it is impossible to endure life." In her voice Des Grieux hears his doom: he cannot resist her. And once again his honour, his family, his career, all are cast into the fire of the love that is strong as death.

ACT IV: *Scene 1*

"Each of the new disorders into which I now lapsed carried me deeper and deeper still down the profound abyss of vice." In the book Des Grieux becomes a cardsharper and his behaviour with Manon is little better than that of a pimp. But Massenet takes us no further than the gaming-tables.

And here is the scene: it is a flashy, disreputable place, crowded with cocottes and sharpers; Lescaut is squabbling with another gamester over a disputed deal, and altogether one gathers that no one is behaving any better than he should. Lescaut tempts Des Grieux to gamble: he is sure to have 'beginners' luck'. Manon joins her cajoleries to her cousin's. They have no money left; what are they to do? With an unusual flash of spirit her lover turns on her:

Ma-non,sphinx é-ton-nant, Vé-ri-ta-ble si-rè — ne!
Ma-non, sphinx as thou art, sy-ren lure to de-struc-tion!

He hates the place they have brought him to, he hates the life they have brought him to, he hates Manon—and loves her. He gambles, savagely, recklessly—and wins. Guillot accuses him of cheating and summons the police. He is supported by Des Grieux Senior (who has suddenly and inexplicably appeared). The young man is arrested and Manon also is dragged away as his accomplice.

ACT IV: *Scene 2*

Manon is being taken to Havre to be deported with a herd of other wretched women. Des Grieux and Lescaut have planned to rescue her at a lonely spot on the road to Havre, but their plot miscarries. They bribe the soldiers to release her for an hour, and at last she and her lover are left alone. She is ill and exhausted, but suffering has purified her heart. She realises now the great love that has driven this man to sacrifice everything for her, and in a broken voice she asks his forgiveness. But her repentance is too late; she is dying. And she sinks down into his arms whispering, "Now is ended the story of Manon Lescaut. . . ."

". . . I sat for some time upon the bank intently gazing on her, and could not command fortitude enough to close the grave over her. At length . . . I committed to the earth all that it had ever contained most perfect and peerless. I then lay with my face down upon the grave, and closing my eyes with the determination never again to open them, I invoked the mercy of heaven, and ardently prayed for death."

GIACOMO MEYERBEER

(1791–1864)

The Huguenots

Libretto by Scribe.
Time: 1572.

First Production,
Paris, 1836.

> 'We are God's chosen few;
> All others will be damned;
> There is no place in Heaven for you,
> We can't have Heaven crammed.'
>
> Attributed to JONATHAN SWIFT.

The Huguenots is the best and most representative work of one who a century ago was the supreme dictator of opera. Since then the wheel has come half-circle and Meyerbeer today is rather like Wordsworth's Lucy, whom there were none to praise and very few to love. The few who love him sometimes maintain that we are foolishly starving ourselves in so seldom taking down from the shelf such mildewed museum pieces as *Dinorah* or *The Star of the North*. Those in the opposite camp either ignore Meyerbeer completely or dismiss him as a purse-proud[1] mountebank who never wrote a line of real music in his life.

The truth is probably midway between these extremes. Meyerbeer may not have been a mountebank, but he was undoubtedly a showman. He was a Jew and a man with a keen flair for the main chance—the two terms are usually synonymous. It may not be true that the hour produced the man, but it is certainly true that the man made the most of the hour. He was the perpetual opportunist. He began life as Jakob Beer, but when his grandfather, Liebmann Meyer Wulf, left him a handsome income on condition that he added Meyer to his name, then Beer became Meyer-Beer. When he decided to make his fortune in Italian opera, he Italianised Jakob into Giacomo. And so on.

In his operas he gave the public what it wanted. He knew his own limitations as a composer and the public's limitations as an audience, and they roughly corresponded. The public wanted thrilling effects, and Meyerbeer could supply them. Wagner described the type of drama Meyerbeer demanded from his *librettists* as 'a monstrous motley,

---

[1] It is harder to tolerate wealth than genius, and Meyerbeer's enemies never forgave him for being a rich man.

91

historico-romantic, diabolico-religious, fanatico-libidinous, sacro-frivo-
lous, mysterious-brazen, sentimental-humbugging dramatic hotch-
potch'. And in substance he was right. Considered in cold blood,
Meyerbeer's operas have their ridiculous side: their action is 'blood-
and-thunder', their emotion is what actors call 'ham'. Yet even the
calculating Meyerbeer occasionally forgot himself and said splendid
things for the mere sake of saying them. *Robert the Devil*, with all its
Monk Lewis–Ann Radcliffe absurdities, has moments of real power,
and we shall see that the music of *The Huguenots* has not only power
and dramatic effect (Meyerbeer could always call spirits from the
vasty deep), but also here and there a haunting and memorable
beauty.

We are in the thick of the religious quarrels of sixteenth-century
France, and the Prelude is built wholly on the great Lutheran Chorale,
'*Ein' Feste Burg*':

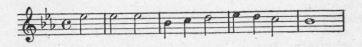

ACT I

The Comte de Nevers (baritone), a gay young Catholic nobleman,
is entertaining some hilarious friends at his château in Touraine.
Dinner is delayed for the arrival of the last guest, Raoul de Nangis.
He is, Nevers explains, a Huguenot, but they must not allow that to
prejudice them. After all, the Royal Family is doing its best to reconcile
the Catholics and Protestants. Raoul (tenor) at last arrives. He is a
young man of romantic ideals, very different from the young bloods
of Nevers's party; and when Nevers proposes a toast, 'Our mistresses',
Raoul tells of a fair unknown whom he rescued one day from annoy-
ance by a band of students. He has seen her only once, he knows
neither her name nor her station, yet she will stay in his heart for
ever. And he vows eternal homage, in one of the most charming and
expressive airs Meyerbeer ever wrote; a viola *obbligato* curls round the
voice-line like spirals of smoke:

There is a little trouble with Raoul's retainer, Marcel (bass), a rough old Lutheran of the sword-and-Bible type, who is horrified at seeing his master in such ungodly company, thunders forth '*Ein' Feste Burg*' at them, and finally trounces the whole Catholic community in the once-famous 'Piff-Paff' *aria*—

Pour les cou-vents,c'est fi-ni! Les moi-nes à ter-re,
The monks and their con-vents we'll hurl down to-geth-er,

—in which he imitates the piff-paff of bullets. Before he can reply to this explosion of rather unmannerly zeal, Nevers is summoned to interview a lady in the garden. The others peer through the window, and Raoul is astonished and dismayed to recognize the woman of his dreams. Nevers, on his return, tells them that she was his betrothed, a lady-in-waiting to Queen Marguérite, but she has now persuaded him to release her. His friends chaff him good-humouredly on this blow to his vanity, and presently Urbain (soprano), the Queen's favourite page, enters. He brings a message to one of their company:

U - ne da - me no-ble et sa - ge,—
From a la - dy fair and love - ly,—

The favoured one is Raoul: he is to be blindfolded and accompany some masked men to a secret rendezvous.

ACT II

In the garden of the Châteaux of Chenonceaux the Queen (soprano) and her ladies are singing of the pastoral beauties of Touraine. Some of the girls are bathing in the stream—a scene to which Scribe and Meyerbeer, who knew their public, did full justice. Presently Raoul is led in, and when he is left alone with the Queen the scarf is taken from his eyes. She exacts his promise to obey her in everything and then tells him she is planning to reconcile Catholics and Protestants by marrying him to Valentine, daughter of the Comte de Saint-Bris, an ancient enemy of his family. Raoul consents at once. Since the shock of discovering the woman he loves to be an associate of Nevers and his dissolute set, he hardly cares whom he marries.

The courtiers, Catholic and Protestant, now enter, and Saint-Bris (bass) brings in his daughter, Valentine (soprano). Raoul starts back. It is she! He is immediately convulsed with jealousy and wounded pride. "She! No, no; I cannot, I will not marry her!" There is a moment's silence; then the rest break out in passionate indignation, and the act ends with the kind of powerful and exciting *ensemble* in which Meyerbeer has such an expert touch.

Act III

Paris. We are in the Pré-aux-Clercs, the great meadow by the Seine. It is early evening and the stage is filled with a noisy crowd— Catholic students and girls, Huguenot soldiers, monks, workpeople, citizens and holiday-makers. Rejected by Raoul, Valentine has been persuaded by her father to accept Nevers after all, and their wedding procession now passes on its way to a chapel nearby. There is some bickering between Catholics and Protestants, but this is interrupted by a troupe of gipsies who dance gaily in and provide the ballet without which opera in the eighteen-thirties was not considered opera at all.

Nevers then comes out of the chapel and tells Saint-Bris that his bride has remained behind in prayer. Saint-Bris is still furious at Raoul's affront to his daughter, and at that moment, as if in answer to his thoughts, Marcel delivers him a challenge from Raoul. Excellent! He will wipe out the insult to his family honour. But his friend Maurevert (bass) points out that he need take no such risk: they will form an ambush and—murder Raoul; and to this the man who is so touchy about his honour readily agrees. But Valentine has overheard the plot, and when Marcel reappears she warns him that his master must not come to the rendezvous alone. The duellists meet; but just as Raoul is about to be overpowered by his enemies, Marcel calls out the Huguenot soldiers to his rescue. There is a violent street fight, which dies down, however, at the entrance of the Queen. A few moments later a gaily decorated barge appears on the river: Nevers has arrived to conduct home his bride. And Raoul at last learns the truth: that he has rejected the woman who truly loves him and who has saved him from assassination.

Act IV

The fourth act is the finest in the opera, if not the finest in all Meyerbeer's works. He is still the showman; he is still providing

excellent 'theatre'. But one almost believes here that the 'theatre' is
accidental and that the showmanship is the unconscious and inevitable
result of art.

It is the night of St. Bartholomew, August 24th, 1572. In a room
in the house of Nevers, Valentine is lamenting 'the miseries of enforced
marriage'. (An air she sings here is usually omitted.) Raoul suddenly
appears. He has come to bid her farewell; but after they have
exchanged only a few words, footsteps are heard. It is her husband
and her father. "Go, go!" she implores Raoul. "No," he replies, "I
will face them and die here." But Valentine begs him to save her
honour, and he reluctantly allows her to conceal him behind a tapestry.
Saint-Bris, Nevers and other Catholic noblemen enter and discuss
their plot: that very night shall see the massacre of the Huguenots.
Only Nevers recoils in disgust from this project: he is a soldier, not
an assassin. Saint-Bris prudently places him under arrest until the
following day. Three monks then enter the room, bearing the white
armbands which are to identify the Catholics, and there follows the
impressive scene of the Benediction of the Poniards:

The conspirators troop out, glowing with pious fervour. Raoul,
horrified at what he has overheard, emerges from behind the tapestry,
and he and Valentine then begin a long duet which rises to the most
passionate pitch Meyerbeer ever reached:

He must hasten away, he says, and warn the Huguenots of the horrible
fate in store for them. Valentine pleads with him not to go; it is
certain death. "Raoul, stay with me! I love you; I shall die if you
leave me!" As she is clinging to him with the strength of despair, the
great bell of St. Germain's booms out. It is the signal for the massacre:
flames are seen at the window, shouts and the clash of arms echo
through the darkness. "Protect her, O God, in this hour!" cries
Raoul, and jumps through the window into the street.

So ends the great fourth act; and, in many productions, so ends the opera. The fifth act is frequently cut, partly because it is something of an anticlimax and tells us little we have not already guessed, and partly because there is inevitably a slight falling-off after the sustained splendour of the fourth. On the other hand, it *does* 'round off' the story, and it has many musical and dramatic merits.

Act V

It is in three scenes. The first is the hall in the Hôtel de Vesle, where the Huguenots, unaware of what is happening outside, are celebrating the wedding of Marguérite and Henri of Navarre. Raoul, bloodstained and dishevelled, rushes in to tell them that their leader, Coligny, is slain and the gutters are running with the blood of their murdered comrades. The men draw their swords and crowd out into the streets.

The scene changes to a Huguenot churchyard in which Raoul and Marcel have taken refuge. Valentine joins them. Nevers has been killed and she is free to marry the man she loves. But Raoul will not turn from his religion. Very well: she will turn from hers and become a Protestant for his sake. Marcel acts as priest and blesses them. In the final scene, on one of the Paris quays, Raoul totters in mortally wounded and supported by Marcel and Valentine. Saint-Bris and his followers appear and challenge them: "Who goes there?" Raoul rallies himself and with his last breath cries out defiantly, "Huguenots!" There is a rattle of musketry, and the next moment Raoul, Marcel and Valentine are lying dead. Saint-Bris is left with the satisfaction of having, in his fanatical zeal, murdered his own daughter, and the curtain falls on the soldiers clamouring for still more bloodshed. "Men never do evil so completely and cheerfully," wrote Pascal, "as when they do it from religious conviction."

MODESTE MOUSSORGSKY

(1839–1881)

Boris Godounov

Libretto after Pushkin's drama.
Time: 1598–1605.

First Production,
St. Petersburg, 1874.

> 'Better be with the dead,
> Whom we, to gain our peace, have sent to peace,
> Than on the torture of the mind to lie
> In restless ecstasy.'
>
> SHAKESPEARE: *Macbeth.*

Boris Godounov is like a huge, ungainly mountain. We come upon jagged pinnacles, we balance ourselves dizzily on razor-like edges of rock. Magnificent vistas break on our vision, making us catch our breath at their beauty, and give way the next moment to stretches of sterile desolation. It seems always winter here; and mysterious lights flash through the falling snow.

Not the best of the Russian operas, but unquestionably the greatest; not even, by conventional canons, a good opera; but one whose greatest moments harrow us with pity and terror as only the greatest art can. At these moments Moussorgsky is in the world of Shakespeare, Dante and Beethoven.

Of the man himself it might be said that he put so much genius into his art that he had none left for his life. His life, indeed, was as untidy as his orchestration: he was a shiftless drunkard and died of epilepsy on his forty-second birthday. Such was the mouse that gave birth to this mountain. He was a nationalist and a realist. As a nationalist he wrote the first really great Russian national opera; and as a realist he wrote it in music that was as Russian as vodka—music that could have come out of no country *but* Russia, coloured with folk influences and catching with unerring felicity the natural inflexions of Russian speech. And, incidentally, he created one of the noblest acting parts in all opera. Boris is not a long part (in the Rimsky-Korsakov version it figures on only sixty pages in three hundred), but it dominates the whole work and calls for the physique and temperament of a Chaliapine. It also calls for a very special type of voice: like those of Wotan in *The Ring* and Sachs in *The Mastersingers*, the part is really high bass', demanding bass tone and gravity, yet occasionally shooting up to F and F sharp. It is, in short, a bass part with a baritone range.

The version which brought *Boris* (and Chaliapine) into world fame was the version rearranged and rather drastically 'ironed out' by Rimsky-Korsakov. Purists prefer Moussorgsky's original score, published in 1928; but I have taken here the Rimsky-Korsakov version because, being the more operatically effective, it is the one we are more likely to hear—if, indeed, we ever have the luck to hear *Boris* again in *any* version!

PROLOGUE: *Scene* 1

The orchestra begins with a dark, wintry little theme (bassoon and cor anglais) which gradually broadens and extends to other instruments and at its climax the curtain rises on the courtyard of a monastery near Moscow. There are two leading characters in *Boris Godounov*: the Tsar and the people; and the people come before us first. They are as listless as a herd of cattle. A police officer (baritone) flourishes his whip over their heads. They must sing; they must plead with Boris, 'their master and father', to accept the crown. Obediently they lift their voices in a dreary chorus. But the Boyard Stchelkalov (baritone) appears and announces mournfully that Boris has refused the kingdom. "Woe to our land!" he sings. "Ye orthodox: pray that heaven may shed light upon the soul of Boris!" The scene ends with a chorus of pilgrims.

PROLOGUE: *Scene* 2

Heaven has shed light upon the soul of Boris. And the first thing we hear is the booming of a great, deep-toned bell. Here Moussorgsky achieves a remarkable effect by the constant repetition of two alternating chords:

The sound grows in volume as other bell-like figures are added—still alternating between D flat and G, clanging, insistent, monotonous. Then the curtain rises on a scene of great animation. It is the courtyard of the Kremlin, and a vast crowd kneels between the Cathedral of the Assumption and the Cathedral of the Archangels. The bells are ringing for the coronation of Boris. The people hail him in a mighty chorus:

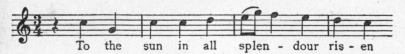

To the sun in all splen - dour ris - en

The bells peal out again, and at last Boris (high bass) appears. On a stroke the brilliant, festal music ceases, as though its heart had suddenly stopped beating. And out of the silence Boris's voice rises in a mournful cadence which sets before us all the dark, haunted soul of the man. He has a premonition of evil; and he prays for strength to rule justly and wisely. Then he seems to recover himself: the shadow passes, and in an altered voice he commands that the people shall all feast with him. The rejoicing bursts forth again as the procession moves on to the Cathedral of the Assumption.

Act I: *Scene 1*

The curtain rises on a cell in the Monastery of the Miracle. It is night; an old monk sits writing by a lamp on the table, a young novice lies asleep in a corner of the cell. The composer has magically caught, in this cold, austere music, the atmosphere of the time and place— the still night, the dimly lit cell, the stone floor worn through the centuries by pious feet. A tenuous, wavering figure in the bass seems to follow the old man's hand across the parchment. Presently Pimen (bass) lays down his pen and meditates on the chronicle of Russian history he has nearly completed. The dawn is near, he says, and his rushlight is failing: he must end his task. The novice, Gregory (tenor), wakes, and Pimen tells him of the last legend he has transcribed: it is the crime of Boris Godounov. When Ivan the Terrible died, his son Feodor became Tsar, and at Feodor's death the crown was accepted by his brother-in-law, Boris Godounov. This happened because Dmitri, a younger son of Ivan, had been murdered in childhood— most people believed by Boris's order. If he had lived, says Pimen, Dmitri would be exactly the same age as Gregory. His words are full of meaning; and Gregory pauses at the door of the cell and makes a vow that Boris shall be brought to justice.

Act I: *Scene 2*

Gregory is now acting on his desperate resolve and has reached an inn on the Lithuanian frontier. On the way he has fallen in with two disreputable wandering monks, Varlaam (bass) and Missail (tenor), and now the three of them are admitted by the Hostess (mezzo-soprano), who has been solacing her loneliness with one of those delightful little songs in Moussorgsky's miniature style. Gregory is anxious and preoccupied with his schemes, but the holy brothers start to get tipsy, and Varlaam roars out a boisterous ballad about the fighting at Kazan:

Long a - go   at Ka - zan where I was fight - ing

Then there is a dramatic interruption: a captain (bass) and some guards burst in. They are chasing a renegade monk, Gregory, who is believed to be making for the Lithuanian frontier. The captain cannot read, so he shows the order to Gregory himself, who quick-wittedly alters the description to fit Varlaam. But Varlaam eventually turns the tables on him, and Gregory leaps through the window into the night just as the guards rush forward to arrest him.

ACT II

Now we are to watch the agony of one who, like Macbeth, 'gave his eternal jewel to the common enemy of man'; and, again like Macbeth, was not great enough—or perhaps too great—to be the complete villain. We are in the Tsar's apartments in the Kremlin. Xenia, his daughter, is weeping over a portrait of her dead lover; Feodor, his son, is studying *The Book of Great Plans*. Xenia (soprano) breaks out into a lament—a bleak, bewildered little melody, each note of which is like a crystal tear that seems to freeze as it falls. The nurse (mezzo-soprano) rallies her, and she and Feodor (mezzo-soprano) combine in some little nursery songs to divert her (again in Moussorgsky's miniature style). While their merriment is at its height the tall, menacing figure of Boris darkens the doorway. He speaks kindly to the children, and the music melts into tenderness, like little clusters of green leaves magically glittering on the boughs of a gaunt, barren tree. Then the black fit falls on him. "I am Tsar of Russia; yet no peace comes to my tortured soul. The people curse me by day; a murdered child haunts me by night":

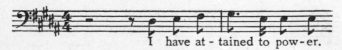

I have at - tained to pow - er.

From this moment to the end of the act, no composer ever surpassed, few composers ever equalled, Moussorgsky in revealing a strong soul in the agony of remorse. Prince Shouïsky comes stealing in to tell the Tsar that a pretender is leading a revolt. He claims to be the boy Dmitri, risen from the grave. Boris staggers; the words clang in his ear like a death-knell. Dmitri! "Tell me, Shouïsky," he cries in a terrible voice, "when that evil deed was done—the boy they buried—was he in truth Dmitri?" Shouïsky tries to reassure him. He watched, he says, by the child's body. The throat was cut, but the face was as fair as in life, and the little hand clutched the toy he had last played with. . . . Boris can stand no more. He shouts to him to be gone. And there, in his own children's nursery, surrounded by his own children's toys, he gives way to the terrors of conscience. He sees the ghost of the murdered child advancing on him through the shadows, the throat dripping blood. A clock begins to chime—inexorably, monotonously, like the tread of doom. He clutches his hair and grovels on the floor, panting for breath. "O God, Who desirest not the sinner's death, have pity on me, the guilty Tsar, Boris!"

Act III

For a whole act the tension slackens; and perhaps it is just as well. One could not live for long at such a pitch of anguish; and in any case the smooth conventionality of what are usually called 'the Polish scenes' serves to throw the main tragedy into sharper relief.

In Moussorgsky's original plan there was no love interest—in fact, the opera had no important woman's part at all. So, under pressure, he added those scenes in Pushkin that show the Pretender being entangled, for political reasons, in a love-affair with the Polish princess, Marina (mezzo-soprano), the entanglement being presided over by a scheming Jesuit, Rangoni (bass). These scenes belong to opera, not to music drama; and their persistent labelling by ostentatiously Polish rhythms soon grows tiresome. Yet, even when he was working against his principles, Moussorgsky could not prevent fine music from breaking in now and then—as in the duet where Gregory (now called Dmitri) and Marina pledge their love:

O Tsar - e - vich, I__ en - treat thee;

Act IV: *Scene 1*

We have seen that there are two leading characters in *Boris Godounov*: the Tsar and the people. This is the great scene of the people. They have gathered in a forest clearing near Kromy, in revolt against the Tsar. We see them taunting and insulting a captured boyard. Presently a crowd of boys drives in the village idiot (tenor), dressed in a white nightshirt and with a saucepan on his head. He sits on a stone and sings, rocking himself to and fro—

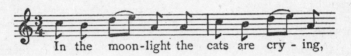

In the moon-light the cats are cry - ing,

—an inane, moonstruck melody, like an echo from some lost, abandoned country of the mind. The boys hammer on his saucepan and snatch away the bright farthing he has been gloating over. "Oh —my little farthing's gone!" he wails. And they laugh at him. Varlaam and Missail join the mob, and eventually the false Dmitri passes on horseback. In ringing tones he promises them deliverance from the tyrant Boris. "To Moscow!" he cries; and they crowd after him, hailing him as Tsar. The Idiot is left alone, crooning piteously to himself: "Woe and sorrow always! Lament, Russian folk—poor hungry folk!"

Act IV: *Scene 2*

It is the last scene. "Better be with the dead . . ." Boris staggers in to a meeting of the Duma. His brain is failing and he hardly knows what he is doing. The ghost of the murdered child still haunts him. "Back, child!" he gasps as he totters in; "I am not thy murderer!" With a tremendous effort he pulls himself together. He stumbles forward and collapses on to the throne. Shouïsky tells him that a holy man waits outside; he has a wondrous story to tell. "Bring him in," says Boris, breathing heavily; "perhaps he brings me comfort." But the holy man is Pimen; and in a few moments we know that he has come merely to twist the knife in Boris's heart. To the kind of meagre, spectral music we heard in the Monastery scene in the first act, he tells of a blind shepherd recovering his sight by praying on the tomb of the Tsarevitch Dmitri, now numbered among the saints of

God. Only a holy man could have timed things with such evil accuracy. Boris falls unconscious into the arms of his boyards. He is in his death-agony. They bring in Feodor, his son; and, rousing himself, he bids him farewell:

Fare-well, my son, I am dy-ing.

"The evil he has desperately embraced," writes A. C. Bradley of Macbeth, "continues to madden or to wither his inmost heart. No experience in the world could bring him to glory in it or make his peace with it, or to forget what he once was and Iago and Goneril never were." We may say the same of Boris Godounov.

WOLFGANG AMADEUS MOZART

(1756–1791)

Il Seraglio

Libretto by Stephanie, after Bretzner's *Belmont and Constance.* First Production,
Time: Eighteenth Century. Vienna, 1782.

'Men may have rounded Seraglio Point: they have not yet doubled Cape Turk.'
MEREDITH: *Diana of the Crossways.*

Il Seraglio is the happiest of Mozart's operas. He was to do far greater things for the theatre: *Figaro*, with its powdered elegance; *Don Giovanni*, with its piercing note of terror; *The Magic Flute*, with its mystic solemnity. But in the *Seraglio* he struck a note of youthful, romantic freshness, the true tone of which he was never quite able to repeat. It is genuine comic opera. The story is 'silly sooth, and dallies with the innocence of love', and the music has just the right careless piquancy. Nothing is overweighted, nothing is stretched beyond that point where one's instinctive taste declares that it should stop. Moreover, in Osmin, the Pasha's major-domo, Mozart has created one of the richest comic characters and one of the greatest *basso-buffo* parts in all opera. Osmin is the supreme example of the old martinet who disapproves of young people because he is no longer young himself. Every bar of his music is completely in character—one might almost say that it has its own distinctive *smell*, so to speak—and could be sung by no one else in the opera. Indeed, it could be sung by very few people in *any* opera: it has an exceptional compass (low D to high F) and was originally written for an exceptional artist—a bass named Ludwig Fischer.

ACT I

The short overture runs straight into an enchanting little song by Belmont (tenor)—

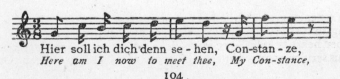

Hier soll ich dich denn se - hen, Con-stan - ze,
Here am I now to meet thee, My Con-stance,

—which is over before we have fully realised its delicate charm. Belmont has come to the palace of the Pasha Selim in Turkey, to seek his affianced bride, Constance, who has been captured by pirates and sold into the Pasha's harem. He catches sight of Osmin (bass), who is working in the garden and singing a lugubrious ditty about the wretched plight of an old man in love with a young girl.

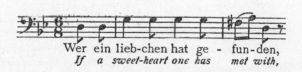

Wer ein lieb-chen hat ge - fun-den,
If a sweet-heart one has met with,

But Belmont can get nothing out of Osmin, who roughly orders him off the premises. The old man grunts and goes on with his work. He is joined by Pedrillo (tenor), Belmont's former servant, who has got a job at the Palace to be near Constance's waiting-maid, Blonda. Now Osmin hates the youthful Pedrillo, partly because he hates youth in any form, also because he wants Blonda for himself. In a vigorous *aria* he curses these young fellows who come sneaking round after the women, the music reflecting, with grotesque humour, his alternating moods of baffled hate and spiteful, elephantine cunning:

Sol-che her-ge-lauf-ne Laf - - - - - - - fen,
Oh! These dandies hith-er roam - - - - - - - ing.

Eventually Belmont and Pedrillo meet. Pedrillo assures him that Constance and Blonda are waiting eagerly to be rescued, and to further their plans he will present Belmont to Selim disguised as an architect. Belmont sings of the joy of meeting his beloved once again:

O wie ängst-lich, O wie feur-ig
O how an-xious, O how ar-dent

Selim (speaking part) has treated Constance with the utmost respect, hoping that she will learn to love him. But Constance (soprano) vows that her heart belongs for ever to Belmont. Later, Selim takes Belmont into his service as an architect, and everyone is pleased—except Osmin.

Act II

Blonda laments her fate: to be pestered by the clumsy advances of a great bear old enough to be her grandfather.

Durch Zärt-lich-keit und Schmei-cheln,
By   ten-der-ness and   kind - ness

Osmin tells her she must obey him. Blonda retorts that she is a free-born Englishwoman and Englishmen don't treat women in that way. Then Englishmen must be mad, is Osmin's sage comment. Meanwhile, Constance also is suffering the disadvantages of having been born beautiful. In case the Pasha should grow a little tired of his old-world chivalry, she vehemently assures him, in a long *aria* of heroic stature, that she cannot love him; neither tortures nor death can make her consent:

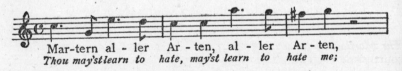

Mar-tern al - ler   Ar - ten, al - ler   Ar - ten,
Thou may'st learn to   hate, may'st learn to   hate me;

But the plans for their escape are rapidly maturing. First, to deal with Osmin. Pedrillo enters with two flasks of wine, and in the course of a riotous duet he makes the old man helplessly drunk.

The act ends with a brilliant quartet by the four lovers.

Act III

All is prepared. Outside the palace wall Belmont and Pedrillo meet by the light of the moon, Pedrillo carrying a rope ladder. He gives the signal—a serenade to Blonda. But—disaster! Just as they are about to get clear, Osmin, having slept off his drunkenness, surprises them. He calls the guard, the two couples are arrested and Osmin gloats over them in a terrific piece of rodomontade, which is also one of the greatest bass airs ever written (listen for the low D held on for eight bars):

Ha! wie will ich tri - um - phi - ren,
Ha! How I will tri - umph o'er you,

The Pasha is summoned and learns that Belmont is the son of his bitterest enemy. At first he exults in this turn of fortune, but after a while he perceives a nobler way of retribution: he despises his enemy too much to revenge himself. Belmont is free, and the four lovers may go in safety. Everyone is pleased—except Osmin.

The Marriage of Figaro

Libretto by Lorenzo da Ponte, after Beaumarchais.   First Production,
Time: Seventeenth Century.   Vienna, 1786.

> 'What guards the purity of melting maids,
> In courtly balls, and midnight masquerades,
> Safe from the treacherous friend, the daring spark,
> The glance by day, the whisper in the dark,
> When kind occasion prompts their warm desires,
> When music softens, and when dancing fires?'
>
> POPE: *The Rape of the Lock.*

The Marriage of Figaro is Mozart's 'Way of the World'. It is the most courtly and elegant of his scores, and the closer one gets to it the more is one convinced that studied grace and conscious delicacy could go no further. There are other affinities with the master-jewel of Restoration comedy: here too we are in an enchanted world, remote from all moral issues; a world of powdered gallantry in which the only fashionable pursuit is a love intrigue and the only unpleasant thing about a fashionable woman is her husband. There is no reality in it, nothing to wound our feelings. They are not men and women, these counts and countesses, amorous pageboys, intriguing valets and chambermaids, any more than Congreve's Millamants and Mirabels: they are like figures treading out a stately measure in some exquisite Watteau pastoral. The Overture, however, is not stately; it fairly bubbles with jollity and seems to express the ready wit and pert and nimble spirit of Figaro and Susanna rather than the languid gentility of their betters.

ACT I

After this racy little introduction we meet Figaro (baritone) and Susanna (soprano) themselves. They are to be married, and Figaro explains why the Count Almaviva has placed their bedroom near his own apartments: it will be convenient, he says, when the Count summons his valet or the Countess her waiting-maid. But Susanna has caught the Count's roving eye, and she has a shrewd idea that this is an arrangement not for master and man but for master and mistress. "Never fear," says Figaro; "I'll outwit him. If he wants to dance I'll make him dance to *my* tune!" Cherubino (soprano), the young page, begs from Susanna a ribbon belonging to the Countess, whom he believes he worships as the moth the star. But in reality he is only in love with love, and confesses that a glance from any fair maid can make his heart beat faster:

Non so più co-sa son, co-sa fac-cio,
I am lost, and scarce know what I'm do - ing —

Cherubino is in disgrace with the Count—probably because of his youth, which, no doubt, wins him greater success in what seems to be the main occupation of everyone in the Casa Almaviva. The Count (baritone) gets him a commission in the Army, and Figaro taunts the wretched youth by telling him that he must give up being a dandy and learn to be a soldier:

Non più andrai, far-fal-lo - ne a-mo-ro - so,
Now no more may we, love-sick, phi-lan - der,

ACT II

In this bewildering world of intrigue and jealousy the Countess (soprano) defies the fashion, and is so ill-bred as to be in love with her own husband. And in her boudoir she laments his coldness and infidelity, to an air that seems almost grievous with its own loveliness:

Por - gi a-mor,   qual-che ri - sto - ro
Sooth - ing spells,   ah love, cast o'er___ me,

Susanna brings in Cherubino. He has with him a little love-song he has written. Will his divinity deign to hear it? His divinity will. So, shyly and timidly, he sings it while Susanna accompanies him on a guitar:

The Count suddenly knocks at the door and they hide Cherubino in the bedroom. The Count is furiously jealous; his wife is concealing a lover, he says, and he insists on searching the rooms. Cherubino jumps into the garden. Figaro appears (most opportunely) and tries to appease the Count with a tissue of ingenious lies; and at the end of the scene they are joined by old Dr. Bartolo (bass), the Countess's former guardian, and Marcellina (soprano), a spinster whom Figaro has promised to marry if he cannot pay a debt he owes her. The act ends with a brilliant *ensemble*, all the characters voicing their individual grievances and emotions and nobody listening—except, of course, the audience.

ACT III

The Count (quite naturally) has a strong respect for the *droit du seigneur*. Having arranged a fête in honour of Figaro's marriage, he resolves to balance things by taking away the honour of Figaro's bride. Will Susanna meet him that night in the garden? Susanna promises that she will. But what of Figaro's promise to marry Marcellina? That is quite lightly and easily disposed of by a comic scene in which Figaro discovers that he is an early mistake made by Marcellina and Dr. Bartolo! Meanwhile, the Countess is again praying that her husband's love may return to her—in another air that seems luminous with tears:

But she and Susanna hit on a more practical plan than prayer. They will write the Count a letter of assignation, purporting to come from Susanna, and the Countess will disguise herself as her maid and keep the appointment:

"Che   so - a - ve   ze - fi - ret - to"—
"Gen - tle   ze - phyr, soft - ly   breath - ing"—

The villagers stream into the castle for the fête, and during a dance Susanna skilfully passes the Count the letter of assignation.

Act IV

We are now in the garden. It is a scented summer evening and masked figures, glimmering in the half-light, pass and repass, now challenging each other, now joining hands and moving away into the deeper darkness. Susanna sings a tender invocation to night and love:

Deh vie - ni, non tar - dar, o gio - ja bel - la,
Ah, come, nor lin - ger more, my soul's — fond trea-sure

Each character mistakes the other for someone else—according to the charming convention of eighteenth-century comedy that if one covers one's eyes with a narrow strip of black velvet even one's nearest and dearest will fail to recognize voice or figure. The tangled couples are at last sorted out, and these airy creatures, whose fancies blow to and fro like thistledown in the breeze, forgive each other as lightly and readily as they took offence.

Don Giovanni

Libretto by Lorenzo da Ponte.   First production,
Time: Seventeenth Century.   Prague, 1787.

> 'I am Don Juan, curst from age to age,
> By priestly tract and sentimental stage:
> Branded a villain or believed a fool,
> Battered by hatred, seared by ridicule,
> Noble on earth, all but a king in Hell,
> I am Don Juan with a tale to tell.'
>
> JAMES ELROY FLECKER.

Don Giovanni has been called the world's greatest opera. One might argue, of course, that the expansion of harmony since Mozart's day has helped to produce greater operas, and one might prefer to say that it was the world's greatest opera at the time it was written—of which there is no shadow of doubt. On the other hand, *Don Giovanni* is not of an age but for all time. There is a demonic power in this music that rises high above the formal, tonic-and-dominant framework enforced by the times. There is real terror in it; and the final catastrophe will always be an astounding revelation of what genius can do with limited harmonic resources, and a salutary shock to those who regard Mozart merely as a writer of pretty tunes. The prevailing tonality is D— festive and glittering in the major, fierce, steely and menacing in the minor; and the first thirty bars of the Overture (in the minor) at once strike the note of doom, reminding us that 'the gods are just, and of our pleasant vices make instruments to plague us'.

ACT I: *Scene* 1

The pleasant vices come first. For this is that Don Juan whose infamous fame has gone out to all lands and enriched the world with a new nickname. When we first meet him he is being chased out of the house by Donna Anna (soprano) and her father, the Commendatore (bass). The two men fight, and Don Giovanni (baritone) unwittingly signs his own death-warrant by slaying the Commendatore. Don Ottavio (tenor), Anna's betrothed, swears vengeance.

ACT I: *Scene* 2

Giovanni and his comic pander, Leporello (bass), a kind of depraved Figaro, overhear a deserted maiden, Elvira (soprano), singing of her faithless lover. The faithless lover is, of course, Giovanni (it always is), and when Elvira denounces the two rascals, Leporello laughs at her. "What are *you* fussing about?" he says. "You're not the only one—not by thousands!" And he sings her the famous Catalogue song, enumerating the Don's world-wide conquests:

Ma-da-mi-na!   Il ca-ta - lo-go e que-sto
Gen-tle la - dy,   *this my ca - ta-logue num-bers*

ACT I: *Scene 3*

We are now in the countryside near Don Giovanni's palace. Rustics celebrate the approaching marriage of Zerlina (soprano) and Masetto (bass). Giovanni, of course, cannot look on so enchanting a girl as Zerlina without wanting to add her to his catalogue. So he gets Masetto out of the way and begins the assault:

Là, ci da-rem la   ma - no!
Hand link'd in hand we'll wan-der,

Don Giovanni tells Leporello to prepare a sumptuous banquet in his palace. "Let wine flow in fountains," he says; "and women—bring all the women you can find, dames from the city, maids from the country; and—I'll do the rest":

Fin ch'han dal vi - no,
Wine flow a foun-tain!

Later we hear Zerlina pleading with Masetto to forgive her for having flirted with Don Giovanni:

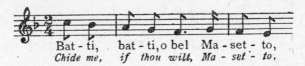

Bat - ti, bat - ti, o bel Ma - set - to,
Chide me, if thou wilt, Ma - set - to,

ACT I: *Scene 4*

While the banquet is at its height Zerlina's voice is heard screaming for help. Everyone, of course, knows exactly what a scream means in Don Giovanni's palace, and Anna, Elvira, Ottavio and the rest prepare to rush to her rescue. Don Giovanni tries to put the blame on Leporello, but this deceives no one; and the act ends with Giovanni defying the crowd and making his escape with drawn sword.

Act II: *Scene 1*

Don Giovanni now resolves to lay siege to Elvira's maid. Even Leporello begins to be perturbed by his omnivorous versatility, but the Don explains that to be constant to one woman is to be unkind to the others, and *that* he cannot bear. So, disguised as Leporello, he pays his addresses:

Deh vie-ni al-la fi - ne - stra,
Ap - pear in all thy beau - ty,

Act II: *Scene 2*

Ottavio and Anna bring indisputable evidence to Elvira that Don Giovanni is a murderer. Ottavio, in one of the most beautiful airs Mozart (or anyone else) ever wrote, renews his pledge to avenge the death of Anna's father:

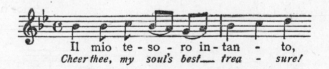

Il mio te - so - ro in - tan - to,
Cheer thee, my soul's best trea - sure!

Don Juans turned novelists tell us that a woman can never quite kill her love for the man who first betrayed her. And the moment comes when Elvira is tempted to desert the hunters and go to the help of the deer. A monster of iniquity; and yet—she loved him once. Perhaps she loves him still—for his very iniquity:

Mi tra - di quell' al-ma in - gra - ta,
In a breast be - tray'd to ru - in,

H

Act II: *Scene 3*

The citizens have erected a statue to the late Commendatore.
There he sits on his horse in the moonlight. Giovanni and Leporello
address him with mocking words. "I invite your Excellency to supper,"
says the Don. "Speak! Will you come?" And the statue nods his head
and says, "Yes!"

Act II: *Scene 4*

He keeps his word. In the midst of laughing revelry the Man of
Marble suddenly appears, like Banquo at the feast. "You invited me
to your banquet: I am here!" He stretches out his hand. Don Giovanni
does not flinch: he grasps it. It is the hand of death. An icy terror
strikes to his heart. Over ponderous chords hammered out in D minor
like the tones of the last judgment, the Statue calls on Giovanni to
repent. But Giovanni will not deny his creed: he has lived his life and
he is ready to meet his fate. In an apocalyptic climax the devils bear
him down to the pit. The gods are just, and of our pleasant vices
make instruments to plague us. . . .

A libertine and a villain; but not a sordid libertine, not a cowardly
villain. He was true to himself. He was a poet; he loved beautiful
things—alive or dead—and he dared perdition for them. There are
worse ways of going to hell.

Così Fan Tutte

Libretto by Lorenzo da Ponte.   First Production,
Time: Late Eighteenth Century.   Vienna, 1790.

> 'A fellow that lives in a windmill has not a more whimsical
> dwelling than the heart of a man that is lodged in a woman.'
>   CONGREVE: *The Way of the World*

Così Fan Tutte is perhaps best translated as 'Thus do all women'. The
story is based on the immemorial tradition that *la donna e mobile*, and
that one either breaks one's heart over this, as in tragedy, or accepts i
with cynical good-humour, as in comedy. This alleged fickleness o
women is, of course, one of the eternal themes of all art; and althoug
life plainly demonstrates that the average woman is by nature mor
prone to fidelity than the average man—indeed, it is the faithf

women who are often the more troublesome!—the vast majority of
poets, dramatists and philosophers have combined through the
centuries to shout down this obvious truth; the most feasible explanation being that the vast majority of poets, dramatists and philosophers
have been men.

Così Fan Tutte is probably the least popular of Mozart's five greatest
operas, and the reasons are fairly evident. The *libretto* is artificial
comedy and rather tedious artificial comedy at that; and one needs a
good stock of patience to sustain interest in the restricted action, the
monotonous reshufflings of the two pairs of lovers and their ridiculous
subterfuges that would not deceive a child of two. In fact, unlike
Figaro, which has real wit, and *Don Giovanni*, which has real drama,
Così would be insupportable without the music. *This* is characteristic
Mozart, abounding in charm and wit, even though it lacks, for me,
some of the variety and freshness of his earlier scores.

The Overture uses only one theme from the opera—

Co - sì fan   tut - te!   Co - sì   fan   tut - te!

—which is sung by the two lovers and the old cynic towards the end
of the second act. The rest of it is just one light rippling *presto*.

Act I: *Scene 1*

In a café in Naples, Don Alfonso (bass), a hard-bitten man of the
world, has been impatiently listening to two young officers, Ferrando
(tenor) and Guglielmo (baritone), praising their mistresses' constancy.
Nonsense, he scoffs; all women are the same—and no better than they
should be. *Così fan tutte*, in fact. Now every lover knows perfectly well
that his beloved is different from all other women, and Ferrando and
Guglielmo are not exceptions. They are exasperated that Alfonso is so
blind to this obvious truth, and when he proposes a wager they
confidently agree to it. A hundred sequins that he will prove their
'Penelopes' frail. Done! But they must give the ladies no warning, and
for the next twenty-four hours they must do exactly as he directs them.

Act I: *Scene 2*

We find the two sisters, Fiordiligi and Dorabella (sopranos), in a
garden by the sea, each contemplating a miniature of her lord. They

are discoursing very fulsomely on their devotion, but there is an
occasional touch of mischief in the music that reminds us that we are
still in the world of artificial comedy. Suddenly Don Alfonso hurries
in to tell them that their lovers have been ordered to join their regiment
for active service. The young men follow him in, and the five of them
express their feelings in a quintet which is a masterpiece of wit and
characterisation:

Sen - to, oh Di - o!   che que-sto pie - de
Cour - age fails me!   *No e - va - sion*

Soldiers and townsfolk march down to the quayside and Ferrando and
Guglielmo embark with the soldiers in a waiting ship. In a brief but
beautifully written trio the ladies and Alfonso implore the winds and
tides to be propitious:

So - a - ve sia il ven - to
O   wind gent - ly   blow-ing

Act I: *Scene 3*

Back at home, Fiordiligi and Dorabella are (avowedly) inconsol-
able. Their maid, Despina, a kind of feminine Figaro, rallies them. Why
these absurd heroics? she asks. Absence causes the heart to wander,
and their lovers are probably having a high old time away from them.
Why don't they do the same? The sisters sweep out of the room indignantly. Soon Alfonso comes in, bribes the maid to help him in his
plot and introduces the two young men, fantastically disguised as
Albanians; and when the sisters return, the 'Albanians' begin to pay
court to them in extravagant terms, each wooing the other's betrothed.
At first it looks as though Don Alfonso will lose his money. Fiordiligi,
for instance, declares that she is—

Co - me sco-glio   im - mo - to re - sta
Firm as   rock   *in   o - cean plant-ed,*

—a pompous burlesque of the grand manner, with great leaps up and down the scale (the original Fiordiligi had a voice of exceptional compass). At last Fiordiligi and Dorabella can bear the impudence of these 'foreigners' no longer and they haughtily leave the room. Alfonso warns his young friends that the game is not yet over, but they laugh at him; and Ferrando sings of his faith and love in a warmly romantic *aria:*

Un' au - ra a-mo - ro - sa
Her eye so al - lur - ing

ACT I: *Scene 4*

The first act ends with a wildly comic scene in the garden, which Mozart builds up with the utmost constructive skill. The 'Albanians', desperate with the pangs of despised love, pretend to swallow poison. Despina, disguised as a doctor, 'mesmerises' them back to life, and the sisters are beginning to feel that after all there is something to be said for men who will kill themselves for love. But when the suicides become more enterprising than men in their condition ought to be, they flare up again in virtuous indignation. The betting is now about even.

ACT II: *Scene 1*

Once again Despina makes gentle fun of her mistresses for their fidelity. They ponder over her words, and when Don Alfonso summons them to the garden where Ferrando and Guglielmo are serenading them with singers and instrument-players, they are not exactly displeased.

ACT II : *Scene 2*

Alfonso and Despina give the lovers a lesson in courtly gallantry. Then the two couples pair off diagonally as in the first act, and before long the disguised Guglielmo has won the heart of Dorabella, his friend's sweetheart. Fiordiligi then comes in, hotly pressed by Ferrando. She dismisses him in a rage whose intensity suggests that she is furious not only with him but with her own weakening resistance. Then she gives way to her remorse in another long and elaborate *aria:*

Per   pie - ta,   ben mio,   per - do - ña
Ah,___ my___   love___ for - give   my___ mad - ness!

It now begins to look as though Don Alfonso will *win* his wager after all; and, incidentally, it is a tribute to the younger men's 'sportsmanship'—or to the charm of wooing a new mistress!—that they do not 'play to lose'.

Act II: *Scene 3*

No, they certainly play to win, alternately elated and horrified at their success. The passionate and highly strung Fiordiligi is soon reduced to the level of her sister, and a wedding breakfast is prepared. The versatile Despina dives once more into her extensive wardrobe and appears this time as a notary. She reads out the marriage contract between 'these noble Albanians and these Ferrarese ladies', which the ladies then sign. But at that moment military music is heard and Alfonso announces that the regiment has returned. They push Ferrando and Guglielmo into another room, from which the conspirators soon emerge in their right clothes if not in their right minds. There is a great deal more byplay and confusion, but matters are straightened out at last; and we are left to reflect, presumably, that although 'thus do all women', the men would find them vastly less interesting if they did otherwise.

The Magic Flute

Libretto by Emmanuel Schikaneder and Gieseke.   First Production,
Time: Legendary.   Vienna, 1791.

> 'And the old man ordered and developed his thoughts in a musical language full of grace and daring. He told of love, of fear, of vain quarrels, of all-conquering laughter, of the calm light of the intellect, of the arrows of the mind piercing with their golden shafts the monsters of Ignorance and Hate.'
>
> **Anatole France**: *The Revolt of the Angels*.
> (Trans. Mrs. Wilfrid Jackson.)

The Magic Flute is no doubt the most fantastic mixture of the sublime and the ridiculous ever put on the stage. We fidget in our seats as one grotesque absurdity succeeds another; and then—something happens: one of these preposterous puppets begins to sing—is, as it were, illumined by song, dissolved into music; and what was before mere pantomime trickery becomes ageless and timeless magic, the very revelation of godhead. What seemed an assemblage of clowns and buffoons becomes a flight of archangels, radiant with the laughter of the spheres and luminous with that compassionate love that moves the sun and all the stars. If ever the toilworn adjective 'divine' could be applied to a work of art it is to *The Magic Flute*. Oh yes, we know that the *libretto* was by a fellow-Freemason, that Mozart was commissioned to compose the music and composed it in a few months in the year of his death. We know also that the actual composition of music, the inking-in of little black blobs on endless sheets of manuscript paper, can be sheer sordid hard labour with nothing romantic or inspirational about it; a weary, brain-fagging, back-breaking job. I am all for realism in these matters; but any man who lives by this kind of work knows that there are days when it is not work at all, days when his brain races along delightedly and the physical labour of giving shape to his ideas becomes an ecstasy of the spirit. Some say it is merely because his physique is in perfect harmony; but there is no really clinching explanation, and we cannot afford to scoff at the old idea of the divine fire descending until we can think of a better one. The fact remains that *The Magic Flute* is a miracle; that the touch of the music heals the *libretto* of every imperfection. In the words of Clutton-Brock, "The silver bells ring from every tree and the enchanted nightingales sing in all the thickets, and the sages and the lovers smile like children; and the laughter passes naturally into the divine beauty of Mozart's religion, which is solemn because laughter and pity are reconciled in it, not rejected as profane."

The Overture, one of the most beautifully balanced in existence, puts us in the proper mood at once, with its darting swallow-dives and busy little themes that flutter like butterflies' wings. We are entering an enchanted world (externally it is ancient Egypt, but fairy-land has no local habitation), and we must suspend disbelief and cast away cold, withering logic. We are going to see fantastic genii, comic blackamoors, vengeful queens, kindly and omniscient priests of Isis and lovers winning each other through ordeals of fire and water and living happily ever after. We must become children again.

Act I

Tamino, an Egyptian prince (tenor), runs on to the stage confused and out of breath. He is fleeing from an enormous snake, and in his haste he stumbles and falls into a swoon. Three ladies-in-waiting to the Queen of the Night (two sopranos, one contralto), black-garbed and mysterious, appear and slay the monster with their spears. They vanish, and Tamino, recovering consciousness, sees a grotesque figure dressed in yellow feathers approaching him. It is Papageno (baritone), who explains his costume by telling us, in a lilting, jingling song, that he is a birdcatcher:

Der Vog-el-fän-ger bin ich ja,
I__ am a fow-ler blithe and gay.

Tamino sees the dead serpent and naturally thinks Papageno is his rescuer. "Why, of course!" says the birdcatcher, and immediately begins to boast of the power of his mighty arm. He is exposed at once: the three ladies reappear and place a golden padlock on his mouth to punish him for lying. To Tamino they give a miniature of the daughter of the Queen of the Night, and at the first glance he falls in love with her:

Dies Bild-niss ist be-zau-bernd schön,
A form ar-ray'd in beau-ty rare,

In a few moments the Queen herself (soprano) appears. She tells the Prince that her daughter Pamina has been abducted by Sarastro, an evil magician, and Tamino passionately pledges himself to rescue her. The ladies take the padlock from Papageno's mouth, saying they hope it will be a lesson to him to speak the truth. They then give him a set of chimes and Tamino a magic flute. The two adventurers must use these as signals of danger in their perilous enterprise.

In Sarastro's palace Pamina (soprano) is being pestered by Monostatos (tenor), a ridiculous blackamoor. Papageno comes on the scene and the Moor scuttles away to plot fresh mischief. Papageno comforts Pamina: a noble prince is hastening to rescue her. And they sing that duet which will for ever bring despair to writers who try to translate its ineffable beauty into words:

Bei Männ - ern, wel - che Lie - be füh-len,
The man - ly heart with love — o'er - flow-ing,

Meanwhile, Tamino approaches a grove in which stand three temples. Ominous voices drive him away from the doors of the first two, but at the third door a priest appears who tells him that the Queen has deceived him: Sarastro is no evil magician, he is the fount of all human wisdom. Tamino plays on his flute and then he hears the chiming of Papageno's bells. They are drawn together, and Papageno brings in Pamina. The three are about to escape, when Monostatos and his slaves run in to intercept them. Again Papageno remembers the virtue of his talisman: he plays a rhythmic, leaping melody on his chimes, and the blackamoor and his slaves are at once charmed out of their wickedness by the power of music. They stop as if petrified, and then dance away stiffly and jerkily like clockwork dolls. It is not great or terrible music that so hypnotises them, just a childlike little tune that has made them children again. Trumpets sound to herald the approach of Sarastro (bass), the High Priest of Isis, before whom all tremble. Tamino and Pamina are brought before him and confess their love. So be it, he says, in music of immense power and gravity: they must pass through the ordeals of probation to prove that they are worthy of the highest felicity.

ACT II

The priests gather in the sacred grove, and Sarastro invokes the aid of Isis and Osiris for the youthful pair who are to undergo their trial—in one of the most sublime hymns that ever expressed at once the humility and dignity of the soul of man:

O I - sis! und O - si - ris! Schenk-et der Wei___
Great I - sis! Great O - si - ris! Strength-en with wis-dom's

Geist dem nev - en Paar!
strength this nov - ice pair.

So the ordeals begin. Papageno is involved too; but he makes no
secret of the fact that all *he* wants to gain is earthly content—plenty to
eat and drink and a pretty little wife of his own nature. Sarastro has
one for him, they say, but he must be patient and prudent. While they
are away, the Queen of the Night finds Pamina and poisons her mind
against the High Priest. There is only one way to salvation, she says:
to kill Sarastro. And she gives her daughter a dagger. It is here that
she sings the great Vengeance *aria*, whose leaping figures dart and
hiss like tongues of fire—

—in D minor, Mozart's favourite key for the discharge of demonic
fury. The Queen of the Night is indeed a remarkable incarnation of
cold, venomous hatred (her very name, Astrifiammante, seems to
strike out stinging sparks as one hears it!), and this *aria*, rising to F
in *alt*, is one of the most brilliant Mozart ever wrote. (The part was
written for his sister-in-law Josepha Hofer, who had a voice of exceptional compass.)

Presently Pamina is found by Sarastro. She protests against what
she thinks is his tyranny, but he explains gently that all is being ordered
for the best. Her mother, he says, is inspired by hatred, and hatred is a
futile weapon that turns upon those who use it. Love alone is all-
powerful and will prevail. And he expounds to her the gospel of Isis, in
a grave and beautiful benediction that sums up the spirit of the whole
opera:

Well, there are mistakes, misunderstandings and complications;
but—love alone is all-powerful and will prevail. Tamino and Pamina
surmount the ordeals and enter into the light of truth and happiness;
Papageno is given his bride, Papagena, a dainty little maiden dressed
in yellow feathers like himself; the wicked Queen and the foolish
Monostatos are shown the error of their lives, and all hates and

rancours are smoothed out and dissolved in the benign key of E flat, in which the opera began. "The silver bells ring from every tree and the enchanted nightingales sing in all the thickets, and the sages and the lovers smile like children; and the laughter passes naturally into the divine beauty of Mozart's religion, which is solemn because laughter and pity are reconciled in it, not rejected as profane."

JACQUES OFFENBACH

(1819–1880)

The Tales of Hoffmann

Libretto by Jules Barbier and Michel Carré,
  after stories by E. T. A. Hoffmann.
Time: Early Nineteenth Century.

First Production,
Paris, 1881.

> 'Now must I these three praise—
> Three women that have wrought
> What joy is in my days.'
>
> W. B. YEATS.

The Tales of Hoffmann—that fantastic box of tricks out of which spring dolls and drolls, angels and demons—was Offenbach's last and finest work. He was in deadly earnest about it. It was to be his final testament, his conclusive summing-up of human life. For years he had written to please the public, this court jester to the Second Empire, this laureate of the Boulevards; now he was writing to please himself, and writing with a burning sincerity. For years he had mischievously lampooned and parodied more serious composers; at last he would try to prove that he could beat them at their own game. He wrote to Carvalho, the director of the *opéra-comique*: "Make haste, make haste to mount my piece; I am in a hurry and have only one wish in the world—to see the *première* of this work." Offenbach died on October 5th, 1880; *The Tales of Hoffmann* was produced on February 10th, 1881. The gods certainly have a sense of humour.

PROLOGUE

Hoffmann, the poet (tenor), and Nicklausse, his friend (mezzo-soprano), are carousing with their cronies in Luther's tavern. Councillor Lindorf watches them balefully. He is jealous of Hoffmann because he finds out that his mistress, Stella, an opera singer, has made an assignation with the poet. Hoffmann begins the song of Kleinzach, a comic legendary dwarf—

Il é-tait u-ne fois à la cour d'Eise-nach!
Now once up-on a time at the Court of Eise-nach!

—but in the middle he breaks off to rhapsodise about a woman he has seen and loved at first sight. The company calls on him for the stories of his love affairs. Yes, there are three, he says, and here is the first:

ACT I

She is a doll, Olympia, made by Dr. Spallanzani (tenor), a famous scientist, who passes her off as his daughter. Guests assemble at his house. They generally appear as a wizened, raddled company, like ghosts of a bygone age, which helps to deepen the macabre atmosphere of the whole opera. Coppelius (baritone), Spallanzani's partner, a queer vulture-like creature, has sold Hoffmann a pair of magic spectacles, and looking at Olympia through these, the poet falls in love with her. She sings to the company:

Les oi-seaux dans la char-mil — — — — le.
Ev 'ry grove with song-birds la — — — — den.

Coppelius returns, livid with rage: Spallanzani has paid him for his work in worthless bank-notes. He smashes the doll, and Hoffmann realises that he has been fooled.

ACT II

We are in Venice, on the balcony of a palace overlooking the Grand Canal. Giulietta (soprano), a courtesan, is giving a magnificent ball, and in the magical stillness of the summer night she and her guests sing the sultry and sensuous Barcarolle:

Bel - le nuit, Ô   nuit d'a-mour,
Love - ly night, O   night of love,

Hoffmann is in love with Giulietta, but she has granted her favours to Schlemil (bass). Again the spirit of evil enters the fable, this time as Dapertutto (baritone), a grotesque magician who steals men's shadows. Hoffmann is his latest quarry, and he sings a song to the magic mirror that is to take away Hoffmann's reflection:

The theft is accomplished by Giulietta, and when Hoffmann looks again into a mirror he sees no reflection of himself. He kills Schlemil in a duel and takes from him the key of Giulietta's room. But in his moment of triumph he hears a peal of mocking laughter and Giulietta in the arms of a new lover passes in a gondola. Hoffmann has been fooled a second time.

ACT III

His third love is Antonia (soprano), a lovely, fragile girl who has inherited a wonderful voice from her dead mother. She is forbidden to sing because of her health, but she cannot refuse Hoffmann, who hears in her voice the music of heaven. Once more an evil influence darkens the house—Dr. Miracle (bass), whom Crespel (bass), Antonia's father, fears and hates, since he suspects him of having caused the death of his wife. By now we perceive a sinister similarity between Coppelius, Dapertutto and Miracle (they are often sung by the same artist), and it is borne on us that they are all evil projections of Hoffmann's own soul—projections which on each occasion poison the pure spring of his love. Miracle hypnotises Antonia into singing, having caused her dead mother to speak to her out of a portrait, and as he capers round her in a devil's dance, furiously playing a violin, she breathes out all her life in her song:

EPILOGUE

Hoffmann has told his stories of the three women who brought him joy and frustration, and they are noisily applauded. By this time he is drunk, and Stella, in disgust, departs from the tavern with Councillor Lindorf, leaving the poet only his memories.

GIACOMO PUCCINI

(1858–1924)

Manon Lescaut

Libretto by the Composer and others after Prévost.
Time: Eighteenth Century.

First Production,
Turin, 1893.

'. . . Ah, Manon, you have sold
The keys of heaven at a vulgar rate.'

WILFRID SCAWEN BLUNT.

Manon Lescaut was not Puccini's first opera. He had already written
Le Villi (*The Witches*) and *Edgar*, but the world at large is unanimous in
ignoring these, and for practical purposes we may regard *Manon
Lescaut* not as the first opera by Puccini, but as the first Puccini opera
—an obvious distinction. It is the work of a young man rejoicing in his
new-found strength, and, as is the way of youth, very prodigal of it.
There is probably more sheer melody in *Manon Lescaut* than in any of
Puccini's other works; in fact it is, if anything, overloaded with melody.
He has not yet learned to discipline his prodigality, to throw his
melodies into higher relief by more frequent interludes of realistic
dialogue or characterisation, as he did so effectively in the *Trittico*
and so superbly in *Turandot*. Open *Manon Lescaut* at almost any page
and you find the same thing: big passionate tunes sailing along the
lines like ships across the horizon. Not very subtle tunes, perhaps, not
always firmly controlled in form and length; but a wealth to singers
and a joy to listeners!

We have already considered Massenet's setting of this well-
beloved story. To me, Puccini's score has a greater power and sweep
than Massenet's and speaks in more impassioned accents. The music,
as music, has a more aristocratic mien. On the other hand, the French-
man shows a sharper psychological insight and an exquisite delicacy
of touch. There is nothing in *Manon Lescaut* that 'melts in the mouth'
so lovingly as the Dream Song in *Manon*, or Manon's farewell to their
little supper-table. Massenet's Manon slips more cosily into the affections than Puccini's, and Massenet has an easier command of that
little woman' type of pathos in which, however, Puccini measurably
surpassed him later.

Writing his opera eight or nine years after Massenet's, Puccini
naturally tried to go over as little of the same ground as possible. He
is more faithful in detail to Prévost in making Lescaut Manon's

127

brother instead of her cousin and in following the deported lovers
to the New World. He is less faithful in spirit, however: for by omitting
the notorious 'Apartment in Paris' (immemorial sanctuary of truant
lovers!) and all reference to Des Grieux's religious avocation Puccini
has somewhat blunted the point of the story. Instead of the clash
between the amoral and religious temperaments we have mere
conventional operatics, the heroine little more than a superior trollop
and the hero a romantic young ninny who can't keep away from what
she gives to him and sells to other men. Still, we can put up with
conventional operatics when our composer is Puccini.

Act I

Puccini's first act is on similar lines to Massenet's. Again we have
the courtyard of the inn at Amiens filled with a lively crowd of
villagers, soldiers, *grisettes* and students, who chaff and rally each
other, to fresh, springtime melodies rich in the unmistakable Puccini
aroma. Out of the diligence from Arras step Manon (soprano);
Lescaut (baritone), who is drawn rather less coarsely than Massenet's
seedy rascal; and Geronte de Ravoir (bass), Treasurer-General, in
whom are concentrated Manon's numerous wealthy admirers. Des
Grieux meets Manon and gives voice to his sudden infatuation:

As in the earlier opera, they escape to Paris, only this time it is
Geronte who has ordered the carriage which, in legal jargon, they
convert to their own use. The old rake is furious; but Lescaut, seeing a
chance of plucking this golden goose, consoles him, saying they will
follow the fugitives to Paris, where Geronte's money will easily outbuy
Des Grieux's devotion.

Act II

So it proves. And here we see Manon installed in Geronte's house,
living in what used to be called 'guilty splendour'. Lescaut lounges in,
appraises the work of dressmaker and hairdresser, and nods approvingly.

Hasn't her good brother done well for her after all? he asks. How foolish she was to elope with that young student; why, he has nothing in the bank! Manon agrees, but there is a far-away look in her eyes. She cannot forget the lover she has abandoned; and, though her life is full, her heart is empty:

In quel - le tri - ne mor-bi - de
In those soft silk - en cur - tains

Singers enter and perform a dainty madrigal composed by Geronte, the quality of which suggests that he is wasting his time in the Treasury. Manon yawns and gives Lescaut a purse to pay them; but that sensitive creature, unwilling to wound the delicacy of artists, pockets the purse himself and dismisses them with a pompous flourish. Geronte comes in with several friends, and a music-master who is to instruct Manon in the minuet. Manon yawns more pointedly than ever; and her intelligent brother, fearing that unless she has a little diversion she may become rash and spoil everything, goes off in search of Des Grieux. And when Geronte and the others have left her she hears a quick step, and there stands her lover—white, grief-stricken and reproachful. At first he curses and reviles her, but her beauty gradually bewitches him again; and there follows a splendid march of music, the melodies falling tumultuously over one another like breakers in a high tide. One triumphant theme—

—(which the fastidious may find a trifle commonplace) is repeated many times later with great emotional effect. But at the climax of their duet Geronte suddenly appears at the door. So! This is the woman he has picked out of the gutter, and this is how she repays him! He stamps away in a fury and the lovers prepare to escape. But Manon lingers, gazing round with a sigh at the luxury she is leaving behind; on which Des Grieux again breaks into passionate reproaches:

Ah! Ma - non,___ mi tra - di - sea il tuo fol - le pen - sier,___
Ah! Ma - non,___ you be - tray me a - gain with that thought,___

I

Lescaut returns. They must take to their heels at once, he says; Geronte is bringing the soldiery to arrest them. Manon, true to type, cannot bear to leave her jewellery behind. The two men implore her to make haste, but she maddens them by rushing round the room and stuffing under her cloak everything she can lay hands on. The delay is fatal; Geronte bursts in with the soldiers and Manon is dragged away.

Act III

She is sentenced to be deported, with other women of loose character. Puccini describes the journey to Havre in an orchestral intermezzo built principally on themes from the love duet in the second act, after which the curtain rises, showing the harbour in the grey light of dawn. Des Grieux and Lescaut are plotting her rescue outside the barracks while the orchestra intones a dolorous melody in D minor. By and by Manon appears at a window in the wall of the barracks. Des Grieux kisses her hands through the window-bars and swears he will never forsake her. Their plans miscarry, however, and as the morning light grows stronger the square is filled with curious townsfolk The women, in chains, are led on to the quayside and a sergeant of marines calls their names, over a dirgelike melody in E flat minor in which we can hear anticipations of *Turandot*. Des Grieux and Manon take a mournful farewell of one another, but when the sergeant is about to pull her away Des Grieux loses all control. To an urgent, hammering theme he implores the captain of the ship to let him sail with her:

Gu̇ar - da - te,   paz - zo   son,   guar - da - te,
Be - hold me,   I__ am   mad!   Be - hold   me,

"All right, my lad," says the captain, with bluff good-humour; "if you want to populate America—I'll take you!" And as Des Grieux joins her in the ship, Lescaut gazes after his sister, shakes his head sadly at the loss of this beautiful source of revenue, and wanders away

Act IV

The last act is (to me) of the nature of an anticlimax. I can almost imagine Puccini, still thrilling with the splendid passion of Act III, squaring his shoulders and saying to himself, perhaps a little resignedly: "Come now; a pity we couldn't have ended there, but obviously Manon has to die (otherwise it won't be a real opera)

Let's make the best job of it we can!" And so we don't whole-heartedly believe in this death scene. It is just a little 'contrived', just a trifle 'stagey'. The springs of melody, too, run rather more slowly, and although earlier themes are repeated with telling dramatic effect, yet their dramatic effect strikes us as a shade too conscious.

It is a short act and consists entirely of dialogue between Des Grieux and Manon. They are threading their way through a vast plain on the borders of New Orleans. The Land of Promise has done them no good. They are poorly dressed and worn out with fatigue. Manon leans heavily on Des Grieux, who supports her only with difficulty. She is parched with thirst, and he leaves her for a moment to explore the countryside. But it is a desert, not a drop of water anywhere. Every moment the darkness deepens. He goes away again to seek for shelter—a cottage, a woodland hut, anything. Left alone, Manon faces the fact that she is going to die; the wildness and solitude of the place begin to overpower her. When Des Grieux returns she clings desperately to him, protesting brokenly that she loves him. And, with the terror of death upon her, the poor soul at last speaks from her heart. "Time will wipe away all my faults," she whispers as she dies, "but not my love."

And so ends 'the first Puccini opera'. Not a masterpiece like *Bohème* or *Butterfly*, but nevertheless so full of the true Puccini fragrance that one feels remorseful at having criticised it. That is the insidious thing about Puccini. He is, in fact, rather like Manon herself: we see his shortcomings but we cannot resist his fascination. As James Wylie says, in *What Every Woman Knows*: "It's that damned char-r-r-m!"

La Bohème

Libretto by Giuseppe Giacosa and Luigi Illica
    after Murger's novel.
Time: about 1830.

    First Production,
    Turin, 1896.

> 'O, lovely days long dead! There falls on me,
> In this dim world I may not understand
> An echo of your sweetness; in my hand
> One frail, sad rose inspires eternity
> With dreams that are no more, and from the sea
> That beats upon this grey perplexéd land,
> Blows rumour of some merry drunken band
> That keeps your revels still in Arcady.'
>
>   RICHARD MIDDLETON.

La Bohème is a testament of youth. For that reason it is an opera one finds very difficult to criticise and almost impossible not to love. It is

the most appealing and companionable of Puccini's operas, because
it speaks to all of us of our own bohemia, no matter where we made it.
In the heart of every man who has adored a Mimi or courted a Musetta,
who has cracked a bottle and a jest with the Schaunards and Collines
of this world, the music of *La Bohème* will always hold a place. It
is not profound music; neither is the heart of youth. If youth but
knew . . . but the whole magic of youth is that it cannot know but can
only feel. To me it is Puccini's perfect score. Elsewhere he was sometimes more intense, more dramatic, more powerful; but nowhere
was he more consistently in tune with his subject. The emotion is
never rank: over it all is that slight sparkle of frost that keeps it fresh,
that faint silvery radiance that seems to cover the music with starry
crystals.

Act I

· The students' attic. Rudolph (tenor), the poet, gazes out of the
window on the roofs glittering with frost. Marcel (baritone), the
painter, is working on his famous picture, 'The Passage of the Red
Sea', which has been submitted to the judges so many times, under so
many different disguises and different names. Rudolph remarks on
the smoke of the Paris chimneys—

—a melody that becomes important later. Yet he and Marcel have
nothing to light a fire with. Well, one cannot work if one's blood is
frozen. "Here," says Rudolph, "let's burn my celebrated drama."
"Great soul!" says Marcel, and they cram it in the grate and set it
alight. Colline (bass), the philosopher, comes in, and the three of them
warm themselves at Rudolph's muse, commenting on the sparkling
phrases and brilliant colours. As the fire flickers and dies there is a
shout, and Schaunard (baritone), the musician, bustles in with errand-
boys carrying food and wine. He has earned some money by pretending
to play a troublesome parrot to death. But, he says, it is Christmas
Eve: they will store the food and go out to dine instead. At that

moment we hear a knock at the door and Benoit (bass), the old land-
lord, comes in for the rent. Marcel shows him the money—and covers
it up. To music that fairly bubbles with wit and good-humour they
proceed to make him tipsy on Schaunard's wine, and at last bundle
him out—without his money. Off now to the Café Momus! But
Rudolph suddenly remembers he has to finish an article. He will join
them later. He has written only a few words when there comes a timid
tap at the door. It is a little seamstress (soprano), his neighbour. Her
candle has gone out, and exhausted by the stairs she now collapses on
a chair. Rudolph sprinkles water over her and then pours her out a
glass of wine. The writing here is of an exquisite fragility. She is just
about to go when she remembers that she has dropped her key. While
they are feeling for it on the floor his hand meets hers:

Che ge - li - da ma - ni - na, se la la - sci ris - cal - dar.
Your ti - ny hand is fro-zen! Let me warm it in - to life.

He tells her of his life and work; and the little maiden in return tells
him her name is Mimi and that for a living she embroiders fine satins
and silks:

Si,   Mi   chia-ma-no Mi - mì
Yes,   They   call___ me Mi - mi

But his friends are tired of waiting for him. They call up from the
street. "Keep places for us," he answers; "we will follow quickly."
And he turns to take Mimi in his arms. A magical thing has happened
to them.

ACT II

Outside the Café Momus. All the uproar and racket of Christmas
Eve in the Latin Quarter. Rudolph introduces Mimi to his friends,
and the five sit down at a table in front of the restaurant. Rudolph has
bought her a bonnet, Schaunard has bought himself a trumpet,
Colline some secondhand books, and they are all hilariously happy
until—there are shouts of acclamation, and 'a pretty girl of twenty,
very coquettish, rather ambitious, with no pretensions to spelling',

trips down the street on the arm of a respectable old gentleman who is trying to recover his youth. It is Musetta (soprano), Marcel's first (and only) love. She sees Marcel and decides on some fun at his expense. The waiters set out a table on the other side of the street, and from there Musetta starts to taunt Marcel. She sings her famous song in praise of light love:

Her escort, Alcindoro (bass), realising that recovering one's youth can be a very embarrassing process, implores her to stop making a scene. She gets rid of him by pretending her shoe hurts and packing him off to get it mended. Then she hops over to Marcel and the bohemian circle is complete. The friends dance off behind a military patrol that marches down the street, and when the poor dupe Alcindoro returns the waiters pounce on him with the bill for the whole party.

Act III

"They are not long, the days of wine and roses." We have had our share of young love and young laughter, and now we begin to see the darker colours of this bohemia which is 'the preface to the Academy, the Hospital or the Morgue'.

It is early morning in February, and at the Barrière d'Enfer the ground is white with snow. As the custom-house officers gather up their things to depart for the day, a fragile figure, shaken with coughing, steals in. It is Mimi, and she is seeking Marcel, who is in the tavern on the corner. He runs out to her. "Mimi! Come inside. It's bitterly cold here." But when she learns that Rudolph is inside she will not go in. She appeals to Marcel: won't he help her? She and Rudolph—they cannot live together, yet they cannot live apart. It is torment. Rudolph's jealousy drives her mad. But suddenly Rudolph comes out and Mimi hides behind a tree. Rudolph then tells Marcel *his* story: he cannot live any longer with Mimi. She is fickle and heartless:

And yet—he is sorry for her: she is so weak and sickly; perhaps she is dying. At last he sees Mimi and rushes to embrace her. But she gently frees herself and bids him farewell. It is wiser, she says; she is returning:

Don-de lie - ta u - sci al tuo gri - do d'a - mo - re,
To the home that she left at the voice of her lov - er,

Marcel and Musetta come in quarrelling. And in a masterly quartet Puccini combines their contrasting farewells—Marcel and Musetta flippant and sarcastic, Rudolph and Mimi aching with the memory of lost happiness.

ACT IV

We are in the attic again. Rudolph and Marcel are working, but we can see that neither of them is really concentrating on his work. At last Marcel takes out of his pocket a bunch of ribbons. Rudolph lets fall his pen and picks up Mimi's old bonnet; and their talk gently drifts into a duet full of yearning for the past:

O,   Mi-mi tu più non tor - ni
Ah,   Mi-mi! false, fick-le - heart - éd

Schaunard and Colline come in and the four proceed to dance and play the fool, but in comparison with Act I the levity seems slightly forced. When it is at its height the door bursts open and Musetta stands there. She had brought Mimi, who has collapsed and has not strength to climb the stairs. Frantic with distress, the men carry her in and lay her on the bed. While Rudolph tries to warm her hands in his, Musetta takes Marcel out to pawn some ear-rings and buy a muff. Colline takes off his old overcoat and looks at it; and we guess what he is going to do:

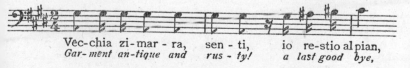

Vec-chia zi-mar - ra,   sen - ti,   io re-stio al pian,
Gar- ment an-tique and   rus - ty!   a last good bye,

He goes out slowly, taking Schaunard with him. Rudolph and Mimi sit together talking of old days, the music poignantly recalling their first meeting. Musetta and Marcel return with the muff, which she pretends Rudolph has bought. Mimi puts her hands in it and sinks back exhausted. Colline comes in very gently and quietly with the money raised on his coat. While Rudolph is putting Musetta's cloak over the window to shut out the strong sunlight, Schaunard suddenly leans over Mimi and whispers: "Marcel! She's dead!" Rudolph turns from the window and stares at them. "What's the matter? Why are you looking so strange?" They cannot speak; and as the truth dawns on him he utters a heartbroken cry—"Mimi!"—and flings himself across the bed.

Tosca

Libretto by Illica and Giacosa after Sardon.   First Production,
Time: 1800.   Rome, 1900.

> '. . . The vile conclusion
> I now begin with grief and shame to utter:
> He would not, but by gift of my chaste body
> To his concupiscible intemperate lust,
> Release my brother; and, after much debatement,
> My sisterly remorse confutes mine honour,
> And I did yield to him: but the next morn betimes,
> His purpose surfeiting, he sends a warrant
> For my poor brother's head.'
>
> SHAKESPEARE: *Measure for Measure.*

Tosca is operatic *Grand Guignol*. The torture scene in Act II might be taken as symbolic of the whole opera: every conceivable device of an artist in pain is used to torment us; every imaginable screw is twisted and turned, and released only when our nerves are on the point of snapping under the pressure. The torture is entirely sensory: we are thrilled, shocked, startled, hurt; but our deeper feelings are not touched. It is the only one of Puccini's serious operas in which the note of true pathos is hardly ever struck. We feel very little pity for Tosca, Cavaradossi and the rest; for the main reason that they are not men and women, but merely figures. Puccini himself gave us the clue when he said that he was forced 'to colour the drama instead of illuminating it from within'. But—it is the colouring of a master. Nowhere is his sense of atmosphere more confident—that uncanny instinct he had for catching and holding the very *smell* of the place and time; nowhere is his melody stronger and more resilient. Not Puccini's most powerful score, but certainly his most forceful; and within its limits a masterpiece.

Act I

Three pounding hammer-blows in the orchestra (the *motif* of Scarpia, chief of police), and the curtain rises on a corner of the Church of St. Andrea in Rome. For a moment the scene is empty. Then Angelotti (bass) stumbles in, dressed in prison clothes, dishevelled and panting for breath. He is fleeing from the 1800 prototype of the Gestapo. He finds a key that has been hidden for him and slips into the Attavanti Chapel. Only just in time: for in comes the old Sacristan (bass). He is followed by Cavaradossi (tenor), who resumes work on a picture he is painting:

Re - con - di - ta ar-mo - ni - a
Strange har - mo - ny   of   con - trasts

Left alone, Cavaradossi hears a noise and discovers Angelotti. They are old friends. He hastily gives him the basket of food he has brought and hides him again as he hears someone approaching. It is Tosca (soprano), Rome's greatest *prima donna* and the painter's secret mistress. She is jealous of the unknown woman who sometimes comes in to pray and whose beauty Cavaradossi has caught on the canvas. But he soon calms her and their dialogue mounts into a passionate and fiery-coloured love duet, of which the main melody—

—is repeated many times later with cunning dramatic effect. When Tosca has gone Cavaradossi lets Angelotti out of the chapel and rushes away with him to hide him at his villa. Choirboys come streaming in for the Te Deum, and while the Sacristan is garrulously telling them their duties the Scarpia *motif* strikes in like a thunderclap and Scarpia himself (baritone) appears—the most feared and hated man in Rome. The trail of the fugitive Angelotti has led him to the church. He strides round the building, the Sacristan and the others cowering away in terror. Who painted that picture? Ha! Cavaradossi: a man suspected. And when Tosca returns in search of her lover he cunningly misleads her into believing that Cavaradossi has disappeared to keep a love tryst. Meanwhile, they are beginning the Te Deum. And while the pure voices rise in a chorus of praise to God, this gargoyle stands gloating over his plot: he will hang Tosca's lover and possess her himself. When the Te Deum reaches its climax he turns a hideous mask of hypocrisy to the altar and lifts his voice with the rest: *"Te aeternum patrem omnis terra veneratur!"*

ACT II

Scarpia sits at his supper-table in a room in the Farnese Palace. His devilish plans are maturing. Cavaradossi has been arrested; Tosca will soon walk into the trap he has laid. Even now she is singing in a cantata in the Queen's apartments below, and the voices float in through the open window. Cavaradossi is brought in. Scarpia accuses him of aiding a fugitive from justice. He contemptuously denies it, and they remove him to the torture-chamber to force his confession. Tosca has entered. Scarpia treats her at first with insidious courtesy, but she quickly grows suspicious; then he alters his tone, and to music that grinds as harshly as the sharpening of an axe he tells her that Cavaradossi is lying in the inner room, his head bound with a circle of steel which tightens until the blood spurts out. "Ah, monster!" she shrieks. "You will kill him!" He laughs sardonically. "Tosca was never so tragical even on the stage!" But at last, with her lover's groans piercing through her head, Tosca breaks down and tells Scarpia where Angelotti is hidden. Scarpia immediately stops the torture. But Cavaradossi must still be shot, he explains; he has been convicted of treason. Tosca suddenly faces him. "Your price, man! Can't I bribe you?" Scarpia laughs, "Oh yes, I am to be bought, certainly; but— not with money." And Tosca realises the snare she has been caught in. Scarpia waits, with cynical patience, for her decision, looking at her quizzically over the top of his wine-glass with the air of a connoisseur in human emotions. She prays to the Blessed Virgin for strength:

News comes that Angelotti swallowed poison when they took him.
" 'Tis well," says Scarpia; "hang up his body on the gibbet!" And—
Cavaradossi? He glances inquiringly at Tosca. She can struggle no
more. She nods her head. Scarpia at once orders his men to prepare a
mock execution—'just as in the case of Palmieri'. He writes out a
safe-conduct for Tosca and her lover, and when he turns towards her
to claim his reward she stabs him in the breast with a knife from the
table. He dies in terrible agony. Tosca looks down at him: "And
yesterday before him all Rome trembled!" She lights two candles and
stands one at each side of his head. She places a crucifix on his breast.
Then she tiptoes out of the room, shutting the door noiselessly behind
her.

ACT III

It is the hour before dawn, and we are on the roof of the Castle
St. Angelo. By one of those little masterstrokes of 'theatre' which were
part of his genius Puccini distracts our minds for a moment from blood
and horror with the tinkling of sheep-bells and a shepherd boy (contralto) singing over gently rocking chords in the orchestra—a simple,
almost trivial song whose simplicity is in touching contrast to the
tragedy that overshadows us. The simple things of life must go on.
The stars grow pale and the dawn breaks to the sound of matin bells.
Cavaradossi is led in, a dim grey figure in the half light. He asks for
pen and paper to write a last farewell to his beloved; and as he writes
he becomes absorbed in the memory of lost happiness:

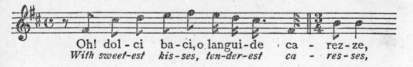

Oh! dol - ci ba - ci, o langui - de ca - rez - ze,
With sweet-est kis - ses, ten-der-est ca - res - ses,

But Tosca has appeared on the platform. Swiftly, breathlessly, she
explains things to him: when the soldiers fire their blank cartridges
he must fall as though shot. Then, when the firing-party has gone, they
will hurry away together from this accursed city and begin a new life.
Laughing excitedly, they make their plans. The soldiers arrive. They
line up and fire. Cavaradossi falls without a cry. He does it splendidly.
"Mario! Mario!" she whispers, "don't move yet. Wait till they've
gone." He does not move; still he does not move. And when Tosca
tries to rouse him she realises that she is holding a dead man. 'Just as
in the case of Palmieri' . . . At that moment Scarpia's officers rush on

to the platform shouting. The murder has been discovered. Tosca leaps on to the parapet—"Scarpia! We shall meet before God!"—and flings herself down into space.

Madam Butterfly

Libretto by L. Illica and G. Giacosa.   First Production,
Time: the present.   Milan, 1904.

> 'And if he ever should come back,
>   What am I to say?
> —Tell him that I watch'd for him
>   All my life away . . .
> . . . And if he should ask me then
>   How you fell asleep?
> —Tell him that I smiled and died.
>   Do not let him weep.'
>
> MAETERLINCK (trans. Frederick York Powell.)

Madam Butterfly is often called the 'Handkerchief Opera', because you must take a handkerchief to the theatre if you wish to enjoy it as Puccini intended you should. It is useless to harden your heart— Puccini will win. In no other opera is his power to draw tears so irresistible; in no other opera is his slightly perverted sense of pity so acute. I say 'slightly perverted' because it always seems to me the product of a kind of sadism, the pity of a man who intensifies his pity by giving pain to the thing he loves. And in *Madam Butterfly* his needle is keener and more incisive than anywhere else. Butterfly herself is his most vital creation—a living, breathing woman whose every line is exquisitely and infallibly in character. Moreover, the *librettists* have cruelly intensified our pity for her by setting her heartrending loyalty against the brutal self-satisfaction of that ogling, swaggering, hip-swinging operatic 'masher', Lieutenant Pinkerton.

ACT I

Pinkerton (tenor) and Goro (tenor), the marriage broker, are talking in the garden of the little house Pinkerton has rented for Madam Butterfly. At the back Nagasaki harbour lies dreaming in the golden haze of the summer afternoon. By and by Sharpless (baritone), the American Consul, joins them, complaining of the steep hill he has just climbed. Pinkerton mixes him a drink and describes the charms of the little Geisha girl he is to marry that afternoon:

A - mo - re o gril - lo,__ dir non sa - pre - i
Is't love or fan - cy,__ I can - not tell you

But, he adds with a knowing wink, he is marrying only 'in Japanese fashion'. Sharpless, a much older man, shakes his head doubtfully: Butterfly trusts him, he says. To him it may be just a light-hearted frolic, while to her it may be a matter of life and death. But Pinkerton laughs it off and actually drinks a toast to his future *American* wife. At that moment the wedding party is heard climbing the hill, Butterfly's clear voice (soprano) soaring above the rest—

....al ri-chia-mo d'a - mor__d'a-mor ben-ni al-lo so - glie
....the sweet summons of love__up - on the threshold stand - ing,

—a melody repeated later in the love duet. Pinkerton and Butterfly are married—a comically brief and simple little ceremony—and eventually the guests begin to leave, Sharpless by now genuinely troubled by Butterfly's obvious sincerity. But nothing can trouble Pinkerton; to him the whole thing is just a huge joke. A moment later there is a sudden outcry and a tall priestlike figure appears. It is the Bonze (bass), Butterfly's uncle. "Where is Cho Cho San?" he cries. "She has renounced her true religion; she has become a Christian!" The relatives are horrified and retreat, howling curses at her. "Well, that's got rid of *them*," says in effect the philosophic Pinkerton, humorously unimpressed by all this fuss. Evening draws in, Butterfly, rather frightened but childishly proud of what she has done, creeps into his arms for protection:

Darkness falls and the sky is thick with stars. Pinkerton eagerly leads his tiny bride towards the house, while their voices rise exultantly in the passionate melody we heard before.

ACT II: *Scene* 1

Three years have passed. Her husband promised to return in the
spring when the robins built their nests. Already they have built
them three times. Suzuki (mezzo-soprano), her servant, says dolefully
that foreign husbands never come back. But nothing can shake
Butterfly's faith: "He will return," she says; "I know it!"

Un — bel di ve - dre - mo
One — fine day we'll no - tice

A shadow falls across the door. It is the Consul. They hail him with
delighted cries. How is he? How is Pinkerton? Is he well? Is he coming?
"Yes—he's—oh, he's quite well," says Sharpless: "in fact, I've a letter
from him . . ." But they are interrupted. Prince Yamadori (baritone)
is crossing the garden. He is in love with Butterfly, but of course the
proud little wife of Lieutenant Pinkerton will have nothing to do with
him. While they are all drinking tea Goro sidles in and tells Sharpless
that Pinkerton's ship is already signalled. The three men whisper
together. "And when they meet again——?" asks Yamadori. Sharpless
shrugs his shoulders. "He doesn't want to see her," he answers. "I have
to break it to her." At last Butterfly and the Consul are left alone and
he begins to read her the letter, over a tender little figure:

Butterfly becomes more and more excited with every sentence. "He's
coming back, isn't he? Tell me! Tell me quickly!" Sharpless tries to
go on reading; she claps her hands and dances, and at length he is so
moved by her piteous eagerness that he cannot speak the words
He jumps up and crushes the letter in his pocket. Then, on a sudden
resolve, he turns to her and takes her hands. "Forgive me if I hurt
you," he says very gently, "but—why not marry Prince Yamadori?"
His words fall like a thunderbolt. At first Butterfly is stunned, then

angry; and then with a shout of triumph she runs into the bedroom and brings back her child. "Tell him that a fine son is waiting for him!" she cries. "What do you call him?" Sharpless asks, taking the little boy in his arms. "His name is Trouble," answers Butterfly, "but tell his father that when he returns his name shall be Joy.' Sharpless promises that he will, and hurries away deeply moved. Butterfly clasps the child passionately to her heart, rocking herself to and fro in grief and indignation. Suddenly there is a distant report: the harbour cannon! They rush frantically to the window and look through the telescope. It is—yes!—Pinkerton's ship, the *Abraham Lincoln*! "They were all liars! Liars!" cries Butterfly. "I've won! My love has come back to me!" Joyously they decorate the house with flowers, to music that curves as gracefully as the curves of rose petals:

It is now quite dark. They make three little holes in the window blind, and Butterfly, Suzuki and the child take up their posts there to watch for the well-remembered figure climbing the hill. Very gently and softly the orchestra begins the music to which Sharpless read the letter, and, as though from an enchanted distance, we hear voices humming the melody and mingling with the sounds and perfumes of the night.

ACT II: *Scene 2*

It is morning. The sunlight gleams through the chinks in the shutters. The scene is precisely as before, except that Suzuki and the child have collapsed and fallen asleep. Butterfly still stands rigid, watching the road to the house. Suzuki wakens with a start and persuades her to take the child and get some rest. As soon as Butterfly has gone there is a knocking at the door. It is Pinkerton and Sharpless. Pinkerton, consistent to the last, has brought his American wife with him. Sharpless explains things to Suzuki in a grave melody that swells into a great trio:

Pinkerton is suddenly overcome with remorse, which takes a thoroughly characteristic turn: he admits he is afraid to face Butterfly, and prepares to go:

Ad - di - o fio - ri - to a - sil
Fare - well___ O hap-py home

Butterfly enters, and at a glance realizes the truth. To music aching with poignancy she wishes Kate Pinkerton (mezzo-soprano) all happiness and says they may have the child if they climb the hill in half an hour. When they have gone she takes down a dagger from the wall and solemnly reads its inscription: 'Death with honour is better than life with dishonour.' She goes behind a screen and—in a moment it is all over. And Pinkerton and Sharpless burst open the door to find the child playing with the American and Japanese flags and Butterfly on the ground, stretching her hands towards him in her death agony.

The Girl of the Golden West

Libretto by Guelfo Civini and Carlo Zangarini after David Belasco.   First Production,
Time: Mid-Nineteenth Century.   New York, 1910.

> 'There's a land where the mountains are nameless,
>   And the rivers all run God knows where;
> There are lives that are erring and aimless,
>   And deaths that just hang by a hair.'
>   ROBERT W. SERVICE.

The Girl of the Golden West brings us a rather different Puccini from the 'happy melodist unwearied' who sang to us in such thoroughly characteristic works as *Bohème* and *Butterfly*. There is a new note, a harsh note, which at first disconcerts us; there is also a new approach to his subject: he is more sparing of melody, more intent on those sharp dagger-thrusts of characterisation which strike home so surely in a work like *Il Tabarro*. Some people, indeed, see in this score a temporary weakening of his powers, a kind of musical constipation. But perhaps a more favourable way of looking at it is that, here as always, he was at pains to catch the essential atmosphere of the drama, and where the situation did not call for a pretty tune he did not write one. The scene is a mining camp in California during the gold fever of 1849–50. Belasco, quoting from an early history of California, says: "In those strange days people coming from God knows where joined forces in that far western land ... struggled, laughed, gambled, cursed, killed, loved and worked out their strange destinies in a manner incredible to us of today. Of one thing only we are sure—they lived!" And for these struggling, laughing, gambling, cursing roughs Puccini adopted a brusque, interjectional style which reflected the rhythm of everyday speech. I do not feel that he was at his best in this style; but I will not deny its forceful effect.

Act I

The 'Polka' is a rough saloon with a bar and a passage at the back, guarded by a stuffed bear, which leads to a dancing-hall. It is evening, and through the window we can see the snowy crests of the mountains, touched with gold from the setting sun. From outside come shouts and mournful strains of song. Larkens (bass), one of the miners, sits on a cask. Nick (tenor), the bartender, walks round lighting the candles, and three or four of the miners come in, talking and laughing. They order drinks and start playing cards. Larkens sits with his head buried in his arms, and they nudge each other sympathetically: he is homesick. Jake Wallace (baritone), the camp minstrel, is heard outside singing as he approaches the saloon—an Indian melody, simple and plaintive, yet with a sort of sunset glow in it:

Che fa - ran - no i vec-chi miei   là lon - ta - no,
I am think-ing of my folk   in the home - stead,

The men join in the chorus as he enters, accompanying himself on his banjo, and at the end of the song Larkens breaks down completely: "Boys, I'm done! I don't care who knows. Send me back home! Send me back home!" The others have a hasty whip-round and collect some passage-money for him. When he has gone, they return to their cards. There is an angry scene when one of them is caught cheating, and a little later Ashby (bass), a transport agent, comes in with news of Ramerrez, leader of a gang of robbers and the terror of the district. Ashby is on his track, and he warns the boys to keep a sharp look-out for him. They drink a toast to Minnie, the young schoolmistress, and Jack Rance (baritone), the sheriff, who is in love with Minnie and savagely jealous, starts a quarrel which ends in pistol-shots. At the

K

height of it Minnie (soprano) rushes in and separates them, snatching the pistols from their hands. The men forget their quarrels and greet her affectionately, offering her little gifts. She admonishes them like children and, opening a Bible, conducts them in a scripture lesson. The postboy enters with letters. Ashby reads his despatch and then turns to Rance. "Sheriff, I'll have this Ramerrez swinging tonight!" and he goes on to explain that the robber's mistress, Spanish Nina, has betrayed him. At last Minnie and Rance are left alone. He tries to make love to her, but she defends herself with a pistol. Bitterly he tells her of his struggles: he has sacrificed everything to his quest for gold, but he would give all his gold for a kiss from her:

Min-nie, dal-la mia ca-sa son par-ti-to
Min-nie, *when I left my lit-tle home*

Minnie is not unsympathetic, but she answers that she will never take a husband unless she loves him. At that moment Nick comes in with a stranger (tenor). Minnie and the stranger start slightly at seeing each other: it is evident they have met before, and Rance, jealous in an instant, begins rudely questioning the other man. The stranger says his name is Johnson; he has called in to rest his horse and perhaps have a game of cards. He and Minnie recall a chance meeting some time before, and we can see from their glances that they are strongly attracted to each other. They begin to dance:

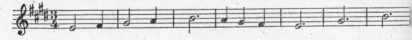

On a false alarm, the miners rush out and saddle their horses to go on the track of Ramerrez. Only Rance hesitates a moment, darkly suspecting the truth: that Ramerrez is Johnson himself. When Minnie and Johnson are alone she invites him to supper at her cabin up the hill. Their growing love is expressed by the waltz theme, which now expands into a broadly flowing, romantic melody.

ACT II

In Minnie's cabin Billy (bass), a redskin, and Wowkle (mezzo-soprano), his squaw, are preparing Minnie's supper. Outside there is a blizzard. Minnie comes in and says the supper will be for two. She then decks herself with a simple and rather pathetic finery, putting roses in her hair and a coloured shawl over her shoulders. The next moment there is a shout of greeting from outside and she opens the door to Johnson, who is dressed in a fur coat and carries a lantern. Shy and confused, Minnie invites him in. They sit chatting about this and that, Minnie telling him artlessly about her life, and the 'Academy' she runs for the boys; but when the Indians have gone, Johnson presses her ardently for a kiss and, unable to resist him any longer, she throws herself into his arms. The door opens and bangs violently and snow is blown into the room. But the lovers stand clasped in a passionate embrace and notice nothing. A new life has begun for them:

The snowdrifts pile against the door. It is fate: Johnson must stay the night. She gives him her bed and wraps herself in a bearskin. But there is a violent commotion outside. Minnie starts up, hides Johnson behind the bed-curtains and opens the door to Rance and the others, who are covered with snow. They have come to warn her against Ramerrez. "And who d'you think Ramerrez is?" asks Rance, with a savage sneer, "why, your fine Mister Johnson! His mistress, Nina, told us!" Minnie is thunderstruck. She hurriedly gets rid of them and drags Johnson from his hiding-place, overwhelming him with contempt. "And I gave you my first kiss of love!" Johnson is tortured with remorse. Yes, he *is* Ramerrez; but from the moment he saw her he has longed to take her away and lead an honest life, praying that she would never discover his past. All is over now. He rushes out into the storm and is immediately shot. His body falls back against the door, and Minnie, forgetting everything but her love of him, pulls him inside again and helps him up a ladder into the loft. Rance comes in with levelled pistol and starts to search the cabin. A drop of blood from the wounded man falls on his hand. "He's here! He's here!" he shouts, and covering Johnson with the pistol, forces him to come down from the loft. Johnson totters to the table and collapses in a faint. Minnie is suddenly inspired by a desperate resolve. "We'll play a game of poker," she cries to Rance; "if you win you take this wounded man and me, but if I win this man is mine!" They play, their abrupt, feverish exclamations accompanied by ominous mutterings in the lower strings. At the third and decisive hand Minnie diverts her opponent's attention and alters the cards. "The game is mine!" she shrieks. "Three aces and a pair!" "Good night!" says Rance, and plunges out into the snow. Minnie bursts into loud hysterical laughter.

Act III

It is a winter dawn on the edge of the great Californian forest. In a clearing flanked by fallen tree trunks Rance, Nick and Ashby are sitting near a fire, gloomy and despondent. They are roused by distant shouting and yelling, like the noise of a pack of hounds, and eventually the miners and camp followers throng in with Johnson in their midst. He has made a desperate fight for it, but he is pale and wounded, his clothes scratched and torn and one shoulder bare. "Hang him, hang him, the scoundrel!" they shout; "string up the curséd Spaniard!" Rance comes forward, blazing with evil triumph. It is *his* turn now! He lights a cigar and blows the smoke in the captive's face, taunting and mocking him. "Please get it over quickly," says Johnson contemptuously. The men close round him, shouting angrily and shaking their fists at him. "Death to the scoundrel! Let's hang him!" After a while they let him speak. He is ready to die, he says; he asks only one thing:

Ch'el - la mi cre - da   li - be - ro e lon - ta - no,
Let   her   be - lieve that   I   have gain'd my free - dom,

It is a short *aria*, but full of all the glow of the old Puccini. Johnson then walks with a firm step to the tree from which the noose is dangling. Six men cover him with pistols, while Rance stands still and watches them, his arms folded. Suddenly there is a piercing cry and Minnie gallops in on horseback. Swiftly she jumps down, and with a pistol in each hand rushes in front of Johnson. "Stand off," she cries, "or I'll kill him and myself too! I claim this man as mine, mine from God. The robber that was died a week ago—in my cabin." The men love Minnie; they cannot resist her appeal.

Il Tabarro
(The Cloak)

Libretto by Giuseppe Adami.
Time: the present.

First Production,
New York, 1918.

> 'In passing by the Morgue we saw a man . . .
> Who had been stabbed and tumbled in the Seine,
> Where he had stayed some days. The face was black,
> And, like a negro's, swollen; all the flesh
> Had furred, and broken into a green mould.'
>
> D. G. ROSSETTI: *The Paris Railway-Station.*

Il Tabarro, the first of Puccini's three one-act operas, is a swift, sordid, brutal drama of passion, jealousy and murder. It contains his sourest music. We shall not meet here the self-wounding sentimentalist, the master of expansive and freely moving melody. There *is* plenty of melody in *Il Tabarro*, but it is more than usually tightened and disciplined to the demands of the atmosphere and action. I myself find, too, a certain detachment about this taut little score. The composer seems to me, as in *Tosca*, to have 'coloured the drama instead of illuminating it from within'. He does not seem to pity the hapless beings who play out his theme. He sets them before us and shows us their hearts, but not his own. He analyses them, but it is the analysis of the crime reporter. And this hard core to the music is one reason why it is so subtly effective. There is an uncomfortable quality about this music; it has a bitter taste of revenge and cruelty.

Its blurred harmonies and slightly acrid flavour at once suggest the scene—the September sunset over the Seine in Paris, the mist rising from the river, the anchored barges, the odours of the dusty, squalid streets. It is essentially *town* music; there is a kind of warm dinginess about it that brings to the mind yellow street-lamps, the noise of wheels on wooden blocks, the smell of smoke and petrol. And through it all sounds a sinister note: there is, figuratively speaking, a dark stain of blood on this cloak, which glows balefully as the light falls on it from the lantern of the barge.

When the curtain rises, Michele, the bargemaster (baritone), a man of about fifty, is sitting by the tiller of his vessel with unlighted pipe, gazing across the wharf at the sunset. His young wife, Giorgetta (soprano), comes up from the cabin. The stevedores have nearly finished their work, she says, and she is going to give them a glass of wine. Michele says they are welcome; but for himself he doesn't want wine, he wants only her love. She does not respond to his kiss, and we immediately suspect—and perhaps Michele suspects too—that she has begun to respond to someone nearer her own age. And when Michele has gone back into the barge and Luigi (tenor), a fine handsome young animal, comes on to the wharf, we see the expressive glance that passes between him and his employer's wife. The tragedy is set.

Tinca (tenor) and Talpa (bass), two of the stevedores, come up from the hold and Giorgetta brings out a bottle and glasses. A passing organ-grinder strikes up a tune (with ludicrously cracked chords) and they dance to it, stopping rather guiltily as the grim bargemaster reappears. The three workmen go back into the hold, and there is some desultory talk between Giorgetta and Michele from which we realise again that they are not on the best of terms. A street-singer comes along, followed by some little milliners, and sings them 'The Story of Mimi', which Puccini points with the Mimi *motif* we remember from *La Bohème*. Talpa's wife, La Frugola (mezzo-soprano), a rag-picker, approaches in search of her man. She and Giorgetta indulge in a long gossip together, Frugola saying that her only real true love is her white Angora cat, Caporale; and when the men join them on their way home she goes on to dream of a cosy cottage in the country with a little garden full of roses. But Giorgetta is a typical child of Paris; and she breaks into a song in praise of the town, with its eternal glitter and fascination. In the main theme—

Ma chi la - scia il sob-bor - go vuol— tor - na - re
But all those who de-part, they crave to re - turn—

—Luigi, infected by her enthusiasm, joins her ecstatically. The group slowly disperses, and when they are left alone Giorgetta and Luigi exclaim bitterly together on the frustration of their desires. It is growing dark. Michele comes up again and is a little surprised to see Luigi still there; but the young man makes some excuse, and Michele, with a grunt, goes back into the cabin to light the lamps. Then follows a passionate duet, sombre and intense, in C sharp minor, the smouldering fire at last breaking free into the key of A:

Vor - rei te-ner-ti strt - ta Co-me u-na co - sa mi - a!
I want to hold you close like i - vy a-round a tow - er!

Luigi promises to come to her later in the night. She will give the usual signal—the striking of a match. He tears himself away just before Michele, carrying the lighted lanterns, trudges up from the cabin.

It is now quite dark. Michele makes a last appeal to Giorgetta: why cannot she love him? Only last year on nights like this they would sleep blissfully in the cabin—they two and the little child that died:

O - ra le not - ti son tan - to fre - sche,
But now the nights are so cool and re - fresh - ing,

He becomes more urgent. "Stay with me—close to me—for ever! As on those nights when I would wrap you in my great cloak." And he grows warm with his memories, while the orchestra plays a gently rocking figure:

But he cannot move her. She is dreaming of Luigi, and she avoids his embrace and passes quickly into the cabin. He looks after her. He knows now! "Vile woman!" he whispers over a grinding change of key from E flat to A minor. Two lovers pass, singing of their happiness. Michele throws his cloak over his shoulders and, leaning against the tiller, stares moodily at the Seine. After a while he takes his pipe from his pocket and strikes a match. It is the signal! And Luigi glides out of the shadows and steps silently on to the barge. Michele recognizes him, and at once his hands are round his throat. "So it is you! Confess that you are her lover! Confess it!" Luigi tries to get at his knife, but Michele prevents him. "Confess it! Confess it—and I'll let you go." Luigi, suffocating, gasps out, "Yes, I love her!" "Again! Again!" says Michele. But the last confession rises to a choked cry, and Luigi hangs clinging to his murderer in the convulsion of death.

"Michele!" calls Giorgetta's voice from the cabin. For a moment the ghastly group on the deck remains as if petrified. Then Michele sits down; the corpse still clings to him, and he covers it with his cloak. Giorgetta comes up on deck. She is strangely frightened and perhaps a little conscience-stricken, a little sorry for that apparently lonely figure. Will he forgive her? May she not creep under his cloak as she used to? Of course she may! Michele throws open the cloak and Luigi's corpse tumbles at her feet,

Sister Angelica

Libretto by Giovacchino Forzano.   First Production,
Time: Late Seventeenth Century.   New York, 1918.

> 'From Eastertide to Eastertide
> For ten long years her patient knees
> Engraved the stones, the fittest bride
> Of Christ in all the diocese.'
>   JOHN DAVIDSON.

Sister Angelica, the second of the three one-act operas Puccini called
his 'Trittico', is a tender interlude between the savagery of *Il Tabarro*
and the ribaldry of *Gianni Schicchi*. It is for women's voices only, and
from the first tinkling bell-like chords the music magically catches the
atmosphere of the little convent wrapped in the blue-and-silver radiance of a spring evening. Not a summer evening; that would call for a
greater richness than Puccini allows himself in these chill, delicate
harmonies. It is also the only opera of the Trittico that reaches true
pathos; *Il Tabarro* is hard and murky and *Schicchi*, of course, is just a
joyous romp. But Sister Angelica is one of those erring 'little women',
to whose hearts Puccini penetrated more surely than any other composer, and who evoked from him music of such porcelain fragility.
His elder sister, Romelde, went into a convent, and it is reasonable to
assume that his affection for her influenced him in writing this work.
We are told that on one occasion he visited the convent and played
the opera over to Romelde and the other sisters, and that afterwards
they paid him the tribute of praying for the soul of Sister Angelica.

The scene is the interior of the convent, showing the little church
and cloister, and farther away the cemetery and vegetable garden.
Among some bushes is a fountain, which sparkles in the evening sun.
We hear the sisters singing in the church:

A - ve, Ma - ri - a,   pie - na di gra - zia,

Two postulants enter, late for prayers. They pass into the church
and, a moment afterwards, Sister Angelica (soprano) follows them.
When the singing is over the sisters come out of the church in twos,
and the Monitor (contralto) announces their penances. For being late
the two postulants must repeat twenty times the prayer for all in need
of absolution; one of the girls is reproved for causing laughter during

the psalms, another for hiding in her white sleeve a bunch of scarlet roses. Sister Geneviève (soprano) points out that the fountain has caught a ray from the sun and the water has turned to gold. It is a smile from the Blessed Virgin, say the sisters, and they give thanks for the spring. They begin to chatter among themselves about their wishes, the Monitor gently chiding them for 'nurturing vain desires'. Sister Geneviève says she used to be a shepherdess and confesses that she sometimes wishes to hold a little white lamb in her arms again. Surely the Lamb of God would forgive her for that wish? Another girl is rebuked for being too fond of good meat and drink—'one of the darkest of sins!'—but when Sister Angelica's turn comes she declares, rather hesitantly, that she has no wishes. "Ah," they whisper, "pray that Jesus forgive her. She has told a lie!" For they know that night and day she is pining to know what has become of her kindred and friends. It is seven years since she entered the convent and she has heard nothing. She was rich and of a noble family. What sin was it that drove her here in her penitence?

Presently two other sisters enter leading a donkey loaded with gifts for the convent—oil, walnuts, flour, lentils, a cheese, eggs and butter. Excitedly they announce that a splendid coach has halted outside the door. A visitor for somebody! And Angelica grows by turns white and scarlet as she hopes and fears that it may be for her. "Sister Angelica," calls out the Abbess (contralto), "I announce you a visit from your aunt, the Princess." The Princess (contralto) is conducted into the cloister, and the aunt and niece are left alone. The Princess is a hard, austere old woman, leaning on an ebony stick, and she greets Angelica coldly and haughtily. She acts as her nieces' guardian in place of their dead parents, and she has brought a document for Angelica to sign, relating to the approaching marriage of the younger sister. "Little Anna Voila to be married!" exclaims Angelica. "Who is the bride-groom?" And the Princess answers: "One who has overlooked the black stain you cast on the family honour!" Angelica reproaches her for her cruelty. The Princess replies that sometimes when she kneels in prayer the spirit of Angelica's mother appears to her:

Nel si - len - zio di quei rac-co-gli men - ti,
In the still - ness of that re - lig-ious soli - tude,

When the vision fades away, her one dominant thought is that Angelica must pay for her sin. The girl answers that she has offered all she had to the Virgin—all but one thing: she cannot forget her son. "Speak to me of him," she cries in a vehement outburst: "why don't you tell me of my son, my darling child?" There is a long pause. "Why don't you speak?" pleads the mother. At last the Princess tells her that the child died two years earlier. Angelica gives a great cry and falls on her face sobbing. The Princess turns away from her, and when the Abbess and the Portress enter with a quill and an inkwell Angelica raises herself and tremblingly signs the document. Then, when she is left alone, she begins an impassioned lament for her dead son:

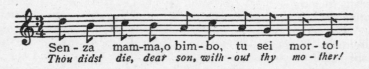

Sen - za mam-ma, o bim - bo, tu sei mor - to!
Thou didst die, dear son, with - out thy mo - ther!

Darkness has fallen and the sisters light the small lanterns on the cemetery tombstones. They draw near to Angelica and comfort her. Then, one by one, the white figures fade away in the darkness. Angelica stands still for a moment, the light of a great resolution in her eyes. She then brings out an earthen jar, kindles a small fire and puts the jar on it, filled with water. She gathers flowers and herbs and drops them into the pot. She sings a farewell to the sisters, saying that her son is calling her from the stars; she will be with him in heaven. In a trance of exaltation she drinks the poison and leans against a cypress, letting the jar fall to the ground. Immediately she is seized with anguish and remorse. "I am lost! I have taken my own life—the blackest of sins!" But a miracle is granted: she hears the voices of angels interceding for her, and the little church beams with mystic light. The door opens and the Madonna appears. In front of her is a child dressed in white, which she gently pushes towards the dying Sister Angelica.

Gianni Schicchi

Libretto by Giovacchino Foranzo.
Time: 1299.

First Production,
New York, 1918.

'That sprite of air is Schicchi; in like mood
Of random mischief vents he still his spite.'

DANTE: *Inferno* (trans. Cary.)

Gianni Schicchi is the fullest and finest expression of that mercurial wit which Puccini scattered in delightful fragments through his other

operas. For this reason, perhaps, it is apt sometimes to be a little
overpraised, particularly by refined persons who wince painfully at
Puccini's sentiment and regard comedy as the only civilising influence.
Gianni Schicchi is not Puccini's greatest work, if only because Puccini
was greater as a sentimentalist than as a wit; but in its own miniature
style it is a masterpiece. Schicchi himself was first immortalised,
incongruously enough, by Dante, that adamantine moralist taking
a deeply indignant view of his rogueries. But Puccini and his *librettist*
lifted him into the sunshine of pure comedy, where moral issues do
not concern us; comedy such as might have come straight out of the
Decameron. Indeed, one almost feels annoyed with Boccaccio for not
writing the story!

A Florentine house in the thirteenth century. On a bed behind
half-drawn curtains lies the body of Buoso Donati, who has died
in the midst of plenty. His nine relatives, a very mixed company of
human vultures, kneel before the bed, rocking themselves mournfully
to a lugubrious figure that, nevertheless, has something gravely
comic about it:

Poor Buoso! What a loss to the city! (The will! The will! Where has
he hidden it?) Poor Buoso! How they all loved him! (It must be
somewhere about; search the room!) Always will they mourn for their
dear kinsman! But such grief is too intense to last, and so they dissolve
their sorrow in action—feverishly turning out drawers and cabinets
and flinging the papers all over the room. At last there is a shout of
triumph from Rinuccio (tenor). He has found the will! They crowd
round to read it—grow rigid—turn pale—and let it flutter to the floor.
Old Simone (bass) angrily blows out all the candles. Buoso has left
everything to the monks! There is a long and tragic silence. Then
suddenly they begin to whisper: "If only it were possible . . . to *upset*
it . . . to *change* it." "Right!" says Rinuccio. "There's only one man can
help us—Gianni Schicchi." And he breaks into a song in praise of
great men—

Fi - ren - ze è co-me un al - be-ro fio - ri - to_____
*Our Flo-rence like a tree is firm-ly plant-ed*_____

—finishing with the name of Schicchi on a triumphant high B flat. Schicchi (baritone), appears ("How glum they all look," he says. "The old boy must be getting better!") with his daughter Lauretta (soprano), whom Rinuccio wants to marry. After much judicial pondering on the case and a dainty little supplication from Lauretta, in which Puccini seems to be gently satirising his own romantic style—

Oh! mio bab-bin - o   ca - ro,
Oh! my   be - lov - ed   dad - dy,

—Schicchi has the idea of the century: no one else knows that Buoso has died; he will take his place and dictate a fresh will. The relatives hail him in a transport of joy and immediately fall to squabbling which of them shall have the three richest treasures—the mule, the villa, and the saw-mills at Signa. "Leave it to me," says Schicchi, putting on Buoso's nightgown and nightcap and getting into the bed—meanwhile secretly promising the three treasures to each of them in turn. But first he warns them: the law says that anyone who falsifies a will loses his right hand and is sent into exile. So if they are found out it will be:

Ad - dio, Fi -   ren - ze,
Fare-well dear   Flo - rence,

There is a knock at the door. It is the notary they have sent for. Schicchi, imitating Buoso Donati's voice, proceeds to dictate the new will. The minor possessions he deals out to them quickly and carelessly ("Thank you, dear uncle!" "Thank you, dear brother!" they murmur dutifully), until at last: "Now we come to the mule, the villa and the saw-mills!"—and they bend forward greedily. "I leave my mule . . . to my devoted friend, *Gianni Schicchi*." (Uproar. What is the rascal about?) "I leave my villa in Florence to my trusty, devoted and affectionate friend, *Gianni Schicchi*." (Stop him! Stop him! The scoundrel!) But the scoundrel pokes his nightcapped head through the curtains and reminds them:

Ad - dio, Fi - ren - ze,
Fare - well, dear Flo - rence,

"The saw-mills at Signa (farewell, dear Florence!) go to my dearest (dear city of great charm!) and most devoted friend, *Gianni Schicchi!*" The notary departs, and at once the relatives fall on Gianni Schicchi like a horde of wild beasts. "Scoundrel! Robber! Traitor! Impostor!" He lashes them with Buoso's stick. "Go! Go! You pack of scavengers! This house is mine now and all that's in it!" —and he drives them out through the door. When he comes back he sees the lovers, Rinuccio and Lauretta, standing on the piazza robed in brilliant sunshine, and he turns to the audience with a smile. "Tell me, ladies and gentlemen, could you imagine a better use for Buoso's money?"

Turandot

Libretto by G. Adami and R. Simone.   First Production,
Time: Legendary.   Milan, 1926.

> 'Back through a hundred, hundred years
> Hear the waves as they climb the piers,
> Hear the howl of the silver seas,
> Hear the thunder.
> Hear the gongs of holy China
> How the waves and tunes combine
> In a rhythmic clashing wonder,
> Incantation old and fine.'
>
> VACHELL LINDSAY: *The Chinese Nightingale*.

Turandot is Puccini's last and greatest opera. I would not call it his most attractive or most characteristic. Certainly it contains the most powerful and splendid music he ever wrote. He has grown in stature and his voice has become louder, more strident, more commanding. He has become trumpet-tongued. Yet I feel that power and splendour are not the chief qualities for which we love Puccini; we love him rather for his tender grace, his miniature pathos, for that romantic sentiment to which we all respond, even though at times we may be slightly ashamed of responding. We shall find these in *Turandot*; we shall find in its intensest form in the character of Liu that strange streak of self-torturing cruelty—almost masochism—which we notice in so much of Puccini's music. But these qualities spring up more or less at random; they are tucked away in corners, overawed, so to speak, by the arrogance and opulence of the rest of the score and by the personality of Turandot herself—a figure of deathlike beauty, as cold and dazzling as an iceberg in the sunlight. A work of indisputable genius. We admire it, we tremble before it, but there are things in it we do not love.

Act I

The opera begins with five piercing notes in the full orchestra, and the curtain rises on the city walls of Pekin reddened by the setting sun. Over chords of a grinding dissonance, punctuated at times by xylophone and Chinese gong, a mandarin (bass) reads the royal decree: Turandot the chaste shall be the bride of him of royal lineage who shall solve her three enigmas; but those who fail shall lose their heads. The Prince of Persia has failed; when the moon has risen he dies on the scaffold. And then we notice poles rising from the bastions, crowned with the gory heads of past victims. Below, a mob demented with blood-lust waits for the moon to rise. Among the crowd Calaf (tenor) comes upon his aged father Timur, King of Tartary (bass), a penniless exile attended only by a little slave girl, Liu (soprano). They recount their adventures, and later the chorus sings an invocation during which the moon rises. It is the signal: "Pu-Tin-Pao!" the people shout to the executioner. "The moon has risen. It is time. Kill him! Kill him!" The funeral procession of the Prince of Persia begins. First come children, singing a song in praise of Turandot—

> Là, su - i mon - ti del - l'est,
> O - ver the hills, far a - way,

—a theme which Puccini borrowed from Chinese music and which is repeated and varied many times in the score. Then the tonality changes to the cold and pallid key of E flat minor, to which the Prince of Persia marches to his doom. Calaf is horrified at this insane cruelty. "Come, show thyself, thou monster, that I may curse thee!" he shouts. Turandot shows herself, and he immediately falls into line with all the others. He is a man bewitched. From that moment he has only one thought in his head: Turandot. He is crazed with desire for her. The three courtiers, Ping, Pang and Pong (baritone and two tenors), grotesque masks in the style of the *Commedia dell' Arte*, try to rouse him from his madness, and finally Liu appeals to him, in music that proclaims her affinity with Mimi, Butterfly, and other pathetic little women of whose hearts Puccini held the secret:

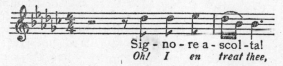

Sig - no - re a - scol - ta!
Oh!   I   en   treat thee,

The Prince tries to pacify her with specious excuses which no one believes, least of all himself—

Non   pian - ge - re, Liù!
Oh!   weep   no more, Liu!

—a theme which rises relentlessly to a clashing climax as he strikes the gong three times—the signal that Turandot has been challenged once again. Liu and Timur sink down in despair, while the three courtiers burst into sardonic laughter at the sight of yet another fool rushing on his death.

ACT II: *Scene* 1

A charming little interlude: Ping, Pang and Pong meet in a pavilion in the Imperial Gardens and bewail the sad fate of China. It is a vicious circle of bloodshed, they say: three strokes on the gong, three enigmas, and off goes another head. Why did they ever come to this accursed court? And softly, as though lost in a dream, Ping begins an exquisite lament over gently rocking chords and smoothly sliding harmonies:

Ho u-na   ca - sa nél - l'Ho - man
I've   a   cot - tage in Kan - sou,

The other two echo his nostalgia in music of a quaint, willow-pattern delicacy. Then their former mood of exasperation returns, to be interrupted at last by drums and trumpets summoning them to the latest trial.

Act II: *Scene 2*

This takes place in the great square before the palace. The court assembles and the people gradually fill the square. At the head of a vast staircase of white marble sits the aged Emperor, a fragile, almost spectral figure. In a thin, ghostly voice he counsels Calaf not to throw away his young life; too much blood has been shed already. But Calaf is inflexible. "Son of Heaven, I claim the right to try my fortune." The children sing their chorus again, and Turandot appears at the foot of the throne. She tells us of her beautiful ancestress who was tortured to death in that very palace a thousand thousand years ago. She has sworn a sacred oath to avenge her:

The Prince defies her, and in a deathly silence she propounds the first enigma: "In the night's dark shadow there hovers a phantom. Everybody invokes it and everybody implores it. It vanishes at dawn, but every night 'tis born again, and every day it dies." There is a long pause. Then the Prince starts up, inspired. "Yes, 'tis born again, and carries me away! For—'tis Hope." A gasp comes from the crowd. He has solved it!

The second enigma: "Like a flame it is flaring, yet it is no flame. Sometimes it is delirium and sometimes languor. If you are losing your life it grows cold, but when you dream of conquest it is flaming." The crowd begins to murmur in feverish excitement. The Prince stands still for a moment. Then his voice rings out: "Yes, mighty Princess! It flames and yet doth languish. It is Blood!" A great shout from the people. He has solved the second enigma! Turandot, with fury flaming in her eyes, comes slowly down the staircase and hovers over the Prince like a great white bird of prey. The third and last enigma: "Ice gives thee fire, and from thy fire more ice is begotten. The force that wills thee free will make thee a slave, yet, accepting thee as a slave, will make thee a king!"

A long dramatic pause. Then the Prince bounds to his feet. "Thou hast told me! My life to thee I owe, and my fire shall dissolve thee 'Tis Turandot!" He has won. The people break into a great song of praise. And now Turandot, this mighty princess, this beautiful monument of ice, begins to shift and palter as contemptibly as any woman of the streets. She will go back on her bargain; she has lost the game, but she will not pay the forfeit. "Never shall man possess me!" The Prince makes a chivalrous gesture. He has solved three enigmas; he will set her one. If she can discover his name by next morning he will consent to die; if not, he will claim her as his bride.

ACT III

In the palace garden the Prince is waiting for the dawn. Turandot has decreed that none shall sleep; on pain of death the stranger's name must be discovered. The Prince ironically echoes her words. Then: "None shall know my name," he sings, "until I whisper it to you, Princess, when the dawn shall make you mine":

Ma il mio mi-ster-ro è chiu-so in me,
With - in my heart my se - cret lies,

Ping, Pang and Pong revile Calaf for his obstinacy. But a moment later a great cry is heard: "Here is the name. It is hidden in the hearts of these two. Torture them! Tear it out of them!" And some soldiers drag in Timur and Liu. They begin to torture the little slave girl, but Liu will not reveal the name—she will rather die; and Turandot, who has appeared before her pavilion, asks wonderingly what it is that gives her such endurance. Liu answers simply: "My love. By my silence I shall give him *thy* love":

Tanto a - mo - re se-gre-to,
Such the love that I bear him,

Just as her endurance is about to snap, she snatches a dagger from a soldier and kills herself. For a moment the people are stupefied; then they lift up the poor little body and bear it away, old Timur muttering broken lamentations and trying to take her hand in his.

And there, as Toscanini declared to the audience at the first performance, 'the Master laid down his pen'. Alfano follows with

L

a long and strenuous duet at the end of which Turandot melts before the Prince's fire and announces to the Emperor that she has discovered the name of the stranger: it is Love. I disagree with other critics in that I think Alfano's music very creditable. It is at least forceful, if not passionate—although the repetition by the chorus of the Prince's song never sounds quite convincing. Nevertheless one feels that not even Puccini himself could have sent us away from this sadistic story with satisfied hearts. When we remember Liu killing herself under the torture, and old Timur wandering away into the darkness, we may well ask ourselves what sort of 'love' it was that Turandot meant.

NICHOLAS RIMSKY-KORSAKOV

(1844-1908)

The Snow Maiden

Libretto by Ostrowsky, after a Russian folk-tale.
Time : Legendary.

First Production,
St. Petersburg, 1882.

> 'What heart could have thought you?—
> Past our devisal
> (O filigree petal!)
> Fashioned so purely . . .'
>
> FRANCIS THOMPSON: *To a Snowflake.*

The Snow Maiden was the third of Rimsky-Korsakov's fifteen operas and, like *The Golden Cockerel*, which we shall consider in the next chapter, is typical of his complete indifference to the problems of the human soul. His operas are fairy-tales in the richest and poorest sense of the term. He wrote them not from the heart, but from the head. They are as magnetic as jewels— as brilliant, as colourful and nearly as heartless. Even his love-scenes have hardly any passion in them. His lovers don't pour out their hearts to each other; they only strike curious and persuasive attitudes, like figures on a tapestry.

On a first hearing, Rimsky-Korsakov's music is wildly fascinating, with its bizarre colours and exotic perfumes. It is only when it becomes familiar that it begins to strike us as—not by any means vulgar, but essentially sterile. It does not develop or propagate; it is continually going back on its own tracks, clothing the old themes in new colours, decking them with new jewels. Each melody has as many skins as a snake. Of all Russian composers, he was the most prone to 'damnable iteration'.

PROLOGUE

On a night in early spring the 'Red Mountain' is shrouded in snow. Snow hangs from the branches of the pine forest growing on its steep side and on the roof of the Tsar Berendey's palace in the village beyond the river. Birds begin to flock to the scene, and soon the Fairy Spring (mezzo-soprano) appears. The birds are shivering in the crystal moonlight, and she tells them that the fault is hers. Sixteen years ago she married King Frost and he treats her like a slave. She

bore him a daughter, Snegourochka, the Snow Maiden, and her also
he keeps a prisoner in the gloomy forest. While the birds are singing—
and dancing 'to keep themselves warm'—there is a sudden snowstorm
and King Frost (bass) makes his appearance from the forest. He
exults in his power, in an impressive *aria*—*staccato* notes that suggest
pin-points of ice, then flowing phrases that whirl round like spirals of
snow:

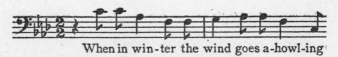

When in win-ter the wind goes a-howl-ing

He must go north, he tells Spring; but the Snow Maiden must
remain hidden, for at the first touch of sunlight and love she will
perish. He summons her forth; and, in one of the most sprightly and
felicitous songs Rimsky-Korsakov ever wrote, Snegourochka (soprano)
sings of her fancy for Lel, the shepherd boy, who makes magic music:

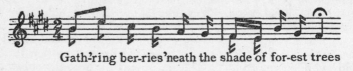

Gath-'ring ber-ries 'neath the shade of for-est trees

King Frost warns her to have nothing to do with Lel. He places
her in the care of an old peasant, and her mother tells her if she is ever
in distress to call on her by the lakeside in the valley. A carnival
procession from the nearby village passes over the mountain and
Snegourochka watches it, hidden in the trees.

Act I

Snegourochka is now living in the hut of Bobil, the peasant in the
Berendey village. In the evening Lel (contralto) dances along, playing
on his pipe, and sings her a couple of songs; but he finds her cold and
quickly leaves her for other maidens, and she prays to her mother,
Spring, that love may enter her heart. Miskir (baritone), a wealthy
young merchant, comes to claim his promised bride, Coupava, but
on seeing Snegourochka he instantly falls in love with her and sends
poor Coupava packing. Coupava returns and, after a passionate
lament, declares that she will fling herself into the river. Lel restrains
her, and the people decide to submit the dispute to Tsar Berendey.

ACT II

In Tsar Berendey's palace a chorus of blind bards sing his praises. When they have departed, the Tsar (tenor) complains to his chief councillor that all is not well with his land: each autumn for fifteen years the corn and fruit are scarcely ripe; summer shrinks every year, and spring is always cold. He decrees that on the day sacred to Yarilo, the Sun God, youths and maidens shall assemble, and when the sun appears their voices shall rise in prayer. Presently the forsaken Coupava enters and tells him her sad story. The Tsar is much moved and summons Miskir to his presence. The court assembles, and Miskir is brought before the Tsar, who sternly reproves him and banishes him to the forest. "There let him live and seek as companions the cruel wolves." "I speak no word against thy judgment, mighty Tsar," murmurs Miskir, "but—ah, couldst thou behold Snegourochka!" At that moment she appears, and the Tsar is dazzled by her beauty:

Oh Na - ture, sa - cred, sweet,

"And who is thy lover, child?" he asks her. She tells him that her heart has not yet awakened to love. He replies that this is a crime against Yarilo—small wonder the god of warmth denies them his grace!—and he turns to the court: "He who shall waken love in this maiden's heart before the morning shall wed her!" The courtiers' wives say that Lel is destined to be the fortunate one, but Miskir also persuades the Tsar to let him stay. The Tsar blesses their endeavours and announces that at dawn he will go to the forest to greet the god of sunlight.

ACT III

In an open glade in the forest the youths and maidens of the village, crowned with flowers, are dancing in the light of the setting sun. Presently there occurs the 'Dance of the Tumblers', which has become so popular in the concert-hall. Meanwhile, Snegourochka, Coupava, Lel and Miskir are passing to and fro among the trees and rallying each other in light-hearted love. Snegourochka at one point prays to her mother, Spring, craving the gift of love. "Oh, Mother, hear my pleading; oh, change me and fashion me like other maids; give me the power to love, or let me die!"

ACT IV

Spring appears to her daughter, and Snegourochka repeats her appeal. Spring then calls up the flowers and bids them endow her daughter with all their graces so that she may know the magic of love. The spell works, and when Miskir appears again the Snow Maiden loses her heart to him. But even while her new exaltation is giving wings to her words, the dawn breaks; a shaft of sunlight pierces her like a sword, and she melts away. Miskir, in his despair, throws himself into the river, and the opera closes with a chorus in praise of the Sun God.

The Golden Cockerel

Libretto by V. Bielsky, after Pushkin.   First Production,
Time: Legendary.   .   Moscow, 1910.

> 'Rather than I'll be bray'd, sir, I'll believe
> That Alchemy is a pretty kind of game,
> Somewhat like tricks o' the cards, to cheat a man
> With charming.'
>
>   BEN JONSON: *The Alchemist.*

The Golden Cockerel can best be explained by saying at once that it is unexplainable—at least, to an English audience. For a Moscow audience in 1910 it may have had some ominous or humorous message; but for us today it resembles little more than a box of grotesque dolls and puppets, whimsically decorated with crude blobs of paint in primary colours, who stand up at the bidding of some invisible sorcerer, sing and dance, make love and war, collapse and die, with stiff, inhuman gestures, and—back into the box again. There is not a moment of reality in it, there is not a spark of human feeling. One might describe it as a fairy-tale not for children. There is evil and cruelty here, a hint of that black magic that must not be spoken of—the fascination of things forbidden. And this is made all the more insidious by the seemingly artless, nursery-rhyme atmosphere of the story, and by the exotic pungency of the music. If a great composer is one that speaks greatly to the human heart, Rimsky-Korsakov was not a great composer. But he had undoubtedly a genius for suggesting the occult and mysterious, for holding us in a witchlike spell with his hypnotic melodies and orchestration—'good, rich, thick, stupefying incense-smoke!'. And nowhere is this genius stronger than in *The Golden Cockerel*.

The introduction opens at once with the Cockerel's call:

It is heard often during the evening, inverted when the dramatic situation demands. Immediately afterwards we hear this phrase—

—which represents the mysterious Queen, and is used so persistently and in so many different forms that we may take it as one of the main seminal forces of the score. A little later there are some tinkling *staccato* notes on the glockenspiel, and the Astrologer (tenor)[1] appears before the curtain, wearing a blue gown embroidered with gold stars. He is a wizard, he sings to a jerky, clockworklike melody, and he will bring before our eyes forms and figures from forgotten legends. It is a fable— yet we can draw a moral from it.

ACT I

King Dodon, a ludicrous, decrepit old man, is addressing his court. He speaks in abrupt, jingling, mechanical sentences that emphasise the unreality of the scene. They are in danger, he says: savage tribes are attacking the land, although they must realise that his fighting days are over and all he wants is peace. He consults his two foolish sons, Guidon (tenor) and Afron (baritone), who apparently have 'intuition'. Their views are coarsely ridiculed by the crusty old General Polkan (baritone), the only professional soldier present, and, while they are wrangling, in comes the Astrologer. In mysterious chromatic phrases he tells the King of his wonderful Golden Cockerel, which he then presents to him. The bird is, apparently, the equivalent of a modern siren: when danger approaches it crows an 'alert'; when

[1] Rimsky-Korsakov wrote the Astrologer's part for *tenor-altimo*, an extremely high voice, but he occasionally wrote in optional notes for him.

danger passes it crows an 'all clear'. Some day, the Astrologer says, he will come for his reward. And he disappears.

All is solved; no need to worry any more. And King Dodon lies down and sleeps on a royal bed which they drag out into the sunlight:

A drowsiness settles over the whole court; but just as everyone has completely relaxed, the Cockerel (soprano) crows an 'alert'. Instant confusion. Trumpets sound, horses neigh and a crowd surrounds the palace. Polkan rushes in to rouse the King, who is disgusted at being disturbed. There is a good deal of argument, but after two or three more 'alerts' Dodon resignedly mounts his horse and leads away the army—from behind.

ACT II

A narrow gorge studded with bushes and flanked by steep rocks. Dodon's two sons lie dead. Some of his soldiers straggle in, then Dodon and Polkan. Dodon laments over his slain sons. Gradually the morning mists disperse, revealing a tent on the hillside. The folds of the tent part, and the Queen of Shemaka (soprano) steps out with her attendants—a creature of pernicious beauty. Some of the soldiers, with a premonition of evil, take flight, but Dodon and Polkan stare fascinated at this apparition. The Queen sings her 'Hymn to the Sun':

Dodon stands open-mouthed, gaping at her in admiration; and, singing all the while in sinuous, undulating chromatics, she deliberately sets out to enslave him. Eventually she makes him sing and dance, and a ridiculous figure he cuts; but he does not care—he is now completely infatuated by this strange, unearthly creature, half woman, half vampire. There is no Golden Cockerel here to warn him of the evil thing that is slowly enmeshing him like a monstrous and beautiful spider's web, and in the end he declares that he will marry her and take her back to his kingdom.

Act III

He keeps his word. Soon after the curtain has risen, festal trumpets are heard and the royal procession approaches the palace, to the well-known 'Bridal March', which ingeniously combines some of the motives of the score. The King's militia comes first, followed by the Queen's retinue, a fantastic crowd, rather like Comus's rout—giants and dwarfs, creatures with one eye in the middle of the forehead, men with horns or the heads of dogs—and last the King and Queen in a golden chariot. The people hail them in wild delight. At that moment the Astrologer reappears. He has come to claim his reward, and he reminds Dodon that he promised him anything he might desire. Very well: he desires—the Queen! There is a general uproar. The King is furious, and after some argument he rises in a climax of passion and strikes the Astrologer dead with his sceptre. All are horror-stricken. Clouds hide the sun, and there is a rattle of thunder. Then silence—broken by a peal of mocking laughter from the Queen. Suddenly the cry of the Cockerel is heard; it flies on to the scene, swoops down on the King and buries its beak in his head. Dodon falls lifeless. There is a violent clap of thunder, the stage grows black and in the darkness we hear again the Queen's mocking laugh. When it is light once more the Queen and the Cockerel have vanished. The scene ends with the people intoning a funeral chant over their 'King and father'. As soon as the curtain is down, however, the Astrologer steps before it, to the same tinkling *staccato* notes as in the Prologue. "Wizard's work is but illusion," he says; "of the shadows you have seen only two were mortal—the Queen and I."

Our first reaction is that surely the exact opposite was the truth. And where is the moral he spoke of? Is it simply that we must keep our promises to beneficent strangers and beware of mysterious queens living in tents? There needs no ghost come from the grave to tell us that! Still, we have had a few wry laughs and steeped our senses in a gorgeously perfumed bath of music. Let us put the dolls and puppets back in the box.

GIOACHINO ANTONIO ROSSINI

(1792-1868)

The Barber of Seville

Libretto by Cesare Sterbini after Beaumarchais.
Time: Seventeenth Century.

First Production,
Rome, 1816.

> 'Why, did you ever hope, sir, committing the secrecy of it to a
> barber, that less than the whole town should know it? You might
> as well have told it the conduit, or the bakehouse, or the infantry
> that follow the court, and with more security.'
>
> BEN JONSON: *The Silent Woman.*

The Barber of Seville is the only opera of Rossini that still holds a firm
place in our affections. Although the music was composed thirty years
after Mozart's *Marriage of Figaro*, *The Barber* is the earlier of Beaumarchais's comedies and tells of the wooing of Rosina by the Count
Almaviva, who behaves so scandalously after marriage, when his voice
has fallen from tenor to baritone and his morals have suffered a
parallel decline. It is tempting, of course, to compare the two operas,
but the most one can say is that each is distinctly representative of its
composer: that Mozart has wings and Rossini has not; that in *Figaro*
there are moments that lift us above time and place, while the heavier,
bolder texture of *The Barber* is entirely of this world and of its own
period. Perhaps it is this lack of a divine something to raise it above its
time that makes much of Rossini's music sound tarnished today, with
its slick facility and wearisome ornamentation. But in *The Barber*
he is at the top of his bent, and the music has such zest and unflagging
energy that we forget to be bored by the conventions of its age. The
first production was a spectacular failure, mainly owing to the machina-
tions of Paisiello, whose own *Barber of Seville* had so far held the
stage and whose followers assembled in force and practically wrecked
the performance. Time, however, has decided entirely in Rossini's
favour.

The Overture to *The Barber of Seville* has the distinction of not
being the Overture to *The Barber of Seville* at all. Rossini is charitably
supposed to have lost the Overture (if he ever wrote it), and the one
we hear now had already done duty for two operas, *Aureliano in Palmyra*
and *Elizabeth, Queen of England*. Still, it does equally appropriate duty
for *The Barber of Seville*.

ACT I: *Scene* 1

It is early morning, and Count Almaviva (tenor) is serenading Rosina outside the house of her old guardian, Dr. Bartolo—

Ec - co ri - den - te in cie - - lo
Day comes with all her ros - - es,

—an air which also was 'lifted' from *Aureliano in Palmyra.* A few moments later a voice is heard carolling blithely along the street, and Figaro, the barber (baritone), struts in. In one of the most splendid and exhilarating *cavatinas* ever written for high baritone—

Lar - go al fac - to - tum del la cit - tà, lar - go!
Room for the ci - ty's fac-to-tum here! Aye, room!

—he tells us that in seventeenth-century Seville a barber's life is one of infinite variety. As we shall see later in the opera, he keeps his hand in by doing a bit of shaving now and then, but his chief talent is for intrigue. If you want a scandal spread about anyone—apply to the barber. If you want to outwit a rival in love—apply to the barber. If you want a love-letter delivered to someone else's wife—apply to the barber. He is the town's factotum, plausible, dexterous, cunning. In fact, what Voltaire said of Beaumarchais himself could very well apply to Figaro: "What a man! He combines everything—pleasantry, seriousness, reason, gaiety, vigour, pathos, all sorts of eloquence, and he strives after none of them; he confounds all his adversaries, and he reads lessons to his judges." Figaro is an old acquaintance of Almaviva's and he promises to help the Count to gain the hand of Rosina; and when Rosina drops a note down to her young lover they feel that success is certain.

ACT I: *Scene* 2

Rosina (soprano) sits dreaming of love. It is definitely a waking dream, for her romantic nature has an astutely practical side to it, and she has quite decided that she will defeat her guardian and marry 'Lindor', as the Count calls himself:

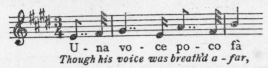

U - na vo - ce po - co fà
Though his voice was breath'd a - far,

An elderly husband or lover was the favourite butt of eighteenth-century comedy, and old Dr. Bartolo (bass) is mercilessly baited throughout the opera for his presumption in planning to marry his ward. To him comes his crony, Don Basilio, the singing master, with news that Count Almaviva is in the town and is wooing Rosina. The prestige of the musical profession was apparently as low in Seville as that of the hairdressing profession was high; for Basilio (bass) is about the most dingy and disreputable scoundrel one could fear to meet—a kind of debilitated Sparafucile. "D'you want to drive this fellow out of Seville?" he asks Bartolo. "Then start a scandal about him." And he sings the great 'Slander Song', remarkable for its gradual *crescendo*, in which the orchestra gobbles and chatters like an ever-increasing hubbub of voices:

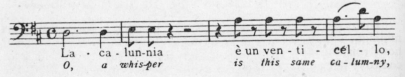

La - ca - lun-nia   è un ven - ti - cél - lo,
O,   a whis-per   is   this same   ca - lum-ny,

(Rossini was rather severe on his basses, and this *aria* is very often transposed down to C major.) Meanwhile, Rosina has given Figaro a note to take to 'Signor Lindor'. Bartolo is suspicious, and he trounces her at great length on her presumption in thinking to deceive a man of such erudition and discernment as himself. Later, the Count, disguised as a drunken soldier, forces his way into the house, telling Bartolo he is billeted on him. But the old man suspects who he is and has him arrested. The Count squares the police, however, and the act ends with a long concerted number in which the characters express their bewilderment at these mysterious happenings.

Act II

Dr. Bartolo having no sympathy with the military, the Count tries another scheme: this time he comes as Don Alonzo, a singing teacher.

The worthy Don Basilio is ill, he says, and has sent him to give Rosina her lesson. Meanwhile, Figaro arrives to shave Bartolo. Amid a good deal of byplay and horseplay, plotting and counter-plotting, Bartolo has his shave and Rosina her lesson. In Beaumarchais's play Rosina sings here a song from a new comedy, *The Useless Precaution*. Rossini did not set Beaumarchais's verses, but with characteristic indifference left his heroine to sing whatever she liked. The 'Laughing Song' from Auber's *Manon Lescaut* is a very usual choice.

Things seem to be going well, when the door opens and, of all people, Don Basilio appears. Everyone is astonished, but with great presence of mind the Count and Figaro rush up to him before he can give the game away, and persuade him he is really ill. "Don Basilio, you are as white as a sheet! You have caught a fever! Get home to bed, man, get home to bed!" Nothing makes one feel ill so quickly as to be told one *looks* ill, and very soon poor Basilio is almost in a state of collapse. They bundle him out of the door:

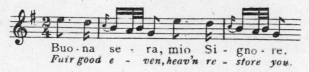

Buo - na   se - ra, mio Si - gno - re.
Fair good e - ven, heav'n re - store you.

There are more complications, including a plan of elopement at midnight and a ruse by Bartolo to make Rosina jealous of the Count—how conveniently credulous people were in seventeenth-century comedy! But all is finally straightened out, and we may fittingly take leave of this comedy of errors with Figaro's final words in the original play: "To tell you the truth, Doctor, when youth and love have agreed to deceive an old man, all that he does to prevent it may well be called 'The Useless Precaution'."

CAMILLE SAINT-SAËNS

(1835-1921)

Samson and Delilah

Libretto by Ferdinand Lemaire.   First Production,
Time: 1130 B.C.   Weimar, 1877.

'The expense of spirit in a waste of shame.'
SHAKESPEARE: *Sonnet CXXIX*.

Samson and Delilah is the supreme example of the right opera by the
wrong composer. It is one of the world's most dramatic stories, and it
has always been a mystery why one of the world's least dramatic
composers chose to set it to music. What had Saint-Saëns, that prim
and rather frigid classicist, to do with this orgy of savage hate and
savage love? Well, he did his best with it, and the surprising thing is
that his best is so good. The stage action always seems slightly petrified,
like dramatised oratorio or the coloured plates in children's Bibles;
but the music is the warmest Saint-Saëns wrote, and here and there
it rises to real passion.

ACT I

Israel is in bondage. In a public square in Gaza they stand,
the conquered men and women, before the Temple of Dagon. Jehovah
has forsaken them and delivered them into the hands of the Philistines.
"Pity, O God, thy people and their sorrow," they sing. "We have
seen our cities overthrown and the Gentiles profane our altars."
Samson appears, and at once his superb presence and inspiring
personality dominate the scene. He rouses them with ringing words
that put fresh heart into them—"Courage, my brethren; bless ye the
name of the God of our fathers"—and we hear in the orchestra a
martial theme that later expands to majestic proportions:

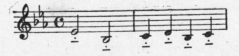

At once Samson has a chance to prove his valour. The Philistine
Abimelech (bass), a typical military bully, strides into the square

174

and mocks at the Israelites and their God in words far more caustic than Saint-Saëns's music. 'And the spirit of the Lord came upon Samson'—

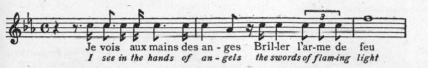

Je vois aux mains des an - ges Bril-ler l'ar-me de feu
I see in the hands of an - gels the swords of flam-ing light

—(a phrase which is repeated in Act III just before the fall of the Temple). Samson contemptuously strikes Abimelech dead with his own sword and, frenzied with triumph, the Israelites surge away into the city, seeking more victims. The High Priest (baritone), an arrogant and sinister figure, bursts out of the Temple doors, sees Abimelech's bloody corpse and curses Israel's leader in a vehement, if rather stiff-jointed, *aria*. For the moment Samson and his men have thrown off their oppressors, and they return thanks to God for their victory; but far greater danger is waiting for them. From the Temple come the Philistine maidens to do homage to the hero:

Voi - ci le prin-temps nous por-tant des fleurs
Fair spring smiles a - gain 'mid beau-te-ous bow'rs

They are led by Delilah, whose glance and voice awake burning memories in Samson. He has yielded to her before, and she tries now to rekindle the old fires. In his agony Samson prays to God for strength. But her voice drowns his prayers—

Prin-temps qui com-men-ce, Por-tant l'es-pér-an - ce
Fair spring is re-turn-ing, Fond hearts now are burn-ing

—and now he has eyes for no one else. He hardly heeds the warnings of the Aged Hebrew (bass), who perceives that Israel will be lost again through her leader's folly. He is a doomed man.

ACT II

Before Delilah's house in the valley. Night is falling and a storm approaching. Delilah calls on the power of love to aid her in making Samson her slave:

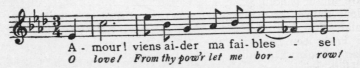

A - mour! viens ai-der ma fai-bles - se!
O love! From thy pow'r let me bor - row!

The High Priest approaches through the thickening darkness. She agrees to help him. Samson will come to her tonight. Together they will crush the chief of Israel, and they swear vengeance in a duet in the same mood (and key) as the High Priest's first *aria*. The High Priest disappears into the night. Samson comes plunging through the trees and stands irresolute, cursing his folly but unable to resist his desire. Delilah approaches him, and then begins a tremendous conflict of wills. Samson hears the Voice of God rebuking him in the thunder, but Delilah at last melts his resistance in this fervid *aria*, with its smouldering fires and highly spiced harmonies:

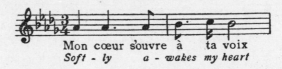

Mon cœur s'ouvre à ta voix
Soft - ly   a - wakes my heart

She taunts him bitterly to reveal the secret of his strength, finally rushing into the house in a fury. Samson hesitates a moment, then plunges after her. It is the signal: slowly and stealthily the Philistine soldiers surround the house. The music and the storm increase and, at a great crashing climax, Delilah appears at the window. "Come, Philistines! 'Tis done!"

ACT III

". . . the Philistines took him and put out his eyes and brought him down to Gaza, and bound him with fetters of brass; and he did grind in the prison house." And as he slowly turns the mill, Samson cries out to God for pity:

Je t'of-fre, o Dieu, ma pau-vre â-me bri - sé - e
My bro-ken   soul here I   of - fer to   thee!

After a short orchestral interlude recalling Delilah's first song,
we are in the Temple of Dagon. The chorus sings No. 4 and the
maidens dance the well-known Bacchanale. Samson is led in by
a child—'his foes' derision, captive, poor, and blind'—and the
High Priest commands him to pledge 'his fair mistress' in wine.
Delilah mocks him with ribald parodies of their love music.
The High Priest and Delilah then sing in canon an invocation to
Dagon. Samson whispers to the child to lead him to the marble pillars.
The final chorus begins, and as the music swells to an exultant climax
Samson grasps the pillars. "O Lord God, remember me, I pray Thee,
and strengthen me, I pray Thee, only this once, O God, that I may be
at once avenged on the Philistines for my two eyes." He hurls down the
pillars and the scene closes in darkness, fire and ruin.

M

BEDRICH (FREDERICK) SMETANA

(1824-1884)

The Bartered Bride

Libretto by Karel Sabina.
Time: Early Nineteenth Century.

First Production,
Prague, 1866.

'Tasting of Flora and the country green,
Dance and Provençal song and sunburnt mirth.'

JOHN KEATS.

The Bartered Bride is the work we usually think of when Czech National
Opera is mentioned, and it is Smetana's most popular work for the
stage. Indeed, it became even too popular: its sensational success
prejudiced the chances of his later and more serious operas, and
Smetana suffered the melancholy fate of the artist who does one thing
so supremely well that the public is unwilling to allow him to do
anything else. He became a disappointed man, began to suffer from
strange delusions and finally lost his reason, dying in a lunatic asylum
at the age of sixty.

There is no bitterness or disillusionment in *The Bartered Bride*
it is a lively, happy little comedy of village intrigue, showing the
sunnier side of the *cavalleria rusticana* of country life. The music i
graceful and felicitous and easy as the flight of a swallow. Yet it has a
hard core and the true healthy rustic tang; there are ground-frosts in
the morning, there is an edge to the fresh spring breeze, and the frui
is not yet ripe.

ACT I

After the sparkling Overture, based on several themes from th
opera and so well known as to need no description, the curtain rise
on the village green. It is the day of the consecration of the church
and the lads and lasses are dancing and singing outside the inn
rejoicing in their health and high spirits and praising God for th
spring. Only two of them are touched with melancholy—the lover
Jenik (tenor) and Marenka (soprano). Marenka tells him that he
parents have already chosen a husband for her, but she will alway
be true to Jenik. Will he be true to her? Or has he found anothe
sweetheart?

178

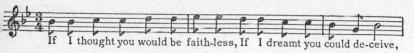

If I thought you would be faith-less, If I dreamt you could de-ceive,

She reminds him that she hardly knows who he is, and Jenik replies that his youth was a sad one: his father married a second time and the second wife's cruelty drove her stepson from home. They swear to be true to each other, and part for the time being. Marenka's parents, Krusina (baritone) and Ludmila (soprano), enter, followed by Kecal (bass), the marriage broker, a voluble scamp bubbling over with typical salesman's 'patter' and as plausible as Autolycus. Kecal obviously enjoys sharpening his wits on these simple peasants, and he almost deafens the old couple with his praises of the prospective bridegroom. It is Farmer Micha's younger son, Vasek, he says. The elder son? Oh, he was a bad lot. He disappeared years ago, and is presumed dead. No, no, Vasek is the lad. When Kecal has talked himself nearly out of breath Marenka comes in and upsets the whole conference by declaring that she is already in love with the handsome youth known as Jenik—and that's that! Even the blustering marriage broker is dashed for the moment. But he quickly pulls himself together, advises the parents to consult with old Micha himself and goes off to find Jenik. "I'll deal with *him*," he mutters fiercely. The villagers troop in again and the act ends with a riotous polka.

ACT II

We now begin to see the drift of the plot. Jenik is the elder son of Micha, Vasek the younger by his second marriage. Marenka's parents have contracted her to 'the son of Tobias Micha', and as the elder son is presumed dead, Vasek is obviously the man. Meanwhile, inside the inn, Jenik and the village youths are drinking. They sing a chorus in praise of beer, of which the commonplace sentiments are redeemed by the abrupt and strongly marked Czech rhythms. Jenik joins the song, but praises love instead of beer; Kecal scoffs at both arguments: money—money is the only thing worth praising. When the inn is empty, a typical country bumpkin comes shuffling in. It is Vasek (tenor), and we see at once why Kecal praised his moral qualities so extravagantly: he obviously has no mental ones. He also has a stammer, which is funny for a few bars but soon grows tiresome. He tells us that 'Mama' has sent him forth to woo, but it is only his terror of 'Mama' that can make him overcome his terror of other women. Marenka comes in and finds out that he is her intended husband. She takes advantage of the fact that he has never seen her before, and warns him that his bride is a flirt and will lead him a devil of a life. But there are others, she adds very archly; in fact, she knows a maiden who is pining for him—

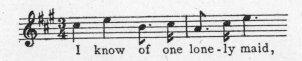

I know of one lone-ly maid,

—and he eventually joins her in one of the most charming numbers in the score. Even a simpleton like Vasek cannot but perceive that this unknown girl is positively throwing herself at him. He swears he will refuse Marenka, and runs off in pursuit of his new conquest as she trips away. Meanwhile, Kecal has been trying on a corresponding game with Jenik, and here they come, the broker expatiating as usual on the virtues of money, to a pompous, laying-down-the-law type of theme. "So don't bother any more with Marenka," says Kecal; "choose an heiress." "An heiress, did you say?" asks Jenik, pretending to be interested. "Yes, an heiress," shouts the broker, "and I've got the very one for you!"—

I know a maid-en with rich-es la-den

—a perfectly delicious duet which skips along to an intoxicating rhythm, Kecal gobbling away below and Jenik echoing his words in the tenor clef. Very well, says Jenik; he will barter his sweetheart for three hundred crowns, but—only on condition Marenka marries no one but Micha's son. Kecal, thinking he means Vasek, clinches the bargain and dances off in high glee. Jenik looks after him with a contemptuous smile, and then drifts into a beautiful *aria* in which he vows to be faithful to Marenka:

How could he ev-er dream that I would bar-ter you, dear?

There are faint echoes of Mozart in this *aria*—although one feels that Mozart would probably have avoided the over-sentimental effect of the D sharp. The villagers enter, and in their presence Jenik signs the paper bartering away his future bride. They are scandalised, and the curtain falls on a howl of execration.

ACT III

Well, as one's nurse used to say when bedtime approached, it all comes right in the end. But meanwhile, Smetana pads out his last act with some comic byplay which enables him to introduce a number of exhilarating Czech tunes. A travelling circus arrives on the village green, and when the comedians have shown their quality in a dance, Vasek, who begins to fear that he has made a mess of his matrimonial affairs, is induced to join them and impersonate the bear. Later, Marenka comes in with her parents. At first she will not believe that Jenik has sold her, but when they prove it she breaks into a passionate lament for her lost love:

Our dream of love, how fair it was!

Jenik prolongs his deception till the last moment, his only imaginable reason being to enable Smetana to provide some lively musical bickering between him and Marenka. When at last she knows that he is Micha's elder son, she throws herself into his arms. Vasek, who reappears as the bear, is brusquely told by his mother that a histrionic career is not for him, and packed off home; and the opera ends with all the village wishing luck to the Bartered Bride.

RICHARD STRAUSS

(1864–)

Der Rosenkavalier
(The Knight of the Rose)

Libretto by Hugo Von Hoffmansthal.
Time: Eighteenth Century.

First Production,
Dresden, 1911.

> 'The adventurous Baron the bright locks admired;
> He saw, he wished, and to the prize aspired.
> Resolved to win, he meditates the way,
> By force to ravish, or by fraud betray.'
>
> ALEXANDER POPE: *The Rape of the Lock.*

Der Rosenkavalier was first planned by Hoffmansthal as a broadly comic piece, practically a farce, the leading parts to be Baron Ochs (indeed, the opera was originally to have been called 'Ochs') and a girl dressed in man's clothes (Octavian). Now the traditional farce has no human feelings and no human characters; it has only situations and types. It depends entirely on a collision of events which throws the follies and frailties of mankind into ludicrous relief. As long as its creators only laugh at the results of these follies and frailties, the thing remains mechanical farce; when they mix pity with their laughter, it rises to emotional comedy. That is what happened with *Der Rosenkavalier*. It began more or less as a piece of comic horseplay. Then gradually the *librettist* and the composer (especially the composer, such is the humanising power of music) began to mix pity with their laughter, and the outcome was the masterpiece of mingled grace and humour and tenderness we know and love today. And the mainspring of this gradual change was the Marschallin, who began as quite a minor character and slowly and irresistibly took possession of her creators, much as Don Quixote took possession of Cervantes, until they were moved to pay their deepest homage to this emblem of the essential graciousness of womanhood.

ACT I

There is a flashing orchestral prelude, passionate and impetuous, in which Strauss leaps acrobatically from key to key like a mountaineer on perilous points of rock. Then the curtain rises on the Marschallin's

bedroom, appointed with all the elegance and luxury of that elegant
and luxurious epoch. The Marschallin (soprano) is in the bed, her
face hidden by the curtains, while Octavian (mezzo-soprano) kneels
beside her on a footstool, like Juan with Julia, 'half-embraced, and
half retiring from the glowing arm'. They are held in a trance of
remembered bliss : the boy at once bold and tremulous in the wonder
of his first love, the woman clinging possessively to each passing moment
of what may well be her last. Their dream is broken by the tinkle of a
bell, and while Octavian hides behind a screen a little black boy
enters with a salver of chocolate. When he has gone they settle down
merrily to breakfast. Their conversation tells us (rather gratuitously,
perhaps) that the lady's husband, the Field Marshal, is away on a
hunting expedition. Again they are interrupted. Can it be her husband?
Octavian draws his sword, swearing he will perish by her side and all
the rest of it; but the Marschallin, damping his ardour with salutary
common sense, pushes him into an inner room. He reappears a moment
later in a serving-maid's dress (which suits him admirably), primly
curtseying to a waltz measure—

—which we might almost call Octavian's *motif*, as it is associated
with him throughout the score. The visitor is the Marschallin's kinsman,
Baron Ochs of Lerchenau (bass). The fact that Ochs means precisely
what it sounds like in English and the leer with which he instantly and
instinctively ogles the supposed serving-maid, give us the worthy
Baron's character at once. He is a kind of middle-aged Tony Lumpkin,
well born but boorish and illiterate, whose main pleasures in life
are eating and drinking and (predominantly) wenching; a reminder,
in fact, that the eighteenth century had its brutal as well as its elegant
side. Ochs is also one of the greatest and most exacting *basso-buffo*
parts in all opera, ranging from bottom C to top F.

    In a long fanfaronade of coarse boasting he gives the Marschallin
to know that he is indeed the terror of the countryside, illustrating
his remarks by vigorous passes at the disguised Octavian (has she
ever been out to supper with a gentleman? When is her night off?
and so forth). But—it is time he married; and his choice is Sophie,
the daughter of Faninal, the wealthy *parvenu*. Will his fair cousin
choose a knight to bear, according to custom, a silver rose to his
betrothed? His fair cousin will; and after the lengthy but lively scene

of the Marschallin's levee, in which a hairdresser, a milliner, a scholar, a singer and others enjoy or compete for her patronage, the Baron goes, and Octavian returns dressed for riding. The Marschallin chooses him to be the Knight of the Silver Rose, and she dismisses him with an almost maternal tenderness, since she knows it is not for much longer that he will desire from her tenderness of another kind. Youth will call to youth and she will fade out of his heart. And, to music of a gentle and expressive melancholy, she sits gazing into a lonely future.

ACT II

At Faninal's house all is bustle and excitement as they make ready to receive the bearer of the silver rose. Faninal (baritone) is bursting with vulgar pride that his family is to be united with the old aristocracy; Marianne, the duenna (soprano), stands at the window watching Octavian's splendid equipage arrive; and even Sophie (soprano), modest and sensible girl as she is, cannot control a certain bubbling agitation at the prospect of becoming a baroness. At last Octavian appears, dressed in white and silver and bearing the rose, which he tenders to Sophie with the most ceremonious gallantry: "From my kinsman, Baron Lerchenau. He begs you to take this from me as token of his love"—and the orchestra whispers mysteriously under his voice:

This figure is followed immediately by a succession of chords—flutes, harps, solo violins and celeste—which fall on the ear like the chiming of some dainty musical toy, and seem to suggest the sprinkling of the rose with the drops of Persian attar that Octavian speaks of:

But Octavian has brought more than the Baron's rose to Sophie: he has brought the rose of life itself, and what the Marschallin so forlornly feared has come to pass. They have looked into each other's eyes, and the rest of the world has ceased to exist. Shyly, haltingly, they begin to speak to each other. Sophie has no modish affectations, and she confesses that the young Octavian pleases her more than any man she has ever met. Into this dream breaks the gross reality: Faninal introduces the Baron, who is followed by four or five lumpish servants. Ochs is nothing if not consistent: he smacks his lips at the sight of this dainty morsel that is to be his, passes his greedy hands over her and tries to make her sit on his knee. Sophie is revolted by her future husband ('he's like a horse-dealer buying a yearling colt!') and Octavian can hardly keep his fists off him. To Faninal, however, these are but the manners of the great, and he wishes the walls could be of glass so that the neighbours might see the 'quality' making thus free with his daughter! When Sophie flares up in her indignation the Baron chuckles more delightedly than ever. He loves a lass of spirit! "Ah," he says, "you'll learn to appreciate me by and by," humming a popular tune—

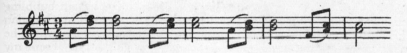

—which is made a great deal of later. He goes out with Faninal to interview the attorney. Sophie and Octavian are left alone, she protesting she will never marry Ochs, he vowing he will save her from him. Their dialogue ends in a passionate kiss, in the midst of which the Baron's spies discover them and raise the alarm. The Baron bursts in, and after a great commotion makes as though to attack Octavian with drawn sword. Octavian wounds him slightly in the arm. Ochs drops his sword (which he has shown only the vaguest notion how to handle) and roars: "Murder! Murder! A surgeon! I shall bleed to death!" and they all crowd round, fussing over him. Octavian hurries away, whispering to Sophie that she will hear further from him, and the distressed girl is led out by her duenna. Meanwhile, the Baron has been reassured that he will not bleed to death. He has also been cheered by a draught of wine and a note from 'Mariandel' (the name assumed by Octavian when dressed as a girl) in which she promises to meet him the following evening. So life has its compensations after all! And he goes out, swaying to his favourite waltz tune, his voice sinking down to a juicy and self-satisfied bottom E as the curtain slowly falls.

ACT III

Octavian's plot is somewhat similar to that of the *Merry Wives of Windsor*, and we may be sure that what hoodwinked the nimblers witted Falstaff will be far too much for a fatuous bumpkin like Ochs-So it proves. Ochs meets 'Mariandel' at an inn (supper laid for two. bed in the corner, all invitingly complete). Primed with wine and confident of success, the lecherous old goat brings into play the method, he has taken a lifetime to perfect, 'Mariandel' coquettishly leading him on and the orchestra capering along merrily to those fascinating waltz measures we often hear in the concert-hall. Then the great sport of baron-baiting begins: weird faces appear, gibbering at windows and trap-doors, and superstitious terror soon freezes the Baron's desires. The climax comes when a woman in mourning breaks in and claims him as her long-lost husband, four children dancing round him and screaming "Papa! Papa!" He roars for the police, but when they arrive he becomes confused, and even tries to pass off 'Mariandel' as his affianced bride, Sophie von Faninal. At that moment Faninal himself appears, having been summoned to rescue his future son-in-law, and of course the poor Baron is in a worse mess than ever. Here he is, not only entertaining a strange young girl in a disreputable inn, but also confronted with a supposed wife and four children! It is hardly necessary to add that this puts the finish to his matrimonial prospects. The final scene is between the Marschallin and the two youthful lovers. Time has brought her to account, and the moment has come when Octavian has eyes for her no longer. She must give place to youth. And she begins the great trio, the climax of the opera:

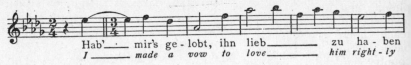

Hab' — mir's ge - lobt, ihn lieb_____ zu ha - ben
I _____ made a vow to love_____ him right - ly

"If I truly love him," she sings softly to herself, "then I must desire his happiness rather than my own." Octavian has found his happiness, and the Marschallin fades quietly and slowly out of their lives. How selfish is young love! They do not even notice that she has gone.

PETER TCHAIKOVSKY

(1840-1893)

Eugene Onegin

Libretto by Modeste Tchaikovsky after Pushkin.
Time: 1820.

First Production,
Moscow, 1879.

> 'Then shalt thou weep, entreat, complain
> To Love, as I did once to thee:
> When all thy tears shall be as vain
> As mine were then: for thou shalt be
> Damned for thy false apostasy.'
>
> THOMAS CAREW.

Eugene Onegin is Tchaikovsky's most attractive opera, and on the whole his best. And here we have a striking paradox: if one were asked to name the two most theatrical composers of symphonic music one would no doubt name Berlioz and Tchaikovsky. Yet neither of them was conspicuously successful with opera. Tchaikovsky especially, so intensely dramatic in the concert-hall—writing, in fact, magnificent 'theatre', the kind of music one might expect some great tragic actor to write, lost much of his dramatic stature when he went into the opera-house. The tiger became tamed indeed, sometimes almost shabby. It is perhaps significant that he called *Eugene Onegin* not an 'opera', but 'lyrical scenes in three acts', and in these pleasant pages we are far more conscious of the Tchaikovsky of the songs and pianoforte pieces than the Tchaikovsky of the symphonies and tone poems. *Onegin* is the tragedy of those who reject love when it is offered and then passionately desire it when it is out of reach. There is a fragrant, melancholy charm about it that brings back, for me, the subtle aroma of Turgenev's exquisite stories of country gentlefolk.

ACT I: *Scene* 1

In the garden of Mme Larin's country house, Mme Larin (mezzo-soprano) and the nurse are recalling old days while the two daughters, Tatiana (soprano) and Olga (contralto), are looking forward to new ones. We see at once the distinction between the two girls—Tatiana, always with a book in her hand and romantic fancies in her heart; Olga, cheerful and healthy, with 'no nonsense' about her. By and by two young men arrive: Lensky (tenor), who is engaged to Olga, and his friend, Eugene Onegin (baritone). Here again is a contrast—Lensky, impulsive, passionate, warm-hearted; Onegin, a cynical young dandy, wrapped up in that fatalistic Byronic pose so fashionable with the young men of that age. Lensky sings Olga a tender little love song—

—while Onegin entertains himself by 'drawing out' Tatiana in heavy and rather patronising 'small talk'.

Act I: *Scene 2*

Tatiana has fallen in love. Onegin, with his aristocratic mien, his disillusioned, slightly disdainful air suggesting a reckless and colourful past, has become the incarnation of the gloomy and ill-starred heroes she has read about, and that night she sits down in her bedroom to tell him so, in a long and passionate letter:

Nowhere outside Turgenev do we get such penetrating insight into the heart of a young girl in the rapturous self-abandonment of first love. We almost feel that we are eavesdropping.

Act I: *Scene 3*

Next morning Tatiana is half-frightened and half-ashamed at what she has written. Not without cause: for Onegin meets her in the garden—what a difference the clear, cruel light of day makes!—and tells her, coldly and calmly, that he has read her letter. He honours her frankness and he will be frank in return. If fate had meant him to be a husband and father, she is the kind of girl he would have chosen. But no, he is a soul apart—and a great deal more of the same sickening sententiousness, to music which is probably apt to the occasion but which I, for one, always find embarrassingly commonplace:

Tatiana evidently finds it so, too, for she says hardly a word in reply.

ACT II: *Scene* 1

It is Tatiana's birthday and they are dancing in her honour. Onegin dances with Tatiana, and the old gossips decide that here is a match—although it is a great pity, they say, that Onegin is such a loose and desperate character. Any Onegin I have ever known would have purred with pleasure at such a description; but Pushkin's hero is unaccountably indignant, and he decides to annoy Lensky and make him jealous by dancing with Olga. This he does so effectually that Lensky loses his temper and challenges him to a duel. The guests are appalled, and even Onegin is a little shaken by the storm he has roused.

ACT II: *Scene* 2

The quarrel begun in the heat of blood the previous night is to reach its tragic climax in the bleak, snow-bound morning. Onegin and Lensky are to meet in a desolate spot by the river, where one of them must die. Lensky stands there in the dawn and sings his farewell to life and love, a heart-rending cry of anguish over 'the ground-whirl of the perished leaves of hope':

The climax comes swiftly: Onegin fires, and his bullet pierces Lensky's heart; and the victor stands for a moment, horrified at what he has done. Such is the end of youthful friendship.

ACT III: *Scene* 1

Six years later we see Onegin at Prince Gremin's house in St. Petersburg. The guests are dancing a polonaise. Soon the hostess enters to receive her visitors, and it is some moments before Onegin

can believe that this gracious, self-possessed, dignified woman is the
shy, ingenuous Tatiana who so impulsively loved him long ago.
Prince Gremin joins him and, serenely unconscious that Onegin has
ever known his wife, tells his guest how happy the love of Tatiana
has made him. She is like a bright star, he says, lighting up the evening
of his life—

—a somewhat wooden melody which suggests that Tchaikovsky, having
introduced a bass, manufactured an *aria* for him mainly from a
sense of duty. On the other hand, such deliberate self-conscious
music is perhaps meant to express an elderly man's idea of love.

ACT III: *Scene* 2

It is the final meeting between Onegin and Tatiana. To the
opening theme of Gremin's song, now transformed into the minor, she
reminds him, quite gently, how she came to him in her youth and
beauty. Love was waiting there for him—and he rejected it. Onegin
bitterly curses his past blindness, and their voices join in an impassioned
lament—"Happiness was once so near us!"—

—but it is too late now. She will not sacrifice her honour to a dream of
the past. And Onegin, realizing that he has thrown away the greatest
treasure of both their hearts, staggers blindly out of the room—and
out of her life.

GIUSEPPE VERDI

(1813–1901)

Rigoletto

Libretto by Piave after Victor Hugo.
Time : Sixteenth Century.

First Production,
Venice, 1851.

'No time to break jests when the heartstrings are about to be broken.'
THOMAS FULLER: *Of Jesting.*

Rigoletto is the crowning peak of Verdi's early period. Before this he had shown pity and tenderness, a gift of abundant melody and a flair for thrilling dramatic effect, but never in one work had he shown all these qualities in such equal power and splendour. Never had his instinct been so sure, his touch so telling; never had the music illumined and electrified the words with such inevitable truth. In every scene of *Rigoletto* we feel that thus and thus only could music express such a situation or emotion. Like many others of Verdi's early operas, *Rigoletto* has had its share of kicks from supercilious persons who sneered at its barrel-organ melodies and their 'Verdi-gurdy' accompaniments. But the more we hear it the more firmly we realise how right Verdi was, and how unerringly he wrote exactly the tune that fitted the moment. Is '*La Donna e Mobile*' vulgar? Perhaps. Is it precisely the type of song a man would sing to himself over a bottle of wine while waiting for a pretty girl? Decidedly.

ACT I: *Scene 1*

Rigoletto begins with nine C's on the trumpets and trombones. That is the Curse *motif*, and we shall hear how it works through the whole drama, like a poison eating through a doomed body. After a few more bars the shadow lifts and we are at a brilliant ball in the Duke of Mantua's palace. The Duke (tenor) is a libertine—and, worse still, a libertine who boasts of his conquests:

Que-sta o quel - la _____ per me pa - ri so - no
In my heart all _____ are e - qual - ly cher-ish'd

Suddenly there is a dramatic interruption to the festivities. Count
Monterone (baritone) rushes in, his hair dishevelled, his eyes flaming
with anger. The Duke has seduced his daughter. He curses the Duke
and curses the Duke's ribald hunchback Jester, Rigoletto (baritone),
who helps him in his tawdry amours. The Duke laughs callously
and dismisses him; but the Jester stands motionless, the mirth dashed
from his lips. A father's curse! And he thinks of his own daughter,
whom he has guarded so fanatically from the contamination of the
court.

ACT I: *Scene 2*

It is late at night. Rigoletto, still troubled by Monterone's curse,
approaches his own house. A dark figure follows him, and, as he
nears the door, mutters something in his ear. It is Sparafucile (bass),
an assassin. Rigoletto starts, and draws away from him. "No, no; I
don't need you." "Very well," whispers Sparafucile; "but—some day
you may. Remember my name—Sparafucile." Their dialogue takes
place over a droning, menacing melody ('cello and double bass) that
seems to enshrine the very heart of darkness. Sparafucile vanishes into
the night; and Rigoletto, after giving vent to his anger and fear in a
passionate monologue, turns into the house to greet his daughter. He is
watchful, anxious, suspicious; but Gilda (soprano) assures him that
she never leaves the house except for the church. She is deceiving
him; for after a few moments the Duke, disguised as a young student,
slips into the courtyard, and when Rigoletto has departed the Duke
and Gilda sing of their secret love in a duet whose buoyant, lilting
measure distils the essence of youthful passion:

E il sol dell' a - ni - ma, la vi - ta è a - mo - re,
Sun of the soul a di - vine in - spi - ra - tion,

They hear footsteps outside, and fearing it is her father, Gilda sends
her gallant away. She looks after him, lost in a dream of love:

Ca - ro no - me che il mio cor_____
Carv'd up - on my in - most heart_____

The footsteps are those of a group of courtiers. They hate Rigoletto, and, thinking he keeps a mistress in this mysterious house, they resolve to carry her off. When Rigoletto returns they persuade him they are abducting the Countess Ceprano, and, to make the jest all the richer, they blindfold him and force him to help them.

ACT II

The Curse has begun its work. The courtiers have carried Gilda off to the palace, and the mantle of Monterone has now descended on to the shoulders of Rigoletto. Maddened with grief, he wanders from room to room seeking her. When the courtiers mock him, he denounces them in an outburst of rage:

Cor - ti - gia - ni,   vil raz - za   dan - na - ta,
Race   of   cour-tiers,   vile rab-ble   de - test - ed,

At last he finds her—grief-stricken, dishonoured, but still hopelessly in love with her seducer. He swears vengeance.

ACT III

This is one of the most powerful acts in all Italian opera. The scene is divided: on one side we see into Sparafucile's squalid tavern by the river, on the other side the lane leading to it. Rigoletto and his daughter crouch in the darkness, watching the house through a hole in the garden wall. Presently the Duke enters the inn and calls for wine. He breaks into a song—

La don - na e mo - bi - le
Plume in   the   sum-mer wind

—a simple trifle in the style of a street ballad, completely spoiled by the elaborate *cadenza* with which most tenors finish it off. We then learn that Rigoletto has hired Sparafucile to murder the Duke and has come to see the deed done. Maddalena (contralto), Sparafucile's

sister and decoy, comes down from the upper room, and the Duke at
once begins to flirt with her. Their byplay gradually develops into
the great quartet—the Duke and Maddalena, Rigoletto and Gilda
all revealing their individual emotions in their music:

Bel - la   fi - glia dell' a - mor - - e,
Fair - est daugh - ter of   the   gra - - ces,

Gilda has seen enough to convince her that her lover is worthless,
but not enough to kill her love. Her father sends her home. She must
disguise herself as a youth and meet him at Verona. A storm is approaching. Sparafucile joins Rigoletto, who counts him out half the blood-
money. He shall have the other half when he has delivered him the
body in a sack. Rigoletto creeps away into the darkness, but in a few
moments Gilda returns, dressed in boy's clothes. She cannot obey her
father, her love is too strong. The storm slowly rises, an invisible
chorus imitating through closed lips the moaning of the wind. The
Duke is now asleep in the upper room and Sparafucile is preparing
to strike the blow; but Maddalena is overcome with pity for the young
man. Why not kill the hunchback instead?—a proposed breach of
contract at which the honest assassin stands appalled. At last he
consents that if anyone else should come in he will kill him and substitute his body for that of the man upstairs—to a fiery, galloping
melody that mingles with the thunder of the storm.

Gilda overhears this and resolves to die for her lover. She knocks
on the door. It is the signal: Sparafucile opens it and she runs in under
his uplifted dagger. . . . Rigoletto tiptoes back to the house, impatient
to see his victim. Sparafucile drags out the sack, pockets the rest of his
money and bids him good night. At last the Jester triumphs! He is
just about to heave the sack towards the river when there occurs the
most dramatic stroke in the whole opera: the Duke's voice rings out
from the house:

La don - na è mo - bi - le
Plume in   the   sum - mer wind

Rigoletto stands petrified: there has been some horrible mistake!
Feverishly he unties the sack and sees the hideous truth. Gilda is dying.
With her last breath she implores him to forgive her and bless her:

Las - su in cie - lo, vi - ci - na al - la ma - dre
From yon - der sky, with the blest an - gels fly - ing,

With a great cry of anguish Rigoletto falls senseless over her body.
The Curse has been fulfilled!

Il Trovatore

Libretto by Salvatore Cammanaro after Guttierez.   First Production,
Time: Fifteenth Century.   Rome, 1853.

> 'The silent room, the heavy creeping shade,
> The dead that travel fast, the opening door,
> The murdered brother rising through the floor,
> The ghost's white fingers on thy shoulders laid,
> And then the lonely duel in the glade,
> The broken swords, the stifled scream, the gore,
> Thy grand revengeful eyes when all is o'er—'
>   OSCAR WILDE.

Il Trovatore has probably been 'guyed' more cruelly than any other
opera. Its salient tunes have become the prey of the barrel-organ,
its characters have been lampooned in the comic papers, its thunderous
heroics have been mercilessly travestied on the music-hall stage. It
has, in fact, become the supreme example of absurdity in opera. No
doubt its complicated plot (much of which is, so to speak, pre-natal) is
partly responsible. Had not Gilbert *Il Trovatore* in mind when he wrote
H.M.S. Pinafore, in which the bumboat woman mixes up the babies
in their cradles? But the chief charge against the plot of this opera is
that it is incomprehensible. I hope to disprove this as nonsense. The
plot becomes perfectly clear with a little attention. True, it has its
absurd moments; but if you are going to be put off by absurd moments
you had better avoid opera altogether. The important thing is that
Il Trovatore is a superb piece of music, full of, brimming over with,
magnificent tunes—'tunes that seem to be hammered out of steel',
as Frank Mullings used to say. It is a gloomy, blood-boltered drama—
reeking of damp dungeons, charnel-houses, sulphurous hates and
the acrid smoke of witches' fires; horror on horror's head. Perhaps
we can afford to smile a little at it; but Verdi could not: Verdi obviously
believed in the thing heart and soul, and attacked it with a blazing
sincerity. Otherwise his score would not have been the masterpiece it is.

Act I: *Scene 1*

First let us get this notorious and much-abused plot straightened
out. What has happened before the opera begins is told in the first
scene by Ferrando (bass), Captain of the Guard in the castle of the
Count di Luna, in a rough and vigorous ballad sung to his soldiers.
Twenty-odd years ago, he relates, the Count's younger brother was
bewitched in his cradle by a gipsy, who was afterwards caught and
burned at the stake. The gipsy's daughter, Azucena, in revenge stole
the boy and flung him into the same fire that had consumed her mother.
Azucena escaped, and the old father died, pathetically nursing the
hope that owing to some mistake his son might still be alive.

Act I: *Scene 2*

In the garden of the Queen's palace the beautiful Leonora (soprano),
a lady-in-waiting, tells her confidante, Iñez (soprano), that she has
fallen in love with Manrico, a troubadour whom she crowned victor
at a recent tourney. He was afterwards banished for political reasons,
but every night he returns to serenade her in the garden. She expresses
her love in a joyous and brilliant *aria*:

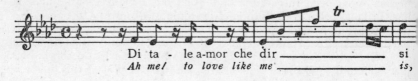

Di ta - le a-mor che dir _____ si
Ah me! to love like me _____ *is,*

But the Count di Luna (baritone), elder brother of the murdered
child, is also in love with Leonora, and when he discovers Manrico
(tenor) serenading her he challenges him to a duel.

Act II: *Scene 1*

Now Manrico passes as the son of Azucena (contralto), living with
her in a gipsy encampment near by; and this scene opens with the
famous 'Anvil Chorus':

Chi del gi-ta-no i gior-ni ab-bel-la?
Who gives the gip-sy a life that's full of plea-sure?

When they are left alone Azucena tells Manrico the horrible story
of her mother's death (which we have already heard from Ferrando),
and urges him to vengeance. She lets slip one vital fact, however:
she stole the child from the castle, but distracted by grief and hardly
knowing what she was about, she threw her own child into the flames
instead of the Count's younger brother. Manrico, therefore, realises
that he is not Azucena's son; and when he tells her that in the duel
he had the Count di Luna at his mercy, but, moved by a strange impulse
of pity, could not kill him, we begin to realise the truth. By and by a
messenger comes to the camp to tell Manrico that Leonora believes
he has been slain in the duel and is to enter a convent. He rushes
away to prevent her.

ACT II: *Scene 2*

But the Count is before him. He plans to carry off Leonora, and,
under cover of darkness, steals to the convent with his retainers.
To a slow and beautiful air he sings of the love that inspires him:

Il ba-len del suo sor-ri-so
Bright her smiles, as when bright morn-ing

The convent bell begins to toll. Leonora, escorted by Iñez, makes
to enter, when the Count and his men spring forward and surround
her. But another figure suddenly stands between them: it is Manrico.
He defies the Count and swiftly hurries Leonora away.

ACT III: *Scene 1*

The Count is preparing to attack the fortress to which Manrico
has taken Leonora. Ferrando brings in Azucena, whom his soldiers

have found wandering near their camp. He is prepared to swear that she is the gipsy who, so they believe, murdered the Count's younger brother. She tells them she is Manrico's mother and is only trying to find her son, who has left her. Manrico's mother! The Count leaps up in triumph. Here is a double vengeance: at one blow he can punish his brother's murderess and revenge himself on his rival! Azucena is dragged away to prison.

Act III: *Scene 2*

The scene changes to Manrico's fortress. He is about to make Leonora his bride; but danger is threatening them: it is useless to conceal it from her any longer. He tries to console her in an expressive *aria*:

Ah si, ben mio;coll'es - se - re io tuo tu mia con-sor - te
Yes, now; thou art my spouse by right, I thine in sight of hea - ven

A moment later their dream is violently shattered: a messenger rushes in: "Manrico! Thy mother, the gipsy, has been captured. See! See! Over there the flames are rising for her even now!" Not a moment is to be lost, and Manrico swiftly gathers his men round him. Then occurs one of those 'absurd moments' from which (to the irreverently realistic) hardly any opera seems to be free. Just on the point of bounding off to her rescue, Manrico pauses to tell the company, at some length, how furious he is about it all. Well, we must accept such a convention, just as we accept the convention that a man shall sing when he is asking the time (*La Bohème*) or inviting a friend to a whisky-and-soda (*Madam Butterfly*). And we accept it the more gladly as this air is one of the most thrilling things Verdi ever wrote. Here, indeed, is a tune 'hammered out of steel'; and how the sparks fly out of it!

Di quel - la   pi - ra   l'or - ren - do   to - co,
Yon-der pile   blaz - ing,   vis-ion ap - pal - ling,

Act IV: *Scene* 1

Manrico has failed in his attempt, and the Count has cast him into prison and condemned him to death. Leonora comes to seek him. She hears the monks chanting the '*Miserere*', the tolling of the death-bell and Manrico's mournful voice from the prison. Their voices join in a duet which has been heard in every country in the world, but which even the barrel-organ cannot rob of its dignity and tragic power:

Quel suon, quel-la pre - ci ·   so-len - ni, fu - ne - ste,
That chaunt-ing so so - lemn,   *and sor-row fore-bod - ing,*

The Count appears. "At sunrise," he tells her, "the son will be beheaded and the mother burnt at the stake!" Leonora forms a desperate resolve. "Spare his life," she says to the Count, "and I will be thy bride." But she adds under her breath that she will poison herself before he can claim her.

Act IV: *Scene* 2

Meanwhile, Manrico and Azucena are together in the dungeon. The old woman begins to wander in her mind. "Let us go home to our mountains, my son, and begin a new life there"—

Ai no - stri mon - ti ri - tor-ne - re - mo,
Once more re - turn - ing home to our moun - tains

—a melody that has often been sneered at for its simplicity; yet in its very simplicity lies its eternal appeal. Is it not precisely the kind of tune to which an old woman, become a child again, would rock herself to sleep? Leonora hurries in: Manrico's life is spared. He must hasten away. But Manrico is troubled at the news. The cost— the cost? Surely she has paid a shameful price for this? Then Leonora tells him the tragic truth: she has bargained with the Count, but

rather than fulfil her bargain she has poisoned herself. She dies in
Manrico's arms. The Count is furious at having been tricked, and
Manrico is dragged away to death. Azucena rises from her straw and
confronts the Count like some terrible avenging angel: "That man
was thine own brother!"

And so this tragedy of blood inexorably burns itself out. "A dismal
opera," I remember (with shame) saying once to Frederic Austin.
"Perhaps it is," he replied; "but only a genius could have written it."

La Traviata

Libretto by Piave, after Dumas *fils*.   First Production,
Time Mid-Nineteenth Century.[1]   Venice, 1853.

> 'You will proceed in pleasure, and in pride,
> Beloved and loving many; all is o'er
> For me on earth, except some years to hide
> My shame and sorrow deep in my heart's core.'
>   BYRON: *Don Juan.*

La Traviata, which means literally 'the misled', was produced
two months after *Il Trovatore*; indeed, Verdi was working on it while
Il Trovatore was in rehearsal. Never were twins in sharper contrast:
the earlier work with its fierce masculine vigour, the later with its
sensitive feminine fragility. Both operas were warm favourites in the
late nineteenth century, but during the last twenty or thirty years—
in England, at any rate—they have declined into a somewhat shoddy
disrepute, which is only deepened by occasional shoddy performances.
Few operas suffer such cruel damage as these two by being crudely or
shabbily put on. The uncomfortable truth is that *Il Trovatore* and *La
Traviata* demand really great singing, if we are to accept in these
sophisticated times the unashamed melodrama of the one and the
unashamed sentiment of the other. And this is not an age of great
singing. Yet, however often we may have seen it humiliated by poor
production, *La Traviata* will always hold for most of us a peculiar and
intimate sweetness—like the charm of an old love letter or a faded
flower pressed between the leaves of a book. That is because it is the
work of a master, whose instinctive refinement of touch never allowed
its sentiment to become tawdry.

[1] Dumas's *La Dame aux Camélias* was, of course, a play of contemporary life and,
consequently, produced in contemporary dress. This partly accounted for the early
failure of *La Traviata*, the audience being used to 'costume' opera. That is why the
opera has frequently been dressed in the period of Louis XIV.

ACT I

Alfred Germont (tenor), an impressionable young Parisian, has fallen in love with the notorious Violetta Valéry (soprano), whose name is not mentioned by the Best People. He is taken to a festive party at her house. At first he is shy and diffident, but when Violetta herself asks him, he sings a buoyant song in praise of wine, in which she joins later:

Li - bia - mo, li - bia-mo ne' lie - ti ca - li - ci
Fill · high! till with wine ev -'ry gob - let brim - ming shall

che la - bel - lez - za in - fio - - ra,
spar-kle with ru - by - like bright - ness

Violetta is consumptive. She knows that she may not have long to live, and she is cynically resolved that if hers is to be a short life it shall at least be a gay one. Alfred is distressed at her callous talk. He implores her to listen to him. He loves her; won't she abandon this mad career for his sake? Doesn't she realise she is killing herself? At first she laughs; but when he has gone into another room she is touched by his love and devotion:

Ah fors' è lui che l'a - ni - ma
Was this the man my fan - cy bright

But no: her mood swiftly changes. Such love is not for her. Only in a crazy whirl of pleasure can she forget the curse hanging over her:

Sem-pre li - be - ra degg' i o fol-leg-gia - re di gio-ja in gio - ja,
Shall I al -ways free - ly rang-ing, Run the course of my ca - reer

ACT II: *Scene* I

But Alfred wins. And here we find him in a house outside Paris, where he and Violetta have been living in quiet contentment for the past three months. He finds out from the maid, Annina (soprano), that Violetta has been selling her jewellery to help towards the expenses of the house, and he goes off to try to raise some money. Later, when Violetta is alone, a visitor is shown in—a grave, aristocratic man of middle age who announces that he is Alfred's father. The elder Germont (baritone) treats Violetta with every courtesy, but it is soon ominously clear why he has come. His son must break off this association; the scandal is ruining Alfred's career and also threatens to ruin the marriage prospects of his sister. Does Violetta truly love Alfred? Does she love him unselfishly enough to sacrifice him? "Can you bear to give him up," he pleads, "for his own sake and the sake of my daughter?" After a bitter struggle with herself, Violetta consents. Germont is deeply moved and perhaps a little ashamed of his victory, but he has done his duty as a father. Violetta writes to Flora Bervoix, a friend from her former life, accepting an invitation to a gay party. An hour ago she would have torn up the invitation. She also writes a note to Alfred, telling him that the call of the old life is too strong for her and that she is deserting him. Later in the scene, a messenger hands Alfred the note when he is alone. He reads the first few words and staggers as though he has been struck in the face. His father, who has entered from the garden, catches him in his arms. "Ah, my dear son," he says, "this is a cruel blow; but surely it is for the best? Come home again—home, where we have mourned for you as for one dead":

Di Pro - ven-za il mar, il suol   chi dal   cor ti can-cel - lò?
From the   land of dear Pro-vence what hath caused thy heart to roam?

But Alfred scarcely listens to him. He can think of nothing but Violetta —Violetta who has betrayed him, fooled him, abandoned him for a rival! He stumbles on Flora's invitation. So: she has gone there, has she? Then he will go there too and revenge himself on her. And he dashes out of the house in a mad fury of jealousy.

Act II: *Scene 2*

The party is a riotous one. Violetta appears with Baron Douphol (bass), who has now undertaken to 'protect' her. Alfred, in a mood of reckless, savage gaiety, is playing cards and winning all the time. "Unlucky in love, lucky at play!" he shouts tauntingly at Violetta. At last, when the other guests have gone in to supper, Alfred and Violetta come face to face. She implores him to control himself. He is angering the Baron, and she is afraid it may end in a duel. Alfred laughs a sneering laugh, and hints that it is the Baron for whom she is afraid. Almost choked with emotion, Violetta nevertheless bravely continues the deception, and declares—yes, she loves the Baron. At that Alfred flies into a frantic rage. He calls in the others from the supper-room. "This woman," he shouts, "helped me to maintain the house where we lived. I, like a miserable slave, allowed it. Be witnesses that I now repay her—twice over!"—and he hurls his winnings at her. His father, who has suddenly entered, gravely reproves him.

Act III

Nature has taken its revenge on Violetta, and she now lies on her death-bed. The Doctor (bass) pretends to reassure her, but as he goes out he tells Annina that there are only a few hours left. As the orchestra plays very softly the melody of '*Ah, Fors' e Lui*', Violetta reads in a broken voice a note from Germont. Alfred has wounded Douphol in a duel, he says; he has been told of her sacrifice, and is coming to ask her to forgive him. But Violetta knows in her soul that it is too late; and to one of the most poignant melodies Verdi ever wrote, she bids farewell to life and happiness:

Revellers pass by the window, singing of the Shrovetide feast. Alfred arrives at last, torn with remorse and vowing he will never desert her. They will leave Paris together and begin a new life far away:

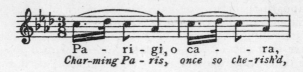

Pa - ri - gi, o ca - - ra,
Char-ming Pa - ris, once so che-rish'd,

But it is a vain dream. Gently she disillusions the young man: he will live and be happy, and if he finds some pure maiden who loves him he will marry her. It is her dearest and last wish. And so the tormented spirit passes.

A Masked Ball

Libretto by Antonio Somma after Scribe.   First Production,
Time: Eighteenth Century.   Rome, 1859.

> 'A good Wife is a hid Treasure, which he that hath found, does well not to brag of.'
>
> DE LA ROCHEFOUCAULD.

A Masked Ball is one of the most interesting of Verdi's scores, since it contains the best qualities of his early style and some striking hints of the greatness that was to follow. It is, in fact, a kind of bridge. His orchestration has gained in richness and significance, there is here and there a touch of sprightly humour, and quite frequently in the turn of a phrase or the outline of a melody we catch recognisable fore-shadowings of the later works—particularly *Aïda*. Unfortunately, the opera has suffered from the absurdity of the revised *libretto* and—in England, at any rate—from shabby and incompetent productions. I myself made my first acquaintance with *A Masked Ball* through a performance that was all but a travesty, and for years the work remained—most unfairly—a laughing-stock in my memory. The casual listener may think that, compared with Wagner or Strauss, the music of Verdi's early and middle periods is easy to sing; the answer is that it is fatally easy to sing badly—a truth which may be tested in England on almost any day of the year.

The revised *libretto* is a typical example of what happens when the official nose pokes itself into the arts. Scribe's drama dealt with the assassination of Gustavus III of Sweden, but the Roman censorship objected to royalty being assassinated (to music); so Gustavus became, most unromantically, 'Richard, Earl of Warwick' (Riccardo in the score), Governor of Boston, Massachusetts; and the two conspirators, Horn and Warting, were rechristened 'Samuel and Tom'. On the sudden apparition in an essentially Italian opera of two protagonists named Samuel and Tom, the only possible comment is: "I ask you!" One is irresistibly reminded of the broker's men in pantomime every time they pop up in the score. Surely there is no valid reason in these times why the original scene and characters should not be restored?

Act I: *Scene* i

There is a short orchestral Prelude having as its main melody Riccardo's love-song, which he sings soon after his first entrance; then we find ourselves in the Governor's audience-chamber, where deputies, noblemen and others are waiting. A brief chorus tells us that, though some of them are loyally devoted to him, others, led by Samuel and Tom (basses), are plotting his murder. Riccardo (tenor) enters. He is a handsome, high-spirited man with some slight affinity with the Duke in *Rigoletto*, though far more honest and chivalrous than that lively blackguard, and sincerely troubled by his guilty love. It is Adelia, wife of his friend and secretary Renato, whom he loves; and when Edgar, a young page (sometimes called Oscar), hands him a list of invitations for a masked ball, he sees her name there and calls up the memory of her beauty in the melody we have already heard:

La ri-ve-drà nell' e-sta-si,
I shall be-hold her form a-gain,

Renato (baritone) comes in, and seeing his chief gloomy and abstracted, says, very meaningly, that he knows the reason. For a moment the Earl is startled. Can he suspect? . . . But Renato immediately relieves his mind: he is speaking of the conspiracy. "Oh, that," says Riccardo lightly; "don't worry about that. I can take care of myself!" They are interrupted by the Chief Justice, who demands that Ulrica, a Negro sorceress, shall be banished from the province. Riccardo, rather flippantly, asks the opinion of his page; and Edgar (soprano) describes the fortune-teller's art in a mercurial ballad:

Vol-ta la ter-re a—— fronte al-le stel-le,
Read-ing the stars on high,—— eyes fierce-ly burn-ing,

Riccardo is amused: she tells fortunes, does she? Why shouldn't they go and consult her, in disguise? Edgar is all for such a piquant adventure, and Samuel and Tom see here a chance to put their design into execution. Renato sees it too, and is gloomily anxious about his chief's safety.

ACT I: *Scene 2*

In her cavern Ulrica (contralto) is calling up the powers of darkness over a smoking cauldron surrounded by village girls and children. The scene has a slightly pantomime flavour but is fully redeemed by the atmospheric power of the music, Ulrica's invocation having the spaciousness of some of the best tunes in *Aida*. Riccardo strolls in disguised as a fisherman. Ulrica tells the fortune of his sailor, Silvano (bass), and a few moments later a servant knocks at the door to announce that Adelia is waiting to consult her. Riccardo is dumbfounded at this and hides himself so that he can overhear their conference. When Ulrica has dismissed her court, Adelia (soprano) steals timidly in. She implores the sorceress to cure her of her fatal love for the ruler of the province. Riccardo cannot stifle an exclamation of joy: his love is returned! Ulrica tells Adelia that she must gather a certain herb at midnight beneath the gibbet outside the city. Riccardo, in his hiding-place, pledges himself to follow her there and watch over her. When Adelia has left by a secret door, Riccardo is joined by Edgar, Samuel and Tom and the others. He tells Ulrica he is a fisherman and asks her to foretell if his life shall be calm or stormy—in a tone of good-humoured banter:

Di tu - se fe - de - le il flut - to m' a-spet - - ta,
De - clare— if to meet storm or calm I am fat - - ed,

Ulrica, not unnaturally, is piqued at his disrespectful attitude towards her art and, perhaps a little spitefully, she warns him that he is near to death. "Indeed," he says lightly; "and who shall slay me?" And she replies, "He who next shakes you by the hand." He laughs at her but the next moment Renato enters and grasps the hand of his friend in greeting.

ACT II

To the gallows at midnight comes Adelia in quest of the magic herb. Her fear and agitation are expressed in short panting phrases which chase each other breathlessly in the orchestra, and later by a broad and beautiful melody in which, in the previous scene, she invoked heaven's protection. Falteringly she stumbles forward in the darkness, seeking the herb that shall cleanse her heart—

Ma dall' a - ri - do ste - lo - di - vul - sa
When at last from its stem I shall sev - er

—an *aria* which ends in an impassioned theme in the major, anticipating the Leonora of *The Force of Destiny*. Suddenly Riccardo reveals himself, and in an ardent duet they confess their love. But at the height of their passion they are interrupted by Renato: he has hurried after the Earl to warn him of the conspiracy against his life. Adelia is terrified at the sight of her husband, but she is veiled and he does not recognise her in the darkness. Riccardo, about to escape, makes his secretary promise to escort the veiled woman back to the city without speaking to her or looking on her face. But as Renato and Adelia are setting forth they are overtaken by the ubiquitous Samuel and Peeping Tom, who, furious at finding Renato instead of his principal, try to tear the veil from Adelia. Renato draws his sword, but Adelia rushes between them and reveals herself. The conspirators burst into mocking laughter at this discovery, while Renato stands horror-stricken at the supposed perfidy of the wife he has loved and the friend he has trusted. In a voice grim with meaning he tells the conspirators to call on him next morning.

ACT III: *Scene* 1

In a room in their home Adelia, crushed and humiliated, lies at her husband's feet. To music of a noble power and integrity he bitterly reproaches her: blood alone can wipe out her sin. She implores his forgiveness: yes, she has sinned, but only in thought. She loves Riccardo, but—he is not her lover:

Mor - ro, ma pri - ma in gra - zia
I die, yet first im - plore thee,

Renato bids her take a last farewell of her son. And when she has gone his eye falls on the portrait of Riccardo. Yes—it is *he* whose death

shall wipe out this dishonour! His music here has more than a hint of
Amonasro, until it passes into the most famous and most expressive
aria in the opera—the '*Eri tu*'. This begins in D minor over relentless,
rhythmic hammer-blows in the orchestra, then softens finally into the
exquisite *cantabile* in which he mourns his broken happiness:

O   dol- cez - ze   per-du - te, O me - mo   -   ria
Oh,   the pangs   of   a joy   aye   de - part   -   ed,

The two conspirators enter. Renato declares that he is with them in
their plot. At first they are amazed at this 'conversion', but they
know him to be a man of honour and they gladly accept him. Whose
hand shall strike the blow? They place their names in a vase, and when
Adelia comes in to announce Edgar, the page, Renato sardonically
decides that *she* shall choose her lover's murderer. The lot falls on
Renato. Edgar enters with invitations to the masked ball. Yes, says
Renato, they will attend; and the three men exchange glances of
terrible significance. The scene ends with one of Verdi's characteristic-
ally brilliant *ensembles*—a quintet, in which the psychology of each
character is expressed with masterly skill.

ACT III: *Scene 2*

Riccardo is alone. He has resolved to stifle his love for Adelia
and is signing an order for her husband to return to England; but
the bitterness of his sacrifice overcomes him and he gives way to
his anguish in an *aria* which, though it has the true note of desolation,
does not wound us so deeply as Renato's outburst of grief in the
previous scene. It may be that Verdi did not quite rise to the occasion
or it may be that he wished to show us that Riccardo had less depth
of feeling than Renato. Either theory is possible.

Edgar hands him a note from an unknown woman warning him
that an attempt is to be made on his life. He is troubled; but it shall
never be said that he was a coward. He will go.

ACT III: *Scene 3*

At the ball the masked figures pass and repass to sprightly music
while the conspirators, like dark spirits of evil, move among them

seeking their man. Renato asks Edgar what the Earl is wearing, but the page, in a nimble, mischievous *canzone*, refuses to tell him :

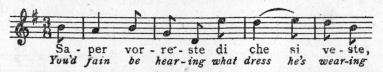

Sa - per vor - re´- ste di che si ve - ste,
You'd fain be hear-ing what dress he's wear-ing

However, in all innocence he gives him a broad hint, and when Renato catches sight of his victim talking to Adelia during a mazurka, his jealous fury shoots up again like a flame. As the dance falters to a close the lovers whisper farewell to each other. "Take *my* farewell, too!" shouts Renato, and stabs him. He is immediately seized and his mask is torn off. But Riccardo raises himself and bids them release him. With his dying breath he swears to Renato that his wife is guiltless and shows him the passport to England.

So ends *A Masked Ball*. Renato, like Shaw's dilemma-ridden doctor, has committed 'a purely disinterested murder'. Yet that is only one instance of the psychological truth of the drama : its characters are not puppets, not heroes or villains, 'blacks or whites'; they are men and women. And Verdi in his music has nobly fulfilled the obligations thus set him.

The Force of Destiny

Libretto by Piave after Rivas.
Time: Eighteenth Century.

First Production,
St. Petersburg, 1862.
(Revised version produced in Milan, 1869.)

'This weapon
Was instrument to my revenge; the reasons
Are just, and known; quit him of these,. and then
Never lived gentleman of greater merit.'
                    JOHN FORD: *The Broken Heart.*

The Force of·Destiny shows Verdi again reaching forward to the more spacious musical world of his last three operas, and, as in *A Masked Ball*, we hear turns of phrase that unmistakably anticipate the shapely melodies of *Aïda*. Brother Melitone, too, is a kind of embryonic Falstaff. In thirty years he was to come to full stature and girth as the richest comic character in opera.

It is a strange anomaly that most composers of opera—perhaps the hardest of all theatrical forms to make intelligible and convincing—

should deliberately handicap themselves by choosing such involved plots, plots that would be difficult enough to follow even without the additional complication of sung dialogue. Perhaps the most striking exception was Puccini, whose plots are admirably direct and concise. Verdi, however, had a strong predilection not only for what the Elizabethans called 'tragedies of blood', but tragedies in which the catastrophe is wrought by elaborate disguises, prolonged misunderstandings and accidents of mistaken identity which we must thoroughly grasp before we can appreciate the dramatic force of his music. It is slightly unfortunate for us that in *The Force of Destiny* he should have given some of his richest melody to a story so complicated that few producers care to tackle it. On the other hand, he did a similar thing in *Il Trovatore*, and *Il Trovatore* remains one of the most popular operas in the world. Which proves once more that one can no more gauge public taste than decide which way the cat will jump.

In *The Force of Destiny* the cat jumps in a multitude of directions. The original play was *Don Alvaro*, by Don Angel de Saavedra, Duke of Rivas, soldier, statesman and considered in his day one of the greatest of Spanish poets. Piave made a workmanlike job of it, but the drama naturally suffered by condensation, and one has to be continually on the alert to follow what is happening.

Act I

After a rather lengthy Overture, built on themes from the opera, the curtain rises on a room in the castle of the Marquis of Calatrava, an old Spanish nobleman. The Marquis (bass) is saying good night to his daughter Leonora (soprano). She is restless, ill at ease. Why is she concealing her true thoughts? Why does she not confide in him? Shaking his head sadly, he blesses her and retires. From what she says to her maid we now learn that Leonora (like Aïda) is torn between love of her home and love of Don Alvaro, with whom she has planned to elope this very night.

Horses' hoofs are heard in the courtyard, and presently Alvaro (tenor) bursts in. It is the hour! He has come to claim her and make her his own for ever. Leonora is at first timid and remorseful at what she is about to do, but Alvaro's urgent passion sweeps away her scruples. At the climax of their duet, however, the door is flung violently open and the old Marquis strides in with drawn sword, followed by servants carrying lights. He is horrified at what he deems his daughter's dishonour. "Your child is pure, I swear it!" shouts

Alvaro. "I alone am to blame. Kill me!" The Marquis retorts that Alvaro is a half-caste and he will not soil his sword upon him. To show that he is sincere, Alvaro then throws down his pistol at the old man's feet. It explodes, and the Marquis staggers back, mortally wounded. Like Don Giovanni, Alvaro has killed the father of his beloved.

ACT II: *Scene* 1

In a village inn muleteers and peasants are dancing and jesting before the evening meal. Among them is Leonora's brother, Don Carlo (baritone), disguised as a student. When they are about to serve the meal, Leonora, in man's attire, enters timidly, starts in terror at seeing her brother, and immediately steals away again. A gipsy girl, Preziosilla (mezzo-soprano), tells them that war has broken out against the Austrians and sings a patriotic song. A band of pilgrims passes by outside. Later, the villagers ask the disguised Carlo for his story, and without, however, telling them who he is, he sings of the great mission of his life: to avenge his father's murder and his sister's dishonour.

ACT II: *Scene* 2

Leonora has fled from the inn, and just before dawn she finds herself outside a Franciscan monastery. Here she will ask for sanctuary, and she kneels in prayer—

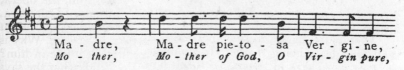

Ma - dre,   Ma - dre pie-to - sa Ver - gi - ne,
Mo - ther, *Mo - ther of God, O   Vir - gin pure,*

—an *aria* that reaches its climax in a noble, far-flung melody, several times repeated:

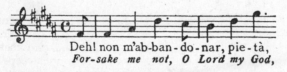

Deh! non m'ab-ban - do - nar, pie - tà,
For-sake me not, O Lord my God,

Brother Melitone (baritone), a gross, paunchy, middle-aged friar, answers her ring at the bell and, grumbling at being roused so early, goes in search of the Father Superior. To the Father Superior (bass)

Leonora tells her secret and the tragedy that has fallen on her family. Her brother seeks her life; surely he, a man of God, will protect her? The Father Superior tells her of a cavern near by where she may live the life of a hermit. He himself will bring her food. And in a scene of great solemnity he calls the brothers together and warns them that no one must enter the hermit's cave.

ACT III: *Scene* 1

The Spanish Army has moved to Italy to fight in the war against Austria and the scene is a wood near Velletri. From the tents comes the noise of soldiers gambling. Don Alvaro enters in the uniform of a Spanish captain. He is lonely and distraught. Leonora! Is she alive or dead?

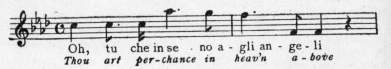

Oh,   tu che in se · no a - gli an - ge - li
Thou   art   per-chance   in   heav'n   a - bove

Suddenly he hears the clash of swords and a cry for help. A young officer is involved in a brawl. Alvaro rescues him. It is Don Carlo but as they have both assumed fictitious names they are, of course unaware that they are avowed enemies, and they swear eternal friendship.

ACT III: *Scene* 2

Destiny has begun to show her force. Alvaro is wounded in battle and fears he is going to die. He summons Carlo and gives into his keeping a package of letters. In them, he says, is hidden the honour of his sweetheart. If he should die, the package must be burned unopened:

So - len - ne in que - st'o-ra   giu - rar - mi do - ve - te
In   this   so - lemn mo-ment   now swear   to   o - bey   me,

Alvaro is carried out, and Carlo, left alone, is strongly tempted to open the package. Alvaro was agitated when Carlo spoke the name of Calatrava. Can it be that his new friend, whom he knows as Don Frederico Herreros, is his father's murderer? He *will* open the package but no—he has sworn to burn it unopened. And yet . . . the seal is open and inside is a portrait. It *is*—Leonora! The truth is now clear to Carlo, and vehemently he renews his oath of vengeance.

ACT III: *Scene 3*

The two men meet again at a camp near Velletri. Alvaro has recovered, and now Carlo tears off the mask and challenges him to a duel. He will kill them both: first Alvaro, then Leonora, whom Alvaro imagined dead. Alvaro makes every effort to avoid crossing swords with the brother of the woman he loves and son of the man he accidentally killed, but Carlo stings him into fury and at last they fight, only to be separated by the patrol, which rushes in at the noise of the duel. Carlo is arrested, and Alvaro, flinging away his sword, vows that he will seek forgetfulness in a monastery.

The camp wakens to a new day. Soldiers, *vivandières*, pedlars, beggars and gipsies mingle in a gay scene, interrupted for a few moments by a glib and unctuous sermon from Brother Melitone. But they will have no truck with the fat old hypocrite. Who is he to talk of an austere life with a paunch like that?

ACT IV: *Scene 1*

In the courtyard of the monastery Melitone is distributing free food to a mob of greedy, yapping beggars. It is a scene of no particular dramatic significance, but interesting musically, since it gives us a foretaste of that racy, humorous, quick-witted style that Verdi finally brought to perfection in *Falstaff*. Presently a visitor is shown in. It is Carlo, and he is searching for his foe, who has entered the monastery and calls himself Brother Raffaele. Alvaro appears in answer to Melitone's summons. He begs Carlo to forswear his oath of vengeance and leave him. He is a monk: he must not shed blood. But again Carlo so lashes him with insults that at last he loses control and they rush away to fight—this time to the death.

ACT IV: *Scene 2*

At the entrance to her hermitage Leonora calls on God to bring peace to her bereaved heart:

Pa - ce,   Pa - ce,   pa - ce, mio Di - o, pa - ce mio Di -   o!
Fa - ther,   Fa - ther,   O heav'n-ly Fa-ther, grant me thy peace at last!

A moment later, however, she hears footsteps and retreats into the cave. From now until the end of the opera the music is overwhelming in its alternate moods of dramatic urgency and heartfelt pity. Don Alvaro stumbles blindly in. The Force of Destiny has been too strong for him: he has wounded Carlo almost to death, and even now the dying man's voice can be heard wailing: "A confessor! A confessor! I'm dying!" Alvaro batters on the door of the hermitage. "Come out for pity's sake! Bring absolution!" The door opens and he is astounded to recognize Leonora. "Don't touch me!" he cries. "I am stained with your brother's blood." Leonora strikes on the bell to summon the Father Superior and rushes to her dying brother. In a moment we hear her shriek, and the Father Superior enters, supporting her. With a last despairing effort Carlo has stabbed her to wipe out what he believes is her dishonour. "Pray," she falters to Alvaro, "God will forgive you"—and she dies with her lover's name on her lips. "She's dead!" cries Alvaro. "She is with God," says the Father Superior. Destiny has ended her sport with these three lives.

Aïda

Libretto by C. du Locle.
Time: Epoch of the Pharaohs.

First production,
Cairo, 1871.
(Commissioned by the
Khedive of Egypt.)

'This lute has out-sung Egypt; all the lives
Of violent passion, and the vast calm art
That lasts in granite only, all lie dead;
This little bird of song alone survives.'

EDMUND GOSSE.

Aïda is Verdi's grandest opera; not his greatest, but certainly his most sumptuous and spectacular. There is something monumental about it—like a pyramid of marble towering into the blue Egyptian sky. It has some of his richest melodies; it has passion, colour and drama—everything but pathos. Perhaps the panorama is rather too vast for pathos; one might liken it to a splendid conflict played out in the clouds, the whole thing just too remote, too colossal, for the softer human sympathies. It was the first of the three great works of Verdi's final period. The two operas that followed were measurably greater, but their germ was in the score of *Aïda*. It has neither the piteousness of *Othello* nor the grace of *Falstaff*, but one can hear in its music foreshadowings of both. And in sheer wealth of melody it fairly overwhelms one: on almost every page some flashing felicity of phrase, some Marlowesque 'mighty line'. Incidentally, it is the only opera in which Verdi uses with real consistency the 'operatic identity-card'—the theme associated throughout with Aïda herself—

... which is the basis of the orchestral prelude.

Act I

Ramphis, the High Priest (bass), meets Radames, Captain of the Guard (tenor) in the King of Egypt's palace, and gives him a very broad hint that he has been chosen to command the Egyptian army against the Ethiopians. Left alone, Radames falls into a dream of renown. He will fight and conquer; and all his glory he will lay at the feet of his beloved Aïda:

Ce - le - ste A - ï - da ____
Heav'n - ly ____ A - ï - da ____

Amneris, the King's daughter (mezzo-soprano), is passionately in love with Radames; but he has eyes only for the Ethiopian Aïda (soprano), who is held as a slave. The three meet in the palace and reveal their hearts to us in a trio; after which the court assembles, and the King (bass) announces that Radames is the new general. The King then leads his subjects in a stirring battle-song:

Su! del Ni - lo al sa - cro li - do
Up! of Ni - lus' sa - cred riv - er

When they have marched away, Aïda gives way to her grief. She is torn between her love of Radames and her duty to her father, Amonasro, King of Ethiopia, against whom Radames is to fight:

L'in - sa - na pa - ro - la o Nu - mi sper-de - te!
Ye Gods watching o'er — me those words deem un - spo - ken!

Radames is consecrated in the Temple—a scene of immense dignity, the chant of the Chief Priestess setting the note of exotic oriental colouring:

ACT II: *Scene 1*

Amneris tricks Aïda into confessing that she loves Radames. In a fit of tigerish jealousy she swears she will crush the presumptuous slave girl. Radames is hers and hers alone.

ACT II: *Scene 2*

Meanwhile, the army has returned in triumph. The people acclaim the victors, who march into the presence of their King:

Among the captives, standing out from the rest by his proud, defiant bearing, is Aïda's father, Amonasro (baritone), King of Ethiopia. He begs the King of Egypt to spare the lives of the other prisoners. The priests, true to type, urge the King to slaughter the lot; but at last Radames himself asks for their freedom and it is granted. Aïda's father, however, (they do not know he is king), must remain as hostage. Amneris is given to Radames in betrothal, and the scene ends with a mighty chorus of praise and thanksgiving.

Act III

This is one of the perfect acts of Italian opera. In concentrated atmosphere Verdi seldom equalled and never surpassed it. It is a moonlit night on the shore of the Nile. Ramphis conducts Amneris into a temple close by on the eve of her nuptials. She must pray to Isis till the dawn. Aïda steals in for her last secret meeting with Radames. The enchantment of the perfumed night enters her heart. She stands 'in tears amid the alien corn' and sings of her bitter-sweet longing for her native land:

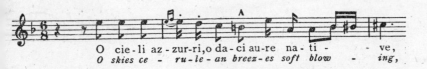

O cie-li az-zur-ri,o da-ci au-re na-ti - - ve,
O skies ce - ru-le-an breez-es soft blow - ing,

Suddenly she sees a dark and menacing shadow among the trees. Her father! He comes to her for help: the Ethiopians are plotting a revolt; but they must know which way the Egyptian army is to march. "Who will discover that?" asks Aïda. "*Thou* shalt!" says her father with terrible significance. "Radames loves thee—get his secret from him!" Aïda recoils in horror from the idea; but her father lashes her with his stinging reproaches until at last, utterly broken in spirit, she consents to all he wishes. And Amonasro slips into the shadow of the trees as he hears Radames approaching. Radames rushes in, and there follows a passionate duet, question and answer alternating in long lines of lovely lustrous melody. To phrases that seem to overflow with honey, Aïda implores him to escape with her to her own country—

Là - tra fo - re - ste ver - gi - ni,
There where the vir - gin for - ests rise,

—and, blinded with love and sickened at the thought of marrying Amneris, Radames impetuously falls in with her plans. From this moment to the end of the act the music sweeps on like a gathering flood, mounting higher and ever higher. At each climax one catches one's breath—"Now he's spent! He can't go one better than that!"

but he does! Not for a single bar right to the last note does the tension slacken. Aïda lures Radames into telling her the army's plans. Amonasro overhears them and reveals himself. There is no time to be lost: they must escape at once. But at that moment Amneris comes out of the temple and denounces them to the High Priest. Radames turns to Ramphis: "Priest of Isis, I yield to thee!" A few swift stabbing strokes in the orchestra and down comes the curtain.

ACT IV : *Scene* 1

Radames is led into the hall of justice to be sentenced by the priests. Amneris, who still loves him, makes a last frantic appeal to him to defend himself—

Gia i sa - cer - do - ti a du - nan-si
Now *to the hall* *the priests proceed*

—but no; he has lost his honour and his love, and life holds nothing more for him. He will not speak a word. And he does not.

ACT IV: *Scene* 2

In the last scene we see the hall of the Temple above, and below a crypt in which Radames is buried alive. A white form glimmers in the darkness. It is Aïda: she has stolen unseen into the crypt to die with her lover. They sing their farewell to the world:

O ter - ra ad-dio, ad - di - o val - le di pian - ti
Fare-well oh *earth, fare - well* *thou* *vale of* *sor - row*

And while the priestesses intone their chant in the Temple overhead, Radames and Aïda seek in death the happiness that life so cruelly denied them.

Othello

Libretto by Arrigo Boïto after Shakespeare.
Time: Fifteenth Century.

First Production,
Milan, 1887.

> 'Jealousy is cruel as the grave: the coals thereof are coals of fire, which hath a most vehement flame.'
>
> OLD TESTAMENT: *Song of Solomon.*

Othello is Verdi's greatest opera and one of the greatest operas in the world. The fastidious may prefer *Falstaff*—none of his other works can challenge comparison—but tragedy is nobler than comedy, and for that reason, if for no other, we must place *Othello* on the higher plane. Its outstanding qualities are a great tragic story, a masterly *libretto* without a single superfluous line or a single lost opportunity, and, above all, music fairly flaming with colour and passion—passion of which the sweep and magnitude make the passion of *Il Trovatore* and *Rigoletto*, splendid as it is, sound in comparison like a child's tantrums. And this from a man of seventy-four!

ACT I

A violent storm is battering the harbour at Cyprus. On the quay, the watchers, drenched in spray and dazzled by the lightning, are scanning the waves, which seem 'to pelt the clouds', and on which Othello's ship is pitching and plunging towards them. They kneel and pray, their voices nearly drowned by the thunder. At last the ship heaves into the harbour. Othello (tenor) springs up the steps on to the quay and tells them that the heavy seas have scattered the Turkish fleet—in a stupendous line of melody that peals trumpet-tongued above the storm:

Iago (baritone), Othello's ancient, and Roderigo (tenor), Desdemona's rejected suitor, are plotting together. "Trust in me," says Iago, "and you shall enjoy her!" By and by, Cassio (tenor), Othello's lieutenant, and other gallants stroll on to the quay and begin drinking outside the tavern. "This Cassio," whispers Iago to Roderigo, "he's your greatest rival. D'you want to ruin him? Good! Mark me: if he drinks he is lost. Let's make him drunk!" And he pledges Cassio in a magnificent drinking-song:

I - naf - fia ___ l'u ___ go - la!
Then let ___ me the can - a - kin clink!

Cassio rapidly gets drunk, and a frantic brawl follows. Othello appears on the scene, and in a storm of wrath dismisses Cassio from his service. When the rest have dispersed, Othello and Desdemona (soprano), gazing towards the sea, which is now calm, sing of their love—a tender and voluptuous duet, in which Boïto, with ingenious economy, introduces part of Othello's address to the Senate:

Già nel - la not - te   den - sa s'e - stin-gue o-gni cla - mor,
Dark is the night and   si - lent, All bla-tant cla-mours cease,

Act II

Iago meets the broken-spirited Cassio in a hall leading on to the castle garden. "Come, don't be downcast," he says. "Why not speak to Desdemona? She'll persuade Othello to forgive you." And as Cassio goes, Iago lets the mask fall. The graceful, caressing little figure in the orchestra suddenly becomes blatant with evil, like a clear stream blackening with some turgid poison. And Iago sings his Credo. The god who created him, he says, was an evil god and created him for evil purposes:

Cre - do in un dio cru - del che m'ha cre - a - to si - mi - le a sè,
Cru - el is he, the god who in his i - mage has fash-ioned me,

When Othello comes in, Iago, with careful carelessness, points out Cassio in the distance, chatting and laughing with Desdemona. A spark is struck, and slowly the flames begin to rise. In the scene that follows Desdemona drops her handkerchief, and Iago swiftly and furtively picks it up. All the while he has been whispering sly hints in Othello's ear, and when his wife has left them Othello breaks out into an anguished farewell to all he holds dear. His peace of mind is shattered for ever; Othello's occupation's gone!

O - ra e per sem-pre ad - dio
And now for ev - er fare - well,

"Villain, be sure thou prove my love a whore!" he shouts, gripping Iago by the throat and hurling him to the ground. He cries out for proof; and at last Iago, with a masterly show of reluctance, tells him that some nights ago he shared Cassio's quarters, and in his sleep Cassio talked of his stolen hours of lust with Desdemona—a sleek, insinuating melody that steals along on tiptoe, so to speak, over soft velvet harmonies:

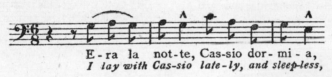

E - ra la not-te, Cas-sio dor - mi - a,
I lay with Cas-sio late-ly, and sleep-less,

Othello explodes like a cannon. "O that the slave had forty thousand lives to lose!" His heart bursts within him: away with love, away with pity! Never shall his thoughts falter, never look back, till a capable and wide revenge swallow them up. He will have blood—blood —blood! And, kneeling down solemnly, they both swear an oath of vengeance, to music that blazes like a bonfire:

Si, pel ciel mar-mo - reo giu - ro!
Wit-ness yon - der mar - ble hea - ven,

Act III

In the great hall of the castle Othello meets his wife, who rushes innocently on her fate by pleading for the disgraced Cassio. The very name is a spark to gunpowder. Othello curses her for a vile godless harlot and flings her away. Left alone, he asks in a strangled voice why God has afflicted him thus, to a starved, forlorn little figure in the orchestra that seems to wilt and droop down to earth in utter dejection. Iago and Cassio appear. Othello conceals himself and watches Cassio showing Desdemona's handkerchief, which Iago had secretly planted in Cassio's lodging. It is the last proof: now she must die. Lodovico (bass) arrives with letters recalling the general to Venice. In the courtyard, before a vast assembly, Othello tries to read them. But he cannot see the words; all he can see is Cassio lying with his wife. And when Desdemona speaks to him he turns on her in a fury and knocks her down. The people exclaim in horror; Desdemona begs his forgiveness in an impassioned appeal, which grows into a sextet with chorus and rises to superb heights of eloquence. Just at its climax Othello blazes out again, and the people scatter in terror and confusion. Othello is now a complete savage. He reels and staggers, clutching at his hair and maddening himself with horrible and obscene visions. Cassio and she! She and Cassio! At last he falls in a convulsion, as the people outside are shouting: "Hail to the Lion of Venice!" At this moment Iago strides forward and points down in devilish triumph to the twitching, writhing body: "Here is your Lion!"

ACT IV

The tragedy sweeps relentlessly to its end. In a dim Gothic chamber Desdemona is divesting herself for bed. She sings 'a song of willow!':

"Pian - gea_____ can - tan - do
"The poor___ soul sat pin - ing

Emilia (mezzo-soprano) speaks words of comfort to her, and when she has gone the frail white figure kneels before the image of the Madonna:

Pre - ga per chia-do - ran-do a te, si pro - stra,
Ah, pray for her who lies in pray'r be - fore thee.

Desdemona gets into bed. There is a pause; and then, over music that speaks with the iron tongue of doom, Othello appears. "Have you pray'd tonight, Desdemona?" . . . In a few moments the dreadful deed is done. And just as the poor victim has ceased to move, Emilia batters at the door. Othello opens it—and lets in the truth. He has been duped, fooled, betrayed! Desdemona was chaste, and Iago an instrument of the devil. The ruin is complete. One thing alone remains —this: and he drives a dagger into his heart, falls to his knees and crawls forward to the music of their early love, stretching his hands helplessly towards the life that those hands have newly stopped.

> *I kiss'd thee ere I kill'd thee: no way but this,*
> *Killing myself, to die upon a kiss.*

Falstaff

Libretto by Arrigo Boïto after Shakespeare.
Time: Fifteenth Century.

First Production,
Milan, 1893.

> 'A blowzed, prodigious man, which talked, and stared,
> And rolled, as if with purpose, a small eye
> Like a sweet Cupid in a cask of wine.
> I could not view his fatness for his soul,
> Which peeped like harmless lightnings and was gone.'
>
> WALTER DE LA MARE.

Falstaff is Verdi's *Mastersingers*. He has 'supped full on horrors'; he has had his bellyful of libertines, changeling children, grief-stricken jesters, midnight assassins and the rest. He has won through, at eighty years of age, to that genial winter sunshine which teaches us that the best way to treat life is to laugh at it. And so, as food for his laughter, he takes the greatest comic character ever created: Falstaff, that tun of man; that round, gloating, glutinous human cheese whose voice comes through a blanket of stale fumes and drips its gorgeous improprieties as fulsomely as a stilton in midsummer. Shakespeare's Falstaff? Not quite, perhaps; this is a gentler buffoon, more nimble in his motions, more graceful in his graceless follies than the 'bolting-hutch of beastliness' we meet in *King Henry IV* and *The Merry Wives*. We cannot always 'view his fatness for his soul'. Perhaps music is bound to purge even Sir John of some of his grossness. Yet, though the characters may be Italianised, the score has (to me) an amazingly English atmosphere for the composer of the most essentially Italian music ever written. "We have heard the chimes at midnight, Master Shallow." Yes—and never did they ring more clearly and mellowly than in the moonlight of Windsor Park in the last act of this opera. "We have lain all night in the windmill in Saint George's field." Yes—and did not the sails murmur to just such tinkling music as that with which Verdi closes the street scene in Act III?

Act I: *Scene* 1

Here he is right away, the Fat Knight (baritone), taking his ease in his inn; baffling the splenetic Dr. Caius (tenor), draining beakers of burnt sherry and lording it over his myrmidons, Pistol (bass) and Bardolph (tenor), to a brisk orchestral figure that bounds and bounces along like the bumping of casks over a cellar floor. Either Pistol or Bardolph (it must have been one of them) has picked Dr. Caius's pocket; and when the excited little man has gone Falstaff gives them the sound musical advice: "Steal gently and—in time" (*a tempo*). But enough of purses; Sir John is out to steal hearts. His followers shall carry two love letters—one to Mistress Ford (Alice), the other to Mistress Page (Meg). But, to his astonishment, the worms turn. They will not help him: 'honour' forbids them. For a moment Falstaff is stupefied. Then he gives the letters to a page, and turns on Pistol and Bardolph with a tremendous outburst—

—into which Boïto ingeniously weaves the greater part of the Honour speech in *King Henry IV*.

Act I: *Scene* 2

The two Merry Wives (soprano and mezzo-soprano) have received the letters and they meet to compare them in Ford's garden, Mistress Ford declaiming the more grandiloquent sentences to a phrase that might have dropped straight out of *Othello*. They plot Falstaff's downfall, in music as light and iridescent as gossamer; and while Pistol and Bardolph are warning Ford (baritone) on the approaching attack on his honour, Nanetta (soprano), Ford's daughter, and Fenton (tenor), her lover, are exchanging kisses:

Lab - bra   di   fo - co!
Lips by   com - mo - tion

Surely the most youthful music ever written by a man of eighty!

ACT II: *Scene* 1

Meanwhile, the old hogshead sits at the Garter Inn, drinking sack and anticipating his conquests. To him comes Dame Quickly (mezzo-soprano). Mistress Ford has read his letter. She is dying of love for him! And—her husband is absent daily:

dal - le due al - le   tre.
from   two un - til· three.

Mistress Page, too, she adds, is breathless with eagerness to meet him; but, sad to say, *her* husband is rarely from home (perhaps that is why he never appears on the stage!). Falstaff rewards Dame Quickly and, left alone, slaps his colossal paunch, telling himself what an abandoned old rip he is. Then occurs one of the most delicious comedy scenes in all opera. Ford calls on Falstaff, disguised as 'Master Brook', and asks his help to win the love of the fair Alice:

Cè a   Wind-sor u - na   da - ma,
In   Wind-sor lives a   la - dy,

"Pooh! She's easy!" says Falstaff. "Why, I've an appointment with her myself—between two and three!" Ford is thunderstruck, and when the knight goes in to change 'into braver garments', he gives way to a storm of jealousy. In a few moments Falstaff, serenely unconscious of his guest's murderous thoughts, swaggers in again, dressed 'to kill' and beaming with fatuous self-satisfaction. They exchange elaborate courtesies and leave the inn together to music that winks as merrily as the bubbles in a glass of wine.

Act II: *Scene 2*

In Ford's house all is ready for the discomfiture of the portly Don Juan. At last, while Mistress Ford sits in a graceful attitude strumming a lute, he enters, singing gaily and as proud as a turkey cock. He begins to pay her the most bejewelled compliments. True, he is advanced in years, and with something a round belly; but ah!—when he was a young page he could have squeezed himself into a thimble:

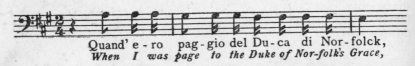

Quand' e - ro pag - gio del Du - ca di Nor - folck,
When I was page to the Duke of Nor-folk's Grace,

But just as he is growing ardent Mistress Page and Dame Quickly burst into the room: Ford is coming, mad with jealousy and with half Windsor at his heels! This was to have been a false alarm, but it turns out to be a true one. There follows a scene of brilliantly organised confusion in which the pace and vitality never falter for a moment, and at the end of which Falstaff is duly pitched into the Thames in the dirty-linen basket.

Act III: *Scene 1*

We begin with a melody in rapid chattering semi-quavers to which we can picture the old man shuddering and spluttering as he shakes the water off himself. And here he sits outside the Garter Inn, restoring his self-esteem with wine. Dame Quickly approaches him. How sorry Alice Ford is, she says, that their last interview was spoiled just when it was getting interesting! At first Falstaff consigns the whole pack of them to perdition, but eventually his vanity again defeats him and he agrees to meet his charmer at Herne's Oak at midnight. He goes into the inn, and as darkness falls Ford and the others discuss their final plans before separating.

Act III: *Scene 2*

Herne's Oak. Midnight. Fenton, wandering in the moonlight, sings of his love—

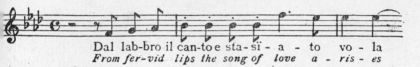

Dal lab-bro il can-to e sta-si-a-to vo-la
From fer-vid lips the song of love a-ris-es

—and is eventually answered by the voice of Nanetta, who joins him dressed as the Queen of the Fairies. The other women come in, carrying cloaks and masks, but disperse as they hear Falstaff approaching. Here he comes, poor deluded old amorist, wearing a pair of antlers; and one feels a touch of pity for his pathetic faith. Alice enters and shamelessly leads him on. But again they are interrupted: a crowd of fairies dances in and Falstaff, in superstitious terror, throws himself down on his face. Nanetta sings her delightful Fairy Song—

Sul fil d'un sof-fio e te-si-o
From se-cret caves and bow-ers

Never did music more magically suggest the rustle of elfin wings in the moonlight. Then these very human fairies pounce on Falstaff, pinching him and scourging him with nettles. He roars for mercy and admits that he has made a fool of himself. Ford, foiled in his design to marry his daughter to Dr. Caius, gives Fenton and Nanetta his blessing; and Falstaff, deciding, like Verdi, that the best way to treat life is to laugh at it, leads the whole company in a brilliant final fugue:

Tut-to nel mondo è bur-la
Jest-ing is man's vo-cà-tion

RICHARD WAGNER

(1813–1883)

IT is manifestly impossible, in this brief handbook, to analyse in detail the complicated musical machinery of Wagner's works. As we know, Wagner built these, particularly the later ones, on an elaborate system of 'motives'—short musical figures identifying characters, objects and emotions, which could be contracted, expanded, inverted or otherwise varied as the dramatic situation required. The four *Ring* dramas, for example, contain nearly a hundred of these figures. It would be impossible to quote them all, but difficult, on the other hand, to decide which to leave out. In the following chapters, therefore, I shall not make a catalogue of motives, but follow my usual method of quoting the first few bars of the more extended lyrical passages as they occur.

In fact, to the beginner in Wagner I would say: just revel in these colossal cloudbursts of tone without worrying about motives. You can easily spoil your enjoyment at first by straining to docket them in your mind, fishing Wotan's spear out of the Rhine or trying to pull Siegfried's sword out of the dragon's tail. No music is more sheerly pictorial than Wagner's, and in time you will recognise the motives as instantaneously as you would recognise a familiar face. If, on the other hand, you *should* wish to make a thorough study of them, you will find plenty of excellent practical guides on the subject.

Nor is it necessary to examine in detail Wagner's theories about music and drama. Wagner was full of theories. He was also, fortunately, full of music; and while few people today are deeply interested in his theories, the whole world is passionately interested in his music. All we need to know is that Wagner's creative life fell roughly into two periods: the earlier period, when he wrote 'grand opera'—with the conventional *arias* and concerted numbers; and the later period when he wrote 'music drama'—in which the shape of the music was governed entirely by the dramatic situation. To use a homely simile, he found that the new wine was too effervescent to stay in the old bottles, so he made new bottles of his own. Hence the vast difference in treatment we notice between, say, *Tannhäuser* and *Tristan* or *The Ring*. Certainly there are detachable 'numbers' in the later operas, particularly *The Mastersingers*. But they are not 'set pieces': they are so woven into the dramatic texture that the action inevitably calls for them.

The Flying Dutchman

Libretto by the Composer.
Time: Eighteenth Century.

First Production,
Dresden, 1843.

> 'Since then, at an uncertain hour
> That agony returns:
> And till my ghastly tale is told,
> This heart within me burns.'

COLERIDGE: *The Rime of the Ancient Mariner.*

The Flying Dutchman is the first opera in which Wagner speaks in his own unmistakable voice. Youthful works like *Die Feen* ('The Fairies') and *Das Liebesverbot* ('The Ban on Love', an adaptation of Shakespeare's *Measure for Measure*) belong to his apprenticeship; while *Rienzi*, although it has some fine galloping tunes and some passages of real beauty—the 'Prayer', for example—is stuffed, for the most part, with the conventional operatic sawdust. The Overture is the only part of it most of us are likely to hear nowadays. In *The Flying Dutchman*, however, we recognise the Wagner we know. To repeat a figure of speech I have already used concerning Puccini, it is not the first opera by Wagner, but the first Wagner opera. It has many defects: the characterisation is often shadowy, and much of the music is formal and rather laborious. It is a long leap, for instance, from *The Flying Dutchman* to the terse epigrammatic style of the *Ring*, by which Wagner could sketch a whole personality—Hagen is an example—in two or three trenchant strokes, somewhat akin to the short, biting phrases of the mature Browning. The score abounds in tamely sequential passages and in melodies that are too conventionally 'rounded off'; and one grows very weary of the rhythmic formula—

—which seems to have obsessed the composer at this time and which recurs again and again in the music of the Dutchman, Senta and Daland. Yet, when all this is said, *The Flying Dutchman* must be recognised as a work of undeniable genius. No one but Richard Wagner could have written its best music. And we perceive for the first time that uncanny sense of atmosphere we get in all his great works. In *Siegfried* it is the world of forests and caverns; in *Parsifal* the naked purity of the spring morning; in the *Dutchman* it is the sea—the wind whistling through the shrouds, the waves crashing on to the beach and rattling back through the shingle. We can positively taste the brine on our lips.

Like most great creative artists, Wagner was an immense egoist, and the Dutchman is, of course, himself: a Wagner at this period frustrated and misunderstood, and yearning, like Vanderdecken, for an all-comprehending love.

The Overture, like that of *Tannhäuser* and *The Mastersingers*, is of the '*pot-pourri*' type, and presents with masterly concentration the scheme of the drama. As I have said, we have not the space to go into Wagner's system of motives, but here it *is* advisable to quote the two themes which form the backbone not only of the Overture but of the whole score. These are the Dutchman's Curse—

—and the theme associated with Senta, the maiden fated to redeem him:

Act I

A violent storm is raging off the Norwegian coast and a ship has just cast anchor in the gathering darkness. Daland (bass), the Norwegian captain, goes ashore and climbs on to a cliff to take his bearings. He finds that he is seven miles from home and will not be able to see his daughter, Senta, that night. After he has gone back into his ship the sea grows more stormy and a ghostly-looking vessel heaves alongside. Her masts are black, her sails blood-red. Silently, like spectres, the sailors cast anchor, and their captain, a dark, saturnine figure, steps ashore. "The term is past," he declaims; "and once more, after seven years, I feel the earth under my feet." Then follows the finest stretch of music Wagner had written up to that time. Over a furious tempest in the orchestra in which we hear the rhythmic crunching of the waves, the stranger (baritone) sings of his wanderings:

Wie oft   in   Mee - res tief- sten Schlünd
Oft   in-to   O - cean's gap- ing maw

He is Vanderdecken, the Flying Dutchman. Once he swore an oath that he would round the Cape, 'though hell should bar the way'. Satan heard his oath and doomed him to sail the seas for ever, without aim, without rest. That is the Curse of the Flying Dutchman. It can be lifted only by the love of a faithful woman; and every seven years the fates allow him to cast anchor and search for her. That is his one hope of salvation. No other is left him; he cannot even die.

Daland now comes out of his ship and approaches the wanderer. He greets him with rough sailorly good nature and is obviously very curious to know who he is and what is in his strange ship. The Dutchman replies that there is the richest treasure imaginable in his strange ship, and at a sign from their captain the Dutch sailors open a chest crammed with jewels. In exchange for these, will Daland let him share his home for a little while? The simple Norwegian stares at the jewels in gaping astonishment and eagerly consents. Then the stranger astonishes him still more by asking if he has a daughter. Daland replies that he has; she is pure and beautiful. "She shall be my wife!" the Dutchman declares. "Do not falter: all my riches shall be yours." Daland consents to this just as eagerly. This is a scene to be endured rather than enjoyed, and, to be really convincing, would need far more exciting music than Wagner has given it. Senta may ultimately redeem the Dutchman; but Wagner hardly redeems the preliminary bargainings. After all, there is something slightly absurd, if not distasteful, in Daland cheerfully selling the daughter he has loved all her life to a sinister stranger he has known only five minutes. However, the bargain is struck, and when the storm has died down the Norwegian pilots the Dutchman along the coast.

Act II

A short orchestral introduction leads us to Daland's house, where Mary (mezzo-soprano), Senta's nurse, and a number of young girls are spinning:

Summ' und brumm' du gu-tes Räd - - - chen
Hum,— my— wheel, the flax now twin - - ing

But Senta (soprano) sings not, neither does she spin. She is gazing in rapt meditation at a portrait of Vanderdecken which hangs on the

opposite wall. And by and by she begins the ballad of the Flying
Dutchman—

Traft ihr das Schiff im Mee - re an,
Saw ye the ship on o - cean main,

—a formal but intensely thrilling song, in which both the Curse and
Senta's own theme are very prominent. At the end she starts up in
wild exaltation and, to a bounding melody which is a kind of dramatic
variation on the Senta theme, declares that *she* will be the one to
redeem him. The other women are terrified at her sudden ecstasy:
surely she is possessed! And they turn to Erik (tenor), her lover, who
has just hurried in: "Help us, Erik; she's lost her senses!" Erik throws
them into further excitement by announcing that Daland's ship is
approaching the coast. Mary bustles about in preparations for his
welcome and the girls troop joyously out of the house, eager to meet
their sailor sweethearts. Erik is not a vital or compelling figure, and it
is a fairly just estimate of much of his music to say that Wagner, having
brought a tenor into his opera, thought he had better give him something to sing. However, he does not trouble us for long: he is appalled
at Senta's resolution and rushes away, leaving the scene free for
the entrance of Daland and the Dutchman. Daland, with more than
a touch of Uncle Pandarus in his manner, brings his daughter and
his strange guest together, fussily anxious that they should please
one another. In a long and rather tedious solo he addresses them
alternately: to Senta he gloats over the Dutchman's wealth, bidding
her behave like a sensible and dutiful daughter; to the Dutchman
he enumerates her charms, rather like a dealer selling a horse at a
fair. Then he decides he had better leave them together, and takes
himself off. And, in truth, we are not sorry to be rid of him. No one
will shake my conviction that Wagner was the greatest operatic composer that ever lived; but it would be injurious idolatry to deny that
in his early works his skill as dramatist and musician is sometimes not
equal to the problems he sets himself.

All this time Senta and the Dutchman, as is so often the way of
Wagner's lovers, have stood stock-still and silent, gazing into each
other's eyes. At last the Dutchman breaks the silence, his *recitative*
expanding presently into a melody in the rhythm that has now become
so familiar:

Wohl hub auch ich voll Sehnsucht meine Blik-ke
Though Sa-tan's power of earth-ly joys be-reft me,

Senta replies in the same rhythm, and the music rises to a love duet whose sweep and passion make us forget the slight monotony of its metre. When Daland returns they join hands and swear to be faithful to each other till death.

Act III

It is a bright summer evening. In the bay outside Daland's house the Norwegian ship and the Dutch ship ride at anchor side by side. Daland's ship is lit up and the sailors are singing a jovial chorus:

Steuer-mann, lass'— die Wacht!
Helms-man, leave— the watch!

The girls come down to the ship with baskets of food and drink, and the sailors hail them merrily. But what of the Dutchman's crew? Will the Dutch sailors not join their party? But on Vanderdecken's ship all is dark, still and silent. They hail it and there is no answer. The girls stare at each other anxiously. What can it mean? Are they all dead? At last, however, a dark-blue flame darts up from the deck of the strange ship, the water round her starts to heave and bubble, and the crew breaks into a grim and mirthless chorus, based on the Curse theme. The ship begins to pitch and roll, and the wind roars through the rigging. For a moment the Norwegians are paralysed with superstitious fear; then they cross themselves and scramble ashore, followed by a peal of devilish laughter from the Dutch crew.

Senta comes forth from the house, followed by Erik. He makes a last appeal to her to break her evil bargain and return to him; and he reminds her that she vowed eternal love to him. But suddenly a menacing figure looms up out of the shadows: it is the Dutchman. He has overheard everything, and in an outburst of terrible despair he cries out that he is lost. "To sea! To sea! Thou hast broken faith with me. Nothing can save me from my doom!" Senta tries to hold him back, but he repels her with a violent gesture: "Thou knowest me

not. I am the Flying Dutchman!" The ship plunges away to sea.
But Senta leaps on to a pinnacle of rock and calls after him: "Praise
now thy redeeming angel. Behold me! I am true till death!" She casts
herself into the sea; and as her body strikes the water the ship sinks.
In the blood-red glow of the dawn we see the clasped forms of Senta
and the Dutchman rising from the wreck and soaring upward.

Tannhäuser

Libretto by the Composer.   First Production,
Time: Thirteenth Century.   Dresden, 1845.

> 'Lo, from the Hill of Venus do I come,
> That now henceforth I know shall be my home!'
> WILLIAM MORRIS: *The Hill of Venus.*

Tannhäuser, in the breadth of its outlook, the intensity of its passion
and the power and sweep of its melody, is a great advance on *The
Flying Dutchman*. Its characters, too, are more strongly defined. Vanderdecken, after all, is little more than 'a lost soul' (to use a common figure
of speech in its true sense), a kind of sombre, shadowy spectre; and
Senta not much more than the incarnation of redeeming maidenhood;
while Daland and Erik hardly take on flesh at all. But with *Tannhäuser*
we are in a rough and exciting world of solid men and women. I feel
that I have known Tannhäuser all my life: the full-blooded man whose
generous animal spirits are constantly wrenching him away from an
austerity of life for which he is constitutionally unfitted—with resultant
bouts of remorse which would be ridiculous if they were not pitiful.
Elisabeth is no mere statue of purity, but an impulsive warm-hearted
woman whose attitude towards Tannhäuser is far more sane and
Christian than that of the stupid knights. Wolfram is rather less
attractive: there is a slightly old-maidish quality about him, and one
can imagine him settling down later in life as an earnest scoutmaster
or a kind of professional bachelor uncle; yet he is a very recognisable
human being. Even the Landgrave has more personality than the
conventional heavy bass of grand opera.

Again there is that striking sense of atmosphere. Just as *The
Dutchman* stands us on a rock surrounded by the seething seas, so
Tannhäuser takes us back in time to mediaeval Thuringia, a country
of shining rivers, hills and meadows, dark forests and the grey turrets
of Gothic castles; indeed, the score itself is like a Gothic castle in its
rugged strength and four-square solidity. Here, too, we have in the

title-part another projection of Wagner himself. At this time he was in one of his periodic revulsions from earthly pleasures; so *Tannhäuser* must symbolize the eternal war between the flesh and the spirit. And yet the case is only negatively put. Ironically enough, Wagner falls into the same devil's advocacy as Milton in *Paradise Lost*, and here, at least, the flesh interests us more than the spirit. It is in the Venusburg music and in Tannhäuser's passion and repentance that we feel the real fire of genius. There is a touch of Meyerbeerian commonplace in the ceremonial passages; also Wolfram's famous 'Evening Star' song has a certain warm dampness about it that I for one find oppressive; and Elisabeth's Prayer strikes me as sensual, almost clammy, in its religiosity. Wolfram's song in praise of love is noble in a rather wooden way, but it is a *dutiful* nobility. One feels that Wagner was *writing* this music; it was not writing itself.

There is immense advantage in using what is known as the 'Paris Version' of *Tannhäuser*. Here the middle part of the Overture leads straight into the first scene, which then begins with the 'Bacchanale', enriched during the *Tristan* period. The Overture in its earlier form, a magnificent tapestry of tone-painting, ending with the grandiose repetition of the 'Pilgrim's Chorus', gives such a complete synopsis of the drama that one feels, after hearing it, that it is almost unnecessary to stay for the opera!

Act I

Deep in the Hörselberg dwells Venus, goddess of love, delighting in her power to lure noble knights into her dark abode, where they sink under her enchantments and forget the world of men. Her latest victim is Tannhäuser, who now lies dreaming in her arms. Naiads bathe in the lake, sirens sing softly from its banks, nymphs and fauns and bacchantes whirl round the grotto, straining and tearing at each other in frenzied and lascivious gambols. Never, we feel, was there music of such searing, maddening voluptuousness. Through rosy mists we see Europa, and Leda with her Swan. Gradually the tumult dies down, the dancers 'wearied with their amorous play'. As though roused by the silence, Tannhäuser (tenor) starts up. He has been dreaming, he says, of the earth—the bells ringing, the bountiful sunshine, the song of birds. The world outside—is it lost to him for ever? Venus draws him back. What is the world, she asks, compared with the wonders and raptures of their love? Is not the world well lost? Fired by her burning words, he springs to his feet, and striking his harp, sings her praises:

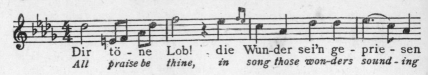

Dir tö - ne Lob! die Wun-der sei'n ge - prie - sen
All praise be thine, in song those won-ders sound-ing

But the song gradually droops and falters as his mood changes, and at the end he breaks out into an impassioned appeal: "O Queen of Love, Goddess, set me free!" Twice more he begins the buoyant, springing melody, and twice more it ends in the desperate cry: "O Goddess, set me free!" Venus realises now that her beauty has lost its power; she can hold him no longer. And with the fury of a scorned woman she curses him: "Go then, traitor to love, go! But no peace shalt thou ever find!" "Yea, I shall find peace," says Tannhäuser, "but not in thee: my hope is in the Blessed Virgin!" Venus gives a wild cry and vanishes. The scene is blotted out and Tannhäuser stands in a beautiful valley bathed in the morning sunlight. Sheep-bells tinkle in the distance, a shepherd plays on his pipe and soon a procession of chanting pilgrims winds slowly across the valley and up the hillside. Tannhäuser sinks on his knees in prayer before a wayside shrine to the Virgin. And in this attitude the Landgrave (bass), Wolfram (baritone) and the other knights find their friend of bygone days as they return from hunting. They recognise him and greet him joyously: "Heinrich, is it really thou—after so long?" Wolfram tells him that Elisabeth, the Landgrave's niece, still loves him and only lives for his return—to a noble, broadly flowing melody:

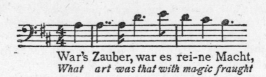

War's Zauber, war es rei-ne Macht,
What art was that with magic fraught

Tannhäuser sees salvation in Elisabeth's love and gladly returns with them.

ACT II

Elisabeth (soprano) comes into the Hall of Song in the castle. She greets the 'beloved place' in an *aria* whose flashing phrases foretell the boundless energy and freedom Wagner was to achieve later:

Dich, teu - re Hal - le, grüss' ich wie - der,
Hail well loved hall,___ so long for-sak - en!

Wolfram leads in Tannhäuser, humble, penitent. He has been wander-ing in distant lands, he falters, but a miracle has led him back to her. Elisabeth impulsively thanks God for the miracle, and they sing of the new life that is dawning for them. Wolfram remains in the back-ground, and from a few words he lets fall we know that he himself loves Elisabeth, but now that she has found her true happiness he will never speak of his love. They now make ready for the Tournament of Song, and knights and ladies enter the hall to a majestic march. The Landgrave announces that Love is to be the theme of their song, and the victor shall be crowned by Elisabeth. The lot falls to Wolfram to open the tournament, and amid an eager silence he grasps his harp and rises:

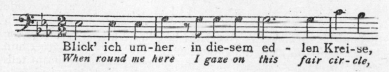

Blick' ich um-her in die-sem ed - len Krei-se,
When round me here I gaze on this fair cir-cle,

Wolfram sings of a selfless love, a love that will sacrifice all for the well-being of the beloved, thinking nothing of its own. And we know that he is singing of his love for Elisabeth, which he is content to cherish in his heart without hope of reward. All this while Tannhäuser has been sitting with a far-away look in his eyes and a secret smile on his lips; and when the court applauds Wolfram with dignified praise he springs impatiently to his feet: "Nay, Wolfram, the love thou singest is a sterile love!" And he breaks into a glorification of physical passion, the music mounting with a fire and vigour that leave Wolfram's sedate measures far below it. There are cries of astonishment from the others, and Biterolf (bass) angrily rebukes him: why, this is blasphemy! And he, for one, is ready to chastise the blasphemer with his sword. But Tannhäuser is now thoroughly roused. What do they know of love, these poor bloodless creatures? O that he could show them what fools they are! And when Wolfram, too, reproves him, he loses all control, forgetting the Hall of Song, forgetting Elisabeth, remembering only the flaming lusts that burnt into his soul for ever in the Hörselberg. And in devilish rapture he bursts forth into his.

song to the Goddess of Love. "There only may ye taste of love—there, in the HILL OF VENUS!"

The assembly scatters in the wildest disorder: the ladies press to the doors and the knights rush forward upon Tannhäuser with drawn swords. The Devil is in their midst! He has polluted their Hall of Song, he has dishonoured the pure name of woman! But Elisabeth remains; and when they are about to slay him she shields him with her body. "Spare him for my sake," she cries. "Would ye rob him of his salvation? I, who loved him, have suffered more than any of you. But it is not for us to judge him; it is for such as he that our Redeemer died." The knights are abashed at her words, and the Landgrave commands Tannhäuser to travel to Rome with the pilgrims and ask absolution of the Pope. At the end of the *finale*, which Wagner builds into a mighty structure of tone, the voices of the pilgrims are heard in the valley beyond. Tannhäuser rouses himself by a mighty effort, kisses the hem of Elisabeth's garment and stumbles out of the hall, shouting, "To Rome!"

ACT III

Before the curtain rises there is a long introduction in which the orchestra warns us that the drama which began in sin is to end in tragedy. We hear the anguished theme of Elisabeth's intercession, but it is answered almost at once by a figure dark with foreboding. This drifts into the gloomier phrases of the Pilgrims' Chorus, and there follows a fanfare of chords rather like the Grail *motif* in *Parsifal*, but stern and relentless in comparison. It is the wrath, not the mercy, of God. We are back in the valley. Daylight is fading. Elisabeth kneels in prayer before the Virgin's statue, and Wolfram, coming down from the wooded height, stops and gazes sadly at her. Then, faintly in the distance, we hear the song of the pilgrims returning from Rome:

Be-glückt darf nun   dich, o Hei-mat, ich schauen,
Oh   joy,   a - gain   now   my home I   may   greet:

It rises to ecstatic heights as the procession crosses the valley and slowly disappears. In an agony of suspense Elisabeth and Wolfram peer eagerly into the pilgrims' faces. In vain: the one they seek is not among them. And as the last man fades into the twilight and the song dies away Elisabeth lifts her voice in fervent prayer:

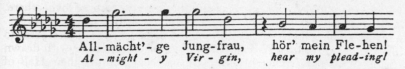

All-mächt'-ge Jung-frau, hör' mein Fle-hen!
Al - might - y Vir - gin, hear my plead-ing!

She moves away, signing to Wolfram not to approach her. The scene gradually grows darker, and he seats himself at the foot of the hill and sings his song to the evening star:

O du mein hol— der A - bend-stern,
Oh star of eve,— thou wel - come friend,

As the last notes of his harp die on the air a figure appears in the deepening darkness: dirty, dishevelled, in rags, with white and haggard face, leaning heavily on his pilgrim's staff. And we know that Tannhäuser's pilgrimage has been in vain. Wolfram challenges him, and he answers in tones of bitter mockery: yes, he has been to Rome! But when Wolfram comes near him he bursts out: "Go back from me! All places where I am are accursed!" And then, in broken accents, he tells the story of his pilgrimage, over the dark, disillusioned figure we heard in the orchestral introduction:

All the way, he tells Wolfram, he scourged himself unceasingly, hoping to shrive his soul by the pain of his body. In Rome, in the blessed morning sunlight, thousands knelt before the Pope and arose, absolved and comforted. And now it was his turn; burning with shame, he confessed the evil lusts that had held him in their power. And the Pope said: "If thou hast dwelt in the Hill of Venus, thou art damned to all eternity! Sooner shall this staff blossom in my hand than thou shalt find salvation!" Blasted by this merciless judgment, Tannhäuser fell senseless. When he recovered consciousness it was night. Songs of joy rose on the air and he cursed them. Was this the mercy of God? Was this Christian love and forgiveness? Then post-haste to hell! To Venus once again! *She* will not reject him. If he is to suffer the tortures of the damned, then he will taste the joys of the damned as well! And now, to Wolfram's horror, he lifts his voice in ecstasy and calls on her to guide him once more to her side. Venus appears in a vision, luring him. "Madman! Blasphemer!" cries Wolfram, wrestling furiously with him. "Remember the angel who prayed for thee! Remember Elisabeth!" At the name Tannhäuser stands as if transfixed. The vision of Venus fades, and a funeral procession comes into sight bearing Elisabeth's body. "Holy saint Elisabeth: pray thou for me!" says Tannhäuser, and sinks beside her in death. The younger pilgrims raise their voices in a solemn chant. A miracle has been wrought, they sing: the Pope's staff has blossomed!

Lohengrin

Libretto by the Composer.   First Production,
Time: Tenth Century.   Weimar, 1850.

> 'For only I saw what I shall see when dead,
> A kingly flower of knights, a sunflower,
> That shone against the sunlight like the sun,
> And like a fire, O heart, consuming thee,
> The fire of love that lights the pyre of death.'
>
> SWINBURNE: *The Complaint of Lisa.*

Lohengrin is the crowning achievement of Wagner's early period, and is nearly as great an advance on *Tannhäuser* as *Tannhäuser* is on *The Dutchman*. It is also the end of an epoch: after *Lohengrin*, Wagner realised that he must no longer write 'grand opera'. He had exhausted its possibilities. His genius could not stand still: it must go forward, and his ideas were expanding beyond the scope of 'grand opera'. To repeat our 'homely simile', the wine was becoming too effervescent for the old bottles. He must make new ones. Useless to go on tamely multiplying *Tannhäusers* and *Lohengrins*; better to wait until he had decided on the form his new ideas should take. So, after *Lohengrin*, he waited six or seven years maturing his plans and working on *The Ring*. The new form was to be 'music drama'.

Lohengrin, then, is the finest expression of Wagner's genius in the old convention; and, in its continuity, its unity of style and atmosphere, it anticipates the new. The old 'props' are still there—*arias*, duets, concerted numbers—but they are bound together more strongly than before by this unity of style and atmosphere, by the heart and life-blood of the mystic legend they commemorate. It is the foreshadowing of that unity which impresses us with such irresistible power in *Tristan* and *Parsifal*. Even the slight monotony which I, for one, am always conscious of in a performance of *Lohengrin* is surely due to this consistent and deliberate 'oneness' of mood.

And the prevailing colour in *Lohengrin* is white—a vast, blinding radiance that seems to descend from another world. This is concentrated in the comparatively short orchestral Prelude which, if Wagner had written nothing else, would have proclaimed him a man of genius. It begins high up in the muted violins, 'pinnacled dim in the intense inane', like a faint beam of sunlight which gradually broadens and brightens until we seem to be bathed in an ineffable purity. But let Wagner describe it for us:

"Out of the clear blue ether of the sky there seems to condense a wonderful, yet at first hardly perceptible, vision; and out of this there gradually emerges, ever more and more clearly, an angel-host bearing in its midst the sacred Grail. As it approaches earth, it pours out exquisite odours, like streams of gold, ravishing the senses of the beholder. The glory of the vision grows and grows until it seems as if the rapture must be shattered and dispersed by the very vehemence of its own expansion. The vision draws nearer, and the climax is reached when at last the Grail is revealed in all its glorious reality, radiating fiery beams and shaking the soul with emotion. The beholder sinks on his knees in adoring self-annihilation. The Grail pours out its light on him like a benediction, and consecrates him to its service; then the flames gradually die away, and the angel-host soars up again to the ethereal heights in tender joy, having made pure once more the hearts of men by the sacred blessing of the Grail."

Act I

King Henry the Fowler (bass) greets his vassals of Brabant under the Oak of Justice in a meadow near Antwerp. There is disunion among them, and he summons Frederick of Telramund to his presence. "I know thee for a virtuous knight: tell how this turmoil arose." Frederick (baritone) then tells the tragic story of Elsa's disgrace. When near his death, the Duke of Brabant appointed Frederick guardian of his two children, Elsa and her brother, Gottfried. One day Elsa wandered with her brother into the forest, and returned alone. Frederick, suspecting she had murdered him, forfeited the right to her hand, which her father gave him, and married Ortrud, a daughter of the Prince of Friesland. Frederick now roundly accuses Elsa of fratricide, and claims for himself the Dukedom of Brabant. The King is startled and distressed at his words; Elsa shall appear and answer the charge. And at the Herald's summons, Elsa (soprano) enters, bowed with grief and humiliation, and moving as in a trance. The King gently asks her what she has to say, and, gazing steadily in front of her, she begins:

Ein-sam in trü-ben Ta-gen hab' ich zu Gott ge-fleht,
Lone-ly in days of sad-ness, bowed by my load of care,

One day, after she had prayed to heaven for succour, she saw in a vision a knight in shining armour, who spoke comfortable words to her. He was sent from God, and she knows that in the hour of need he will come to her again and be her champion. The King thereupon decrees a trial by the judgment of God, and Frederick draws his sword and declares that he will vindicate his honour in combat.

Twice the Herald (baritone) sends forth the challenge: "Who will do battle here in Heaven's name for Elsa of Brabant, let him appear!" Elsa falls on her knees, praying for her deliverer. Suddenly there is a rustle of excitement in the crowd, and those nearest the river begin to exclaim in wonder: "'Tis a boat—drawn by a swan! And in it stands a knight. How bright shines his armour! The eye is dazzled!" A miracle! Elsa's prayer has been answered. The Knight (tenor) makes his obeisance to the King and declares that he is sent hither to defend a maiden's good name. Elsa kneels to him in rapture. "If I conquer in this fight," he asks her, "will thou be my wife?" She answers that she is his, heart and soul. But he makes one condition: she must never ask his name or whence he has come. And to this also Elsa, who is as one in an ecstasy, consents. The King then prays to God that right may prevail in this combat—

Mein Herr und Gott, nun ruf' ich dich,
O Lord our God, on thee I call;

—a measure of great dignity, which swells into a majestic *ensemble*. The two champions fight and Frederick is struck down. The stranger spares his life: "God has decreed to me thy life; I grant it thee. Make thy peace with Him!" The people, led by Elsa, acclaim the victor in a great chorus:

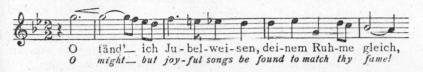

O fänd'— ich Ju-bel-wei-sen, dei-nem Ruh-me gleich,
O might— but joy-ful songs be found to match thy fame!

Act II

It is night. On the steps of the church opposite the Palace of the Knights sit Frederick and his wife, Ortrud (soprano), disgraced and in rags. Over dark and sombre orchestral harmonies, principally in F sharp minor, Frederick savagely reviles his wife: was it not on her sworn testimony that he believed Elsa guilty and fought for that belief? And now God has spoken and proved her a liar. "God?" asks Ortrud with terrible scorn. "Ha! Ha! Give me *thy* strength and I will show thee how much God hath to do with it!" Then she reveals a plan of vengeance: she will wreck this marriage by persuading Elsa to break her promise and ask the Knight his name. Frederick, on his part, shall accuse the stranger of sorcery, and if that fails, murder him. When Elsa appears, Ortrud speaks to her, humble, pitiful and suppliant. Elsa is moved by her wretched plight, and Ortrud takes advantage of her sympathy to warn her against the mysterious stranger. Is she wise to trust all her future to him? Surely it was by magic he came to her; may not magic take him away again? Elsa's troubled face shows that the poison has begun to work. When day breaks, Elsa's bridal procession begins to move towards the church. The two conspirators make desperate attempts to wreck the proceedings: Ortrud claims the right to enter the church before Elsa, but the bridegroom quells her with some contemptuous words. Frederick thereupon accuses his rival of sorcery, but public opinion is against him, and he is finally driven away. Before he goes, however, he contrives to whisper to Elsa that if he can wound but a finger of her bridegroom the Knight will reveal his identity and henceforward be true to her for ever.

Act III: *Scene* 1

This opens with the jubilant epithalamium so familiar to concert-goers:

Then follows the equally famous bridal chorus—

—which has been the prey of innumerable parodists, not entirely without reason. At last the lovers are left alone, and there begins a long duet—in its lyrical freedom and variety one of Wagner's finest achievements up to that time:

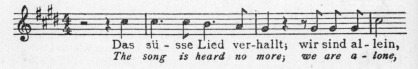

Das sü - sse Lied ver-hallt; wir sind al - lein,
The song is heard no more; we are a - lone,

But Elsa is troubled: she cannot forget the sinister warnings of Ortrud and Frederick; and eventually her reserves collapse. She breaks her promise and pleads with the Knight to tell her who he is. Considered in cold blood, it seems a fairly reasonable question for a young girl to ask a man to whom she is going to entrust the rest of her life. Yet perhaps, to pervert Horatio's expression, 'twere to consider too coldly, to consider so. They are not reasonable young girls, these Elsas, Sentas, Elisabeths. Like most of Wagner's characters, they are recognisable human beings; but they are also creatures in the grip of a great destiny, and, as with most of Wagner's characters again, there is something about them larger than life and higher than reason. And it is their music that so enlarges and exalts them: so compulsory is the hypnotic power of this music that it is only when we emerge from its spell that we are conscious of the absurdity of such situations.

When Elsa has asked the fatal question we know that their happiness is doomed. All is over between them. At that moment Frederick and four other knights break in with drawn swords. Ortrud has told him that if the Knight is wounded he will lose his supernatural power. Elsa sees them and acts swiftly: she hands her husband his sword, and drawing it from its sheath, he strikes Frederick dead. Then he gives Elsa into the care of her women and turns sadly away.

ACT III: *Scene 2*

We are again in the meadow by the River Scheldt, as in Act I. The King and his nobles are preparing to wage war on Hungary. They await Elsa's champion, who has been made Guardian of Brabant. But when he appears he tells them that he cannot lead them in the campaign. He points to Frederick's body, which has been borne on: "This man sought my life. Was I right to slay him?" They pronounce in his favour. He then turns to Elsa, who stands mute with grief before him. "This wife, whom God hath given me—she hath proved false!" And he recalls to them her pledge, which she has now broken. He will reveal the truth to them:

In fernem Land, un-nah-bar eu - ren Schritten,
A   dis-tant land, where none may come un-bid-den,

He comes from Montsalvat, where the Holy Grail is preserved, and whose Knights are pledged to protect the innocent and redress their wrongs. He is the son of Parsifal, and his name—Lohengrin. And now he must depart from them for ever. The Grail calls him and he must go. While the others are pleading with him to remain, the swan appears on the river, drawing the empty boat. Elsa is distracted with grief. Lohengrin bids her farewell in the deepest sorrow; if only she had waited a year, he says, he could have restored her brother to her. He hands her his sword, horn and ring, and bids her, when her brother returns, give them to him in token.

Just before the curtain falls, Wagner indulges in one of those 'transformation' scenes for which he cherished throughout his career what we might call an adolescent enthusiasm. Ortrud breaks through the crowd and declares that the swan is really Elsa's brother, whom Ortrud has changed into that shape. Lohengrin bows himself in prayer, and by and by the white dove of the Grail flies down and hovers over the boat. The swan sinks, and in its place appears Elsa's brother, Gottfried, to be hailed by all as ruler of Brabant.

Elsa sinks lifeless into her brother's arms as Lohengrin steps sadly into the boat and moves away down the river. The majestic music saves the situation, perhaps, yet one cannot help wishing that the mystery had been solved in a way that left more to the audience's imagination. One marvels that that gigantic intellect should continually stoop to devices that come so dangerously near the absurd—until one remembers that the folly of great men is usually in direct proportion to their greatness.

The Ring of the Nibelung

I—The Rhinegold

Libretto by the Composer.
Time: Legendary.

First complete Production,
Bayreuth, 1876.

> 'Anon out of the earth a fabric huge
> Rose like an exhalation, with the sound
> Of dulcet symphonies and voices sweet—
> Built like a temple, where pilasters round
> Were set, and Doric pillars overlaid
> With golden architrave.'
>
> MILTON: *Paradise Lost.*

The Ring of the Nibelung is one of the monuments of the human spirit, one of those great acts of faith by which man has triumphed over time and mortality. It is not perfect; it is too vast to be perfect. But its very vastness, its colossal audacity, its subjugation of 'things unattempted yet in prose or rhyme' make Wagner's achievement akin to the achievement of Prometheus.

Masses of commentary have been written about this work. It has been symbolised almost beyond recognition; it has been twisted to suit every man's theory of the universe. And the sensible thing is to ignore all these symbolisms and ideological theories and saturate ourselves with the drama and the music. There *is* a 'moral' to *The Ring*, and it is such an obvious one that we don't need to read anything *but The Ring* to find it. The moral is that the forces of nature become evil when man uses them for the purposes of his own greed; or, to express it differently, that man is incapable of putting nature's gifts to wise uses. We shall see how the Gold, innocent and beautiful in its natural setting in the bed of the Rhine, becomes an instrument of evil as soon as it is fashioned for corrupt ends, and, like Frankenstein's monster, destroys those who so fashion it, poisoning their lives and loves and bringing them, each in turn, to disaster. If it were written today it would probably be called 'The Atom Bomb'.

That, then, is the moral of *The Ring*; and to point this moral Wagner creates a crowded panorama of life, as rich in human interest as Dante's Divine or Balzac's Human Comedy. Yes—it *is* human interest; for, although Wagner calls some of them gods and goddesses, giants and dwarfs, dragons and water-nymphs, they are all instantly recognisable human types. We can meet them every day—the idealist whose purposes are frustrated by a temporary moral system, the woman who cannot see beyond that moral system, the man who forswears love for power, the honest labourer who is shocked at those whom intellect has made corrupt, the dolt who murders for money and then makes his own life wretched with the responsibility of it. And they live for us in their music, which is Wagner at the absolute height of his creative genius. True, his expression of sheer emotion became intenser in his later works; but for concentrated force of characterisation *The Ring* stands alone in music—almost alone in art. Even Shakespeare seldom surpasses Wagner in putting a man's whole personality into one or two swift and mordant strokes. One other point we should remember: Wagner wrote the poems of this work 'backwards', so to speak. He conceived it first as one drama, *Siegfried's Death*, in which Siegfried's *life* was recalled by various characters during the action. Then he decided that it needed an introductory drama and wrote *The Young Siegfried*, in which, again, previous episodes were narrated. But the subject continued to grow until a third work was necessary, harking still further back and telling of Siegfried's parentage. To this he added *The Rhinegold*—the starting-point of the whole legend—and thus the work became a prologue and three music-dramas. This, of course, explains the redundancies—those occasionally wearisome passages in which some character or other tells us what we have already heard in an earlier opera, but which Wagner had not the heart to cut out. It also partly explains why *The Rhinegold*, there being no previous opera to explain, is the shortest of the four!

The Rhinegold was described by Aubrey Beardsley as 'Wagner's brilliant comedy', and indeed it is the least emotional of the four dramas, partly because there are no normal human beings in it. It is introductory, pre-human, so to speak: gods, giants, dwarfs and Rhine-maidens set the stage ready for the men and women who are to play out their tragic destinies upon it. The orchestra begins with a low E flat which is sustained for no fewer than sixteen bars and seems to ooze from the primeval mud at the bottom of the river. It is the very 'chaos of pre-ordination and night of our fore-being', out of which the first minute germs of life are to rise. And slowly they begin to rise. The music climbs up sluggishly and laboriously, in the common chord of E flat, broadening and thickening bar by bar, until the curtain lifts and we are in the depths of the Rhine, surrounded by shimmering green water. The Rhine-maidens, Woglinde, Wellgunde and Flosshilde (two sopranos and a mezzo-soprano), are swimming round joyously:

Wei - a! Wa-ga! Wo-ge, du Wel-le, wal-le zur Wie-ge!
Wei - a! Wa-ga! Wan-der-ing wa-ters, swing ye our cra-dle!

Alberich (baritone), the Nibelung dwarf, comes blundering down among the rocks. He is a hideous, gorilla-like creature, and when he clumsily tries to make love to the maidens they taunt and mock him. Soon the sun penetrates the waters and lights up the massive mound of gold in the middle of the river. The Rhine-maidens greet it with rapturous cries, and tell Alberich that whoever forges from the gold a Ring shall be master of the world; but only he who renounces love can do this. Alberich springs up in savage glee. They will have none of his love; they have spurned and laughed at him. Very well, he will renounce love for gold. And he wrenches the gold from the rock and vanishes with it in the depths. Darkness blackens the waters, and Alberich's mocking laughter mingles with the wail of the Rhine-maidens as they lament the loss of their treasure. The waves gradually dissolve into clouds, and the scene changes to an open space on a mountain height. A castle with glittering pinnacles stands on a cliff on the farther side of a valley, at the bottom of which the Rhine flows. Wotan (high bass),[1] chief of the gods, and Fricka (mezzo-soprano), his consort, are sleeping on a flowery bank. We perceive that Wotan lacks one eye: this he has forfeited in order to marry Fricka. Later events may incline us to consider this not only a one-eyed but also a one-sided bargain. Wotan soon rouses himself and gazes proudly across at the castle:

Vol - len - det das e - wi - ge Werk!
A - chieved the e - ter '- nal___ work!

[1] I have labelled Wotan in *The Ring* and Sachs in *The Mastersingers* 'high bass' because both parts demand a special type of voice which is something between bass and baritone, having the darkness and gravity of the one and the high *tessitura* of the other.

It is to be called Valhalla, and it has been built for him by the giants, Fasolt and Fafner. As guerdon he has promised them Freia (soprano), the goddess of youth, who now runs in, terrified at the giants' approach. Wotan reflects that without Freia and her golden apples the gods will droop and wither, and he is even now seeking some means of eluding his bargain. Fasolt and Fafner (basses), huge, brawny, stupid creatures, now come shambling in. They have done their job; they demand their wages. But Wotan hedges, and the simple workmen stand amazed at the treachery of those in high places. While they are wrangling, Loge (tenor), the god of fire, comes in. He is the politician among the gods, and the flickering instability of his music constantly suggests his knavish, darting intellect. There is one chance, he tells Wotan: the Nibelung, Alberich, has forsworn love for gold. Would not the giants forswear it, too? Eventually, the giants agree to take the gold instead of Freia, and Wotan and Loge descend into the earth in search of Alberich.

In Nibelheim, in the bowels of the earth, Alberich, now a captain of industry, lashes the slaves who toil at the anvils in his monstrous smithy. They have fashioned the Ring from the gold, and Mime (tenor), Alberich's brother, has made him the Tarnhelm, by which the wearer can change his shape or become invisible. Wotan and Loge appear and persuade Alberich to show off the wonders of this ingenious toy. Alberich, bursting with pride, dons the Tarnhelm and turns into a gigantic serpent. "Wonderful!" says Loge; "but canst thou also change thyself into something small?" Alberich laughs delightedly and collapses into the form of a toad. In an instant Wotan sets his foot on him, and Alberich, restored to his natural shape, is at their mercy. They bind him and drag him back to the mountain top. At Wotan's command the dwarf touches the Ring on his finger and the Nibelungs bring up the gold. Wotan wrests the Ring from Alberich and roughly bids him take himself off. The poor brute, almost in tears with his impotent rage, curses the Ring—

Wie durch Fluch er mir ger-ieth, ver-flucht sei die-ser Ring!
As by curse came it to me, ac-curst be aye this Ring!

—a theme that appears again and again with terrible significance throughout the cycle. Alberich slinks away, and Froh (tenor) and Donner (baritone), the thunder god, join Wotan and the others. The giants insist that they must have enough gold to hide Freia from their sight, and it is now heaped into a monument to screen her. The

Tarnhelm is thrown on to the pile, but there is still a tiny chink through which they can see one of her eyes. The Ring would exactly fill this, but Wotan at first refuses to yield it. At that moment, however, the scene darkens ominously and Erda (mezzo-soprano), the earth-goddess, rises and warns Wotan to give up the Ring and so escape its curse. After a moment of tortured indecision he drops the Ring on the hoard and Freia is released. At once the curse begins to work: the giants quarrel over the spoil, Fafner strikes Fasolt dead with his staff and tears the Ring from his finger. Donner climbs to a high rock and smites it with his hammer. There is a vivid flash of lightning and a loud thunder-clap; the clouds disperse and reveal a rainbow-bridge stretching across to the fortress. Wotan greets it to the same majestic music as in the first scene, and leads the gods into Valhalla. Loge remains behind for a moment. "Fools!" he says with a cynical smile; "they are hastening to their doom!" And from the valley below rise the lamentations of the Rhine-maidens:

The Rhinegold has already brought death and suffering into the world.

The Ring of the Nibelung

II—The Valkyrie

'Ah! gentle pair, ye little think how nigh
Your change approaches, when all these delights
Will vanish, and deliver ye to woe—
More woe, the more your taste is now of joy.'

MILTON: *Paradise Lost.*

ACT I

The Valkyrie opens with a storm. We hear the rain pattering through the leaves of the dark forest, drumming steadily on the roof, rhythmic, monotonous, relentless, in the gaunt key of D minor. We seem to see the tongues of jagged lightning followed by the rattle of thunder. Then the storm begins to fade, and we find ourselves in a hut in the depths of the forest, a hut built strongly round the trunk of a sturdy ash tree.

It is night. Footsteps are approaching. Someone is running, running for his life. We can hear, in the orchestra, his panting breath, the padding of his feet as he crashes through the undergrowth; and next moment a splendid warrior-like figure (tenor), broad-browed, fair-haired and dressed in skins, staggers into the hut and falls exhausted on to a rug. "Whoe'er own this hearth, here must I rest me." A sweet-faced woman with golden hair (soprano) enters from the inner room, and exclaims on seeing a stranger. The man cries out for water and she brings him a cooling draught. There is a long silence, in which they look into each other's eyes, and see there a light they have seen in no other eyes on earth. The music melts into ineffable tenderness. The stranger tells her he was disarmed in battle and forced to flee. He asks her where he is; and she answers that this is Hunding's dwelling and she is Hunding's wife. They look at each other again—and after that they cannot look elsewhere. They are still standing as in a trance when the atmosphere changes harshly and abruptly. The orchestra blares forth a fierce trampling theme and a heavy tread is heard outside. It is Hunding (bass), leading his horse into the stable. In a moment his shadow darkens the doorway: a huge, oxlike man, slow, surly and uncouth. He glances at the stranger and raises his eyebrows. "Faint this man lay on our hearth," falters his wife; "I gave him water to revive him." Hunding glances at them both again, then hangs up his shield and spear. "Set the meal," he growls. As the woman prepares the supper Hunding keeps darting suspicious glances at the warrior from under his shaggy brows. "Strange," he mutters to himself; "he and my wife are very like one another." Over supper the guest tells them he is of the tribe of 'Wolfings'. In bloody feuds long ago he lost his parents and the twin sister he has not seen since childhood. The scene is mainly *recitative*, but how magically different in its limpid flow and unity of colour from the *recitative* of the earlier works! And every now and then comes a little gush of tenderness, like the sudden gleam of a wayside flower, as the wife and the stranger meet one another's eyes. Hunding announces that he is sworn foe to the Wolfings. His guest is safe for the night, but in the morning they must meet in combat. He brusquely orders his wife to bed and follows her after a few moments. The guest, left alone, sits staring at the smouldering logs on the hearth. He is to fight at dawn, and he is without a weapon. Then he remembers:

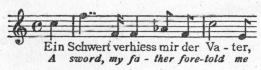

Ein Schwert verhiess mir der Va - ter,
A sword, my fa - ther fore-told me

The sword! Where is it? Suddenly the logs crumble together and a bright flame darts up. It gleams on the ash tree's stem, and there we can dimly see the hilt of a sword. In a few moments Hunding's wife steals in again. She tells him that she has drugged her husband's drink. "Now," she whispers, "a weapon I will show thee." And she relates that, when Hunding wedded her, an old man clad in grey, with one eye hidden, came to the feast and buried a sword in the tree-trunk. None of the heroes gathered there could pull it forth, and there it has remained ever since. Surely it is for him; surely he is the warrior fated to use it—he, the hero sent to deliver her! Impetuously, he clasps her in his arms, while the music races along in passionate ardour. The door at the back of the house swings open and the room is flooded with moonlight. "See! Spring has entered the house!" he cries:

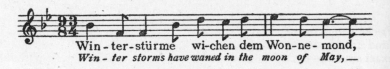

Win - ter-stürme   wi-chen dem Won-ne - mond,
Win - ter storms have waned in the moon of May,—

She responds to him with joyous abandon; and then begins a love scene that is surpassed in sweetness only by the second act of *Tristan and Isolde*:

O süs - ses-te Won-ne!   se - ligstes Weib!
O sweet-est en-chant-ment!   *Wo - man most blest!*

In contrast to Wagner's later lovers, these lovers are very much of this world. They laugh for the joy that has lit up their hearts, they chatter excitedly together like children. Then suddenly the woman pauses, mystified: her lover's face—surely it is the face she has seen as she bent over the stream? And his voice . . . Yes! She has heard it as the echo threw back her own voice in the woods! "Tell me," she cries, "who art thou? Surely thou art Siegmund?" "Yes, I am Siegmund the Wälsung," he answers, "and the sword is mine!" And with a mighty effort he wrenches the sword from the tree. She breaks out in rapture: "Sieglinde am I—thy long-lost sister!" Siegmund laughs boisterously as he waves the sword in the moonlight. "Bride and sister be to thy brother," he shouts. "So flourish the Wälsungs for aye!"

Act II

The orchestra crashes at once into a stormy galloping Prelude, and when the curtain rises we see Wotan and Brünnhilde, leader of the Valkyries (soprano), standing together in a rocky pass. They are preparing for the combat between Siegmund and Hunding. Brünnhilde shall shield the Wälsung, says Wotan. As for Hunding— he cares not what becomes of him. Brünnhilde climbs up the pass, halloing her war-cry:

Ho-jo-to-ho!— Ho-jo-to-ho!—

Fricka comes on the scene, and from her ensuing quarrel with Wotan (and from what Wotan tells Brünnhilde afterwards) we learn the exact situation at this stage of the cycle. By Erda, Wotan has begotten nine daughters—the Valkyries—who carry to Valhalla the bodies of slain heroes to form a guard for the gods. He is also the father, by a mortal woman, of Siegmund and Sieglinde. Now Wotan is anxious to recover the Ring from Fafner, but Erda has warned him that if he himself accomplishes this the gods are doomed. His hope, therefore, lies in Siegmund, who has found the magic sword and whom the gods will protect in the fight with Hunding. But Fricka lacks the imagination to follow Wotan in his daring flights, and cannot see beyond the letter of the law. She is the champion of wedlock, furious at her husband's strategic adulteries and more furious still that he condones the incestuous love of a brother and sister. Siegmund must die, she insists; and she so batters Wotan with her invective that, at last, utterly broken in spirit, he gives way. Miserably, angrily, he tells Brünnhilde of his change of plan: it is Siegmund she must strike down, not Hunding. And he storms away, leaving her lost in amazement.

Siegmund and Sieglinde presently appear in the pass. She is weary with travel, and in a long and tender scene he consoles and encourages her. Brünnhilde appears and bids him prepare for death. When he is slain she will bear him to Valhalla. And will he meet Sieglinde there? When Brünnhilde says he will not, he scorns Valhalla. He is not afraid to part with life, but he will not part with love. Brünn-hilde is so shaken with pity for the forlorn pair that she resolves to disobey Wotan, and, promising Siegmund she will fight for him, gallops swiftly away. Storm-clouds gather, lightning cuts across the scene,

and Hunding's horn sounds above the crash of thunder. Siegmund
rushes away to meet him. Sieglinde, who has fainted, now recovers,
and stumbles towards the fighters, but the lightning flares into her
eyes and she staggers away as if blinded.

On the dark mountain top Siegmund and Hunding meet face to
face. Brünnhilde appears, protecting Siegmund with her shield.
But suddenly there is a red glare of light and Wotan strides forward
holding his spear in front of Siegmund's sword, which shivers into
fragments. At once Hunding plunges his spear into the disarmed man's
breast and Siegmund falls dead. Brünnhilde dashes forward, swings
Sieglinde on to her horse and bears her away. Wotan stands for a
moment, gazing bitterly on the hero whose death has been forced upon
him. "Go, slave," he shouts to Hunding; "tell Fricka that Wotan's
spear hath done her will!" But the sight of the victor, still panting from
the excitement of his triumph, is too much for Wotan. All his baffled
fury blazes out at the great, blundering oaf who has unconsciously
wrecked his plans; and he destroys him with a gesture. Then he
remembers Brünnhilde and her defiance. "Brünnhilde! She shall
not escape my wrath!" And he vanishes into the lightning.

Act III

The Valkyries are riding! Against the scudding clouds they
thunder over the mountain top on their wild horses, the bodies of
slain warriors hanging from their saddles:

Never was sheer brute energy so forcefully conveyed as in this music,
with its vaulting rhythm and its skirling, whinnying trills. By and by
Brünnhilde appears, half-leading, half-carrying Sieglinde. She
implores her sisters to protect them, but they are all terrified of the
wrath of Wotan. Sieglinde breaks in: "Do not dare danger for my
sake. Let me die, as I should have died when Siegmund was slain!"
But Brünnhilde rallies her and gives her the broken pieces of Siegmund's
sword. "Dost thou not know, woman," she says, "that thou bearest
in thy womb the world's most glorious hero? He shall forge his father's
sword anew; and his name shall be *Siegfried*!" And Sieglinde hastens
away, exultant in her great destiny.

Black thunder-clouds begin to roll round the mountain top,

and the sky between glows an angry red. These are the portents of Wotan's wrath, and in a moment his voice is heard calling on Brünnhilde. The other Valkyries crowd round and try to hide her from him as he strides towards them in terrible fury: "Come forth, Brünnhilde. Thou canst not hide thyself from me; thou canst not escape thy punishment!" Bowed with shame and tremulous with fear, the guilty one slowly separates herself from the group. "Pronounce my sentence," she murmurs, her eyes cast down. "I?" retorts Wotan bitterly. "I sentence thee not; thou hast sentenced thyself. Thou, my best-loved one, my second self, the inner light of my spirit—thou of all in this world hast betrayed me!" And in gathering rage he renounces her for ever. She is Valkyrie no more; let her seek out a husband and sit and spin by the hearth at home, derided by all her clan. The Valkyries set up a wail of anguish at his words and scatter in confusion.

Wotan and Brünnhilde are alone on the mountain top, she prostrate at his feet, he leaning on his spear and gazing sorrowfully down at her. And we enter on one of the noblest and most moving scenes in all opera. After a tense silence Brünnhilde finds her voice: surely, she says, her crime was not so shameful? for, although she disobeyed the command of his lips, she interpreted the wish of his heart—that Siegmund should survive. Surely she was right to do so, and surely Wotan was distracted out of himself when he reversed his decision and ordered her to fight for Hunding? Wotan will not deny her words, but he cannot change her fate. She must lie bound in slumber on the mountain height; what man finds and wakens her, he shall win her for wife. "Ah, no!" cries Brünnhilde, "let not a coward win me: surround the mountain top with a girdle of flame, that only he who knows not fear will dare to approach!" Wotan at last grants her desire, and in a long and impassioned *aria* he bids her farewell:

He kisses her eyes and they close in sleep. Then, while the orchestra softly recalls the slow, solemn themes of his farewell, he stretches her on the mound, closes her helmet over her face, and covers her form with the great steel shield of the Valkyrie. He then strikes the earth with his spear: "Loge! Loge! Appear! Come, waving fire, and wind thee in flames round the fell!" The music hisses upward like tongues of flame and we hear the seething, sibilant figures associated with Loge.

The tone swells to a mighty conflagration, and at its climax Wotan raises his spear: "He who fears not the sharpness of my spear, only he shall pass through this fire!" And, when the orchestra answers his challenge by thundering out the theme to which Brünnhilde foretold the birth of Siegfried, we know who is fated to do this. Slowly, and with infinite sorrow in his demeanour, Wotan strides away, while the music draws to a close like a vast fiery sea sinking to an eternal calm.

The Ring of the Nibelung

III—Siegfried

> 'His fair large front and eye sublime declared
> Absolute rule; and hyacinthine locks,
> Round from his parted forelock manly hung
> Clustering, but not beneath his shoulders broad."
> MILTON: *Paradise Lost.*

ACT I

Siegfried begins with a deep sustained murmur in the orchestra that suggests the murk and menace of the great forest. By and by we hear the tapping of Mime's hammer interrupted by the encircling thirds associated with the Ring, and the curtain rises on a rocky cavern in the forest in which is a smith's forge with large bellows. Mime (tenor), the Nibelung, whom we met in *The Rhinegold* toiling for his brother, Alberich, sits at the anvil hammering at a sword. He is a shrivelled, wizened, monkeyish creature, faintly pitiable, but with a gleam of cunning in his little eyes. Soon he stops working, and throws the hammer down petulantly. "Heart-breaking bondage!" he cries. "Toil without end!" And he complains that every sword he forges the 'insolent boy' breaks in mockery. One sword there is—'Nothung'—that he would not be able to break; but Mime has not the strength to weld together the shattered pieces. He thinks of Fafner, the giant, who gained the gold by murdering his brother and has turned himself into a dragon to guard it. If Siegfried could slay the dragon, then Mime would seize on the gold; but only Nothung could prevail against Fafner; and Mime cannot forge it. Siegfried's horn-call is heard—

—and a moment later Siegfried (tenor), the perfect embodiment of youthful strength, grace and beauty, comes bounding in, leading a bear, which he drives at Mime, shouting with laughter at the dwarf's terror. His entrance is like a boisterous breeze, and changes the whole atmosphere of the place. Siegfried is sheer animal energy personified, a grown-up child, a creature of unfettered instincts and impulses, with no emotion besides delight in his own exuberant health. Mime is hideous and deformed: therefore Mime must be taunted and laughed at. Mime is weak and helpless: therefore Mime must be beaten and bullied. He snatches the new sword from the dwarf. "Why, what trash is this?" he roars, and shivers it on the anvil. Mime whines and whimpers. He has done his best; is this gratitude for all his work and care? He has tended Siegfried since he was a baby and this is his reward. Why cannot the boy love him? Siegfried answers, quite simply, that he loathes the sight of him. Then he asks Mime who his mother was. In the forest he has seen the birds and the other wild creatures mating, and they have revealed to him the wonders of love and parenthood. Mime is nonplussed for a moment, but eventually tells Siegfried that he is his father and mother in one. The youth rightly considers this an insult to his intelligence. He loses his temper and flies at Mime, gripping him by the throat. Half-strangled, Mime at last tells him the truth: that his mother was a woman called Sieglinde, whom he found wandering in the forest and who died in giving birth to a boy. She told Mime to name him Siegfried, and left him in the dwarf's care. She also left the broken pieces of his father's sword, Nothung, which Mime now shows him. Siegfried orders him to refashion the sword and takes himself off into the forest. Mime is left alone, half-sobbing at his own helplessness.

Then occurs one of those scenes in *The Ring* which, despite the power and variety of their music, are apt to try our patience a little. As we remember, Wagner wrote the dramas in reverse order, and here he consequently had to acquaint the audience with the events leading up to *Siegfried* and now set forth in *The Rhinegold* and *The Valkyrie*. This he now does by a device which even my idolatry finds rather clumsy. Wotan, disguised in a heavy cloak and a huge hat and calling himself the Wanderer, comes into the cavern, and he and Mime indulge in a kind of reciprocal 'quiz', asking one another questions about the gods, the giants and the Nibelungs, and the sword with which Siegfried

R

shall slay Fafner. Each stakes his head on his replies; but the Wanderer's last question, "Who shall forge the sword anew?" Mime cannot answer. "I will tell thee," says Wotan; "he who knows not fear. Thou hast lost the wager and thou owest me thy head, but I will leave it to the fearless one to sever!" And he strides away, leaving the dwarf fairly gibbering with terror. Siegfried bursts in again. Where is the sword? he asks impatiently. Mime now grows cunning and tries to teach Siegfried the meaning of fear so as to avert the doom the Wanderer foretold for him, but Siegfried simply cannot understand what he is talking about, and again demands the sword. Mime querulously admits that he is not equal to the task. "Off with you, then!" shouts Siegfried. "My father's sword yields but to me; by me shall it be forged!" From now until the end of the act the music leaps and bounds along like the blood in the arteries of youth, springing higher and higher in sheer exultation of power. To a mighty, swinging melody, Siegfried blows the fire with the bellows:

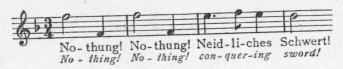

The orchestra grinds and clangs like a multitude of anvils as he strikes the sparks out of the steel. "Ho ho! Ha hei!" he sings. "Now, Nothung, thou blushest red with the fire. Ha! The merry sparks—how they gladden my heart! Laugh now to me!" Meanwhile, Mime crouches in a corner, plotting how he shall drug Siegfried, slay him with his own sword, and then possess the treasure. At last Nothung is finished. "See, Mime, see, thou smith," cries Siegfried, brandishing it round his head; "so sunders Siegfried's sword!" And with a tremendous blow he splits the anvil from top to bottom.

Act II

Before dawn, in the depths of the forest. In a short Prelude the orchestra warns us that the evil forces released by the Ring are again at work. We hear the giants' theme 'dragonised', as it were, and later the notes of Alberich's curse; and when the curtain rises we see the dark form of Alberich himself lurking near a cave. It is Fafner's cave. He has wrested the treasure from his murdered brother, but, having no imagination, all that the great stupid creature can think of is to change himself into an unwieldy dragon and sit guarding that which has become a burden and a misery to him, but which he cannot bear to relinquish. Alberich is joined by the Wanderer, who presently suggests that the Nibelung shall warn Fafner of Siegfred's approach. Perhaps Fafner will give Alberich the Ring as a reward! The dwarf calls into the depths of the cave, but Fafner only answers that he will eat the boy when he arrives, and the Wanderer moves off, sardonically amused at Alberich's failure. The day breaks. Siegfried and his foster-father appear, Mime pointing out the dragon's lair. "Here shalt thou learn fear," he says. Siegfried drives him away, and as he goes Mime mumbles spitefully to himself, "Fafner and Siegfried, Siegfried and Fafner: would that each the other might slay!"

Siegfried stretches himself under a lime tree. "That's no father of mine," he murmurs, gazing after Mime's misshapen figure as it disappears through the trees; "surely Mime's son would be like Mime?" He falls into a deep meditation, trying to imagine the face of his mother. And now follows one of the most enchanting stretches of music Wagner ever wrote. All the life of the forest is here—the beauty of the flowers and foliage, the innocence of birds and beasts, in whom there is no evil because they live by nature alone. Soon, above the murmuring of the woods, we hear fragments of a bird's song:

Siegfried tries to reply to it, first by cutting and blowing through a reed, then with his horn, on which he winds a long blast to the melody we have already heard. There is a rustle in the undergrowth and the sound of ponderous footfalls. But it is not the bird who responds to his call, it is the dragon. He crawls heavily to the front of the cave and after an exchange of violent threats Siegfried plunges his sword into Fafner's heart. With his last breath the monster warns his conqueror that he who urged him to this deed designs his death. And as he dies we hear once again the notes of Alberich's curse; the Ring has claimed yet another victim. Siegfried licks the blood from his hand, and at once he can understand the language of the wood-bird. The bird (soprano) tells him of the Ring and Tarnhelm, and the youth runs eagerly into the cave to get them. When he emerges again Mime steals back and tries to coax him to drink the poison he has prepared. But Siegfried sees through his treachery, and in a sudden fury of loathing he kills him. One more ill-fated one! And we cannot resist a sort of crooked pity for the wretched dwarf—eternal type of the down-trodden, resentful little man, who embarks on crime without the skill or courage to carry it through. But the bird's voice (soprano) is heard again through the branches: he is telling Siegfried of a glorious bride who awaits him. She sleeps on a rocky mountain top girdled by fire, but he who is without fear shall break through the flames and rescue her. "Why, I am he!" shouts Siegfried, in a transport of delight; "lead on and I will follow." And he runs into the wood, the bird's voice guiding him.

ACT III: *Scene* 1

After a wild and tempestuous Prelude we are shown the base of a mountain. It is night, lit up now and then by forks of vivid lightning, while thunder mingles with the orchestra. Wotan enters, and striding towards the mouth of a cave, summons Erda:

The goddess slowly rises from the earth. Why has Wotan broken her sleep? He craves help from her infinite knowledge, but she can no longer aid him. What of the maid she bore to him who was the incarnation of his purest thought? And Wotan tells her how he punished Brünnhilde for her defiance. The gods are doomed, he says, but that troubles him no longer. Siegfried holds the Ring, and he and Brünnhilde will redeem his ruined world. This, again, is in the nature of an 'explanation'; it certainly holds up the dramatic action, and would be tedious if it were not for the powerful and stimulating music, which boils like a witches' cauldron. Soon another day breaks. Siegfried appears on his way to Brünnhilde's rock, and the death-knell of the old order is definitely struck when his sword, Nothung, breaks the spear which Wotan holds out to bar his way. No one can stay him now, and he plunges joyously towards the fire, which surges up in the orchestra into the vast conflagration that closed the final scene of *The Valkyrie*.

ACT III: *Scene* 2

Fire, clouds and mists all gradually disperse, and at last we see Brünnhilde exactly as we left her at the end of *The Valkyrie*—sleeping beneath the fir tree, and covered by her long steel shield.

Siegfried climbs over the rocks and starts on seeing what he takes to be a warrior in armour. He removes the helmet and exclaims at the richness of the loosened hair; and when he lifts off the breastplate the truth is revealed. This, then, is the bride the bird promised him. In his emotion he begins to tremble violently. At last he has learned fear; and it is a sleeping woman who has taught him! How to awaken her? He bends over her and softly kisses her on the mouth. Brünnhilde opens her eyes, half rises, and to music of an elemental majesty, music that seems to be shot through and through with shimmering sunbeams, greets the light of day. She knows her deliverer to be Siegfried, and they gaze rapturously into each other's eyes. It is a moment big with fate. Presently, however, Brünnhilde draws back from Siegfried's ardour. She is immortal, and shrinks from sacrificing her godhead in the arms of a mortal lover:

E - wig— war ich, e - wig bin— ich,
E - ver— lived I, e - ver live— I,

But Siegfried's passion sweeps away her reluctance, and at last, in wild abandonment, she bids farewell to Valhalla and the gods, and joyously embraces her destiny. From now until the final curtain the music flings up fountain after fountain of volcanic energy until we are fairly drenched with the beauty and wonder of it all. Love music it is, but far different from the simple, tender, human love of Siegmund and Sieglinde. Rather let us call it the love of titans, whose voices speak across mountains and whose encounters 'make rock the orbéd world'.

The Ring of the Nibelung

IV—The Twilight of the Gods

'O miserable of happy! Is this the end
Of this new glorious World, and me so late
The glory of that glory? Who now, become
Accursed of blessed, hide me from the face
Of God, whom to behold was then my heighth
Of happiness!'

MILTON: *Paradise Lost.*

The Twilight of the Gods is the twilight of a doomed world. The air is dark with impending tragedy, and its creatures seem to move perpetually in the shadow of death. And this even though much of it takes place in daylight; for it is an angry, menacing daylight, made angrier by the blood-red glare of strife and murder. Never, we feel, did music so balefully suggest the wreck of youthful hopes and ideals, the corruption of faith and love, and 'that sense of ruin which is worse than pain'. We are to see the grace and purity that flashed to such superb heights in *Siegfried* gradually poisoned by jealousy and greed, and heroes and heroines dwindling to sordid hucksters. The powers of nature are nearing the climax of their slow and terrible revenge on those who mishandled them.

And the staggering, knockout-punching, breath-stopping marvel of the whole thing is that Wagner, after piling up the titanic climaxes of *The Valkyrie* and *Siegfried*, should still have reserves of strength to crown the whole cycle with a grandeur that transcends everything that has gone before. Well may one exclaim, as one totters out of the theatre after the trumpeting *finale* of *Siegfried*: "This is the end: what can possibly rise to greater heights than this?" The answer is the *finale* to *The Twilight of the Gods*.

PRELUDE

We are on Brünnhilde's rock once more, shrouded in the darkness before the dawn. The three Norns (soprano, mezzo-soprano and contralto) are weaving the threads of fate. They tell us that the doom of godhead is near and that Wotan and the other gods have cut down the world's ash tree from which Wotan's spear was fashioned, and heaped the faggots around Valhalla. When the end comes they will perish in flames. The Norns then try to peer into the future, but the thread breaks and they vanish into the earth as day slowly dawns. Then for a space we are back in the fresh, sunlit world of *Siegfried*. Siegfried and Brünnhilde emerge from a cave, their love fulfilled, and the light of hope in their eyes. He places the Ring on her finger and she gives him her horse to carry him to fresh adventures. They join in a jubilant duet, in which Siegfried's horn-call and a caressing theme denoting a new aspect of Brünnhilde's love—

—are very prominent. Then the hero gallops away on his journey. Every stage of it is followed by the orchestra in that magnificent stretch of tone-painting often heard in the concert-hall: Brünnhilde anxiously following him with her eyes, the notes of the horn fading into the distance, the surging of the Rhine as he crosses it, and at last the ominous darkening of the whole texture of the music as he approaches the Hall of the Gibichungs, where the evil forces of betrayal and murder lie in wait for him.

ACT I: *Scene* 1

In the Hall of the Gibichungs, Gunther (baritone) and his sister, Gutrune (soprano), are conferring with Hagen (bass), his half-brother. The music tells us that Gunther is an amiable fool as clearly as that Hagen is a detestable knave. Hagen, indeed, is one of Wagner's most striking characterisations. We need only a few bars of his iron-tongued music to know that his nature is as harsh as his name, and that a blonde Hagen would be as unthinkable as a black Siegfried. Gunther and Gutrune are both unmarried, and Hagen suggests that a fitting bride for his half-brother would be Brünnhilde herself, who can be approached only through a ring of fire. Why should not Siegfried, who fears not the fire, win Brünnhilde for Gunther and marry Gutrune? Soon Siegfried's horn is heard, and Hagen, peering out on to the Rhine, watches him ride towards the castle. He enters, and the three conspirators welcome him. Gutrune gives him a goblet of wine and he drinks to Brünnhilde. But the next moment he is a changed man: for in the goblet Hagen has dropped a magic potion which now causes him to forget Brünnhilde and fall in love with Gutrune. Eagerly and blindly he agrees to all their plans. He and Gunther swear blood-brotherhood, and set off together towards Brünnhilde's rock. Hagen is left alone. He slowly seats himself with his back to a pillar and begins a monologue packed so tightly with various themes and motives that it is difficult to digest on a first hearing:

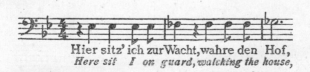

Hier sitz' ich zurWacht, wahre den Hof,
Here sit I on guard, watching the house,

From this we learn that Hagen's father is the Nibelung Alberich, and that he is determined to do what Alberich failed to do: regain the Ring.

ACT I: *Scene* 2

At the entrance to her cave Brünnhilde sits contemplating the
Ring, which Siegfried has given her as a pledge of love. Soon a sound of
thunder is heard, and Waltraute (mezzo-soprano), one of her sister
Valkyries, alights on the rock and comes towards her in great agitation.
She tells Brünnhilde of the approaching doom of the gods. They are
awaiting the end there in Valhalla. One thing only would serve to lift
the curse from gods and men: if the Ring were restored to the
Rhine-maidens. But this Brünnhilde passionately refuses to do. "This
Ring is the love of Siegfried," she exclaims; "never will I remove it,
though Valhalla's splendour fall into ruins!" Waltraute violently
reproaches her sister, but cannot move her. She rides away in despair.
Then follows a scene that never fails to wring one's heart with a kind
of secret shame, when one remembers what has gone before. The
fire shoots up more brightly over the rocky wall, and Brünnhilde,
sensing Siegfried's return, springs forward to meet him with a glad cry.
It is indeed Siegfried; but he is wearing the Tarnhelm, and appears
in Gunther's form. "Betrayed!" shrieks Brünnhilde, and shrinks
back in horror. In a hoarse, unnatural voice he tells her he is Gunther
the Gibichung, and that she must be his bride. She stretches out the
finger on which flashes the Ring: "Thou shalt not force me to shame as
long as I wear this." But against Siegfried the Ring cannot protect
her, and after a furious struggle he tears it from her. He then forces
her into the cave, but pledges himself to lay his sword between them.
It is for Gunther he has won her, not for himself.

ACT II

Once again it is the darkest hour before the dawn. On the shore
of the Rhine, in front of the Gibichungs' Hall, Hagen lies asleep.
The moon suddenly shines out, and in its eerie light we see a dark
figure crouching with its arms on Hagen's knees. "Sleep'st thou,
Hagen, my son?" It is the voice of Alberich. He reproaches his son:
he is letting time slip by. The Ring! The Ring! Let him but secure
the Ring and they two will be lords of the world. Hagen replies in a
distant voice, motionless, as in a trance. "The Ring will I gain me,"
he intones softly. "Rest thou in peace." A shadow begins to cover
Alberich, and he seems to dissolve gradually into the darkness. The
morning light gleams over the river, and Hagen, with a convulsive
shudder, starts into full wakefulness. Siegfried enters, and tells Hagen

and Gutrune of his capture of Brünnhilde. He is now in his own form, and the bride is being brought to the hall by Gunther. Hagen bounds on to a rock, winds a blast on a cowhorn, and calls up the Gibich vassals to welcome Gunther and his bride:

Hoi-ho!— Hoi-ho - ho-ho! Ihr Gib-ich-mannen,
Hoi-hol— *Hoi-ho - ho-ho!* *Ye Gib-ich vas-sals,*

The boat draws up bearing Gunther and Brünnhilde, and the vassals greet them with a boisterous chorus. Gunther, Brünnhilde, Siegfried and Gutrune come face to face, and in the long scene that follows we perceive the subtlest and most demoralising effects of the Ring's Curse: not mere strife and bloodshed, but love betrayed, faith dishonoured and those we knew as gods and heroes degraded by petty spites and vilifying each other in vulgar, malignant brawls. Brünnhilde violently abuses Siegfried for his perfidy; but he, having drunk the potion of forgetfulness, does not recognise her as his former bride, and at length abandons the problem and laughingly leads away Gutrune to marry her. It is Hagen's moment. "Only one thing can avenge us," he cries; "Siegfried's death!" And they echo him: "Siegfried's death!" But it is not in open combat that Siegfried shall die: he shall be stabbed in the back (his only vulnerable part), by Hagen during a hunt, and it shall be said that a wild boar killed him. To this level of sordid subterfuge has the Ring brought its devotees! As if to strengthen their resolve, the bridal procession of Siegfried and Gutrune now passes triumphantly before them.

Act III: *Scene* 1

We now have one of those occasional oases in this desert of crime and suffering, a charming interlude that delights us like the discovery of a fresh spring on a barren hillside. Siegfried, out hunting, comes to a bank of the Rhine, and there meets the three maidens, who first sang to us in *The Rhinegold*. They are still lamenting the loss of the gold:

Frau Son — ne send - et lich-te Strah - len;
Fair sun - light send - eth rays of splen - dour;

Just as Nibelheim in *The Rhinegold* exhales stifling darkness, and Brünnhilde's awakening in *Siegfried* pours out the very soul of sunlight, so this limpid, laughing music expresses nothing but water. We can almost feel it splashing into our faces. The Rhine-maidens tell Siegfried that (as we already know) there is a curse on the Ring, and urge him to restore it to them; but Siegfried refuses, and they leave him with solemn warnings of his fate. There is not much dramatic point in the scene, but we should be grateful that Wagner evidently thought there was—otherwise he might have cut it out! Gunther, Hagen and the vassals now appear on their way back from the hunt. They lie down on the sward and take out wineskins and drinkhorns. "Now sing to us," says Hagen, and Siegfried tells them the story of his adventures —Mime, the dwarf, who fostered him; Nothung, the sword, which he forged; Fafner, the dragon, whom he slew. Hagen then crushes a herb into his drink which restores his memory of Brünnhilde, and he tells how he won the Valkyrie for wife. Gunther starts up, dismayed at this fresh evidence that Siegfried has cheated him—however unwittingly. At that moment two ravens fly out of a bush, hover over Siegfried's head and dart away. "What say those ravens? Canst tell?" Hagen sardonically asks him; and as Siegfried turns to look after them: "Vengeance is their word!" thunders Hagen, and plunges the spear into his back. The others are horror-stricken. "Hagen, what deed is this?" they ask in trembling voices. "It is the reward of treachery," he answers, and moves away towards the heights. Siegfried dies with Brünnhilde's name on his lips. The vassals raise the slain hero as he lies on his shield, and bear away the body into the rising mists. And they bear it away to that transcendent Death March which seems the requiem, not of one man, but of all the vanished glories of the world.

ACT III: *Scene 2*

At last we have reached the climax of this cosmic drama. In the Hall of the Gibichungs Gutrune is watching anxiously for Siegfried's return. She hears a voice, and starts forward. But it is not Siegfried: it is Hagen—with terrible tidings. He points to the funeral procession, which now enters with her bridegroom's body. Gutrune screams, and throws herself on the corpse. She flings back the story of the wild boar with withering contempt, and curses her brothers. "Yes, 'twas I who slew him," says Hagen; "he was a traitor. And I claim the Ring!" But Gunther bars his way. They fight, and Hagen, to the terrible curse theme, strikes his half-brother dead. He then tries to grasp the Ring on Siegfried's finger, but the dead man's hand rises threateningly. All stand motionless with terror. All except Brünnhilde.

She advances now to the front, calm and august in her sorrow, with all things revealed to her. She turns to the vassals:

Star-ke Schei-te schichtet mir dort
Might-y logs I bid you now pile

And we now enter on the final scene of *The Ring of the Nibelung*. No words can justly describe this overwhelming peroration which sweeps with such power and passion to its climax. On its way it passes in retrospect the whole history of the Ring:

> *The accumulated pageant of the past*
> *That clangs and flashes for a drowning man.*

The body of Siegfried is laid on a funeral pyre by the river. Brünnhilde takes the Ring and draws it on her own finger, snatches a firebrand from one of the vassals, lights the pyre and rides into it on her horse. "Siegfried! Brünnhilde greets thee in bliss!" The music seems to shoot up in great fountains of flame. The hall is filled with fire, but in a moment the Rhine overflows its banks and pours in, the three Rhinemaidens leaping on the waves. One of them holds the recovered Ring aloft, and when Hagen plunges in after it they drag him down to the depths. The heavens break out into fire, and in the distance we see Valhalla crashing down in flames over the gods.

So ends the mightiest saga ever put on the stage. The gold is restored to its primal state of nature, and we are to assume that the world (or what's left of it) is at peace again until man discovers some other means of destroying himself.

Tristan and Isolde

Libretto by the Composer.
Time: Arthurian period.

First Production,
Munich, 1865.

> 'Love that is fire within thee and light above,
> And lives by grace of nothing but of love;
> Through many and lovely thoughts and much desire
> Led these twain to the life of tears and fire;
> Through many and lovely days and much delight
> Led these twain to the lifeless life of night.'
>
> SWINBURNE: *Tristram of Lyonesse.*

Tristan and Isolde is the intensest expression in all music of the love of man and woman. That, by now, is a truism. It is also the work of

Wagner that approaches nearest to perfect unity in thought, feeling and construction. The story is rigidly concise and simple; there are no tiresome disguises, tedious misunderstandings, complications or irrelevances. The verse is not perhaps in the highest vein of poetry, but it is vivid and pliant, and ministers perfectly to the white heat of the music. And this music? There are thoughts that do often lie too deep for tears, there are emotions that shake one beyond human expression, and there is music that one despairs of translating fitly into words. Such is the finest music of *Tristan and Isolde*. One can only marvel, a little breathlessly, at its morbid concentration, its magical unity of mood from the first bar to the last. If one dared make one criticism it would be to point to that insidious weakness which gradually grew on Wagner towards the end of his career and is most noticeable in *Parsifal* : his occasional inability to make his voices as interesting to us as his orchestra. There are signs of this in the conversation pieces in the first act, and—at the risk of being hooted to death by Wagnerian fanatics—I will confess that I prefer to listen to the *Liebestod* in the orchestral version. That vast cathedral of tone is wholly orchestral in conception. The orchestra tells us everything, with its immense advantages over the human voice, which, within its limited compass, has to dart in whenever it hears a chance and harmonise as best it can. That, however, is one man's view.

There are many reasons why we long to live our youth again, but perhaps the strongest is the desire to recapture the thrill of our early discoveries : to share Keats's wonder on first looking into Chapman's *Homer*, to discover Marlowe's 'Mighty Line', to feel again the irrevocable magic of first love—and to hear *Tristan and Isolde* for the first time !

The opening phrase of the Prelude is among the most famous and instantly recognisable beginnings in all music :

It is just possible that the first four notes might slip by unrecognised, but at the sound of that unmistakable chord fifteen centuries fall away and we are enshrouded in the cold mists of legend. That chord is the core of *Tristan and Isolde*.

Act I

After the Prelude has scaled its heights of ecstasy and agony and throbbed away into silence, the curtain rises on the deck of Tristan's ship, which is bearing the Princess Isolde from Ireland to Cornwall to become the bride of King Mark. Isolde (soprano) lies on a couch, her face buried despondently in the cushions. Brangäne (mezzo-soprano) is looking over the ship's side. A curtain hangs across the deck, screening them from the stern of the vessel. We hear the voice of a young sailor singing a jaunty song about an 'Irish maid'. Isolde starts up at the words; they are mocking her! "Where are we?" she asks her maid. Brangäne replies that the ship is sailing merrily on, and by nightfall they should land in Cornwall. But Isolde breaks out into fury at the name, and calls on the winds and waves to wreck the ship. Her rage almost chokes her, and Brangäne draws back the curtains to let in the freshening breeze. At the stern, sailors and knights are clustered round the mast. Tristan (tenor) gazes out to sea, while Kurwenal (baritone), his faithful friend and follower, squats at his feet. "See him there, the insolent knight," cries Isolde; "he is too craven to meet my eye! Command him to approach and do homage to me!" But Tristan tells Brangäne that he cannot leave the helm. Kurwenal barks out a few uncouth remarks to her, and she hastens back to her mistress, closing the curtains again. Isolde then tells Brangäne the reasons of her anger against Tristan:

Er - fur - rest du mei - ne Schmach,
Thou know - est now all my shame,———

Morold, her cousin and betrothed, went to Cornwall to claim tribute from King Mark, but Tristan slew him. Later, Tristan himself, sorely wounded, landed in Ireland under the name of 'Tantris'. Isolde discovered that he was the slayer of Morold, but took pity on him and healed his wounds. Now he brings her back as a bride for his king. Better death—death together! We now gather that Tristan and Isolde are, subconsciously no doubt, in love with one another. This, of course, explains his avoidance of her presence on the ship and her fury at his seeming indifference. Isolde resolves on a desperate plan: she opens a golden casket and, taking out a phial of poison, bids her maid pour it into a goblet. At that moment Kurwenal bursts in through

the curtains, saying that they are near land, and she commands him
to summon Tristan. The knight enters, and for a few moments they
stand gazing at each other, over music in which we can almost hear
the beating of their hearts. She recalls his slaying of Morold, and he
impetuously offers her his sword, bidding her take her revenge. But
Isolde rejects the sword and hands him instead 'the draught of atone-
ment'. They drink from the goblet, and the music tells us that Brangäne
has filled it not with death but with love. We hear again the opening
phrases of the Prelude as Tristan and Isolde stand transfigured and see
kindling in each other's eyes the love 'that is blood within the veins
of time'. They cling mortally together like lost and bewildered children.
The world has ceased to exist; and when the ship touches land and
King Mark and his followers step aboard amid the shouts of the
sailors, the royal bride and the knight who has brought her stand
bewitched and stupefied, not knowing where they are.

Act II

We know what the scene will be long before we see it. The orchestra
spreads for us the 'close curtain of love-performing night' in a Prelude
of rapid pulsating figures and dusky harmonies heavy with the perfumes
of the summer darkness. A tremor of expectancy thrills through it
like the throbbing of Isolde's heart. When the curtain rises, Brangäne
stands on the steps that lead to Isolde's chamber, looking out over the
garden and listening to hunting-horns which echo from the forest.
Isolde comes out in feverish excitement. Have the hunters retreated
far enough? Is it time to give the signal? Brangäne implores her to
take care: she can still hear the horns. But lovers hear only what they
wish to hear, and Isolde impatiently urges her to quench the torch
at the door—the signal for Tristan to approach. Brangane is fearful:
she warns her that spies are on the watch to betray her to King Mark,
and pleads agitatedly for the light to be left burning. Isolde laughs
at her fears, and in a climax of joyous defiance seizes the torch and
casts it to the earth. Brangäne, nervous and distressed, goes to keep
watch on the battlements. Isolde is alone with the night, and we hear
again the pulsating figures and dusky harmonies of the Prelude. She
waves a scarf into the darkness, slowly at first, then more rapidly as
the music rises in passion. On a crashing climax Tristan rushes in,
and they fall into each other's arms, speaking in short, panting,
disjointed sentences, while the orchestra blares out a triumphant
theme—

—which is often repeated. The music increases in power and brilliance, then gradually sinks as the lovers' first exultation dies down. Tristan draws Isolde down on to a flowery bank and kneels at her feet, and slowly, serenely, like the moon rising out of a wreath of mist, there glimmers into being the greatest of all love duets:

O sink' her-nie-der, Nacht der Lie - be,
O sink up - on us, night of love,

It is the utter absorption of two human souls in one another. The music blooms and blossoms into an almost stifling richness, until one seems to be wading through a sea of 'dark bluebells drenched with dews of summer eves'. Now and again Brangäne's voice breaks in from the distance over long flowing melodies. But the lovers only smile at her warnings. They are lost to everything; there is no heaven or earth; there is no life or death. There is only Tristan and Isolde—made one. And now begins the crowning glory of the scene:

So star-ben wir, um un - ge-trennt,
So should we die no more to part,

Slowly it rises from key to key like a gradual flame, blazing up at last into a veritable pyre of passion, and just as we feel that we cannot bear the tension any longer, the whole thing is scattered into ruin. Brangäne screams; we hear a frantic shout, "Save thyself, Tristan!" from Kurwenal, who dashes in with drawn sword. Behind him come King Mark (bass), Melot (tenor) and the other courtiers in hunting-dress. Isolde crouches down with averted face, and Tristan tries to hide her shame with his cloak. For a few moments Mark stands in utter dejection, contemplating the perfidy of his queen and his friend; then he grievously reproaches Tristan, in a long and dignified mono-

logue which some find tedious, but which is nevertheless very noble
and moving in its gravity. Tristan bows his head in humiliation. Then
he turns to Isolde. Will she follow him to the land where there is no
sunlight? Isolde replies as one in a trance. She will follow him anywhere;
her life is his. Tristan kisses her gently. Melot starts forward: "Dost
thou see this, O King?" There is a short, sharp encounter, but Tristan
lowers his sword and falls beneath a desperate thrust from Melot.

Act III

We hear 'the league-long roller thundering on the reef'. It is
the garden of Tristan's castle on a cliff in Brittany, weed-grown and
neglected. The music rises on a tapering, spiral figure, and dies away
high in the violins. Again the distant roll of the breakers; again
the tapering figure which dissolves like a wisp of smoke into the golden
air and leaves us to the dizzy immensity of sea and sky. No bird
cuts across this sky; no sail shimmers on this sea. Time seems to
hang suspended. It is as though it has always been thus, as though
it will be thus for ever. Tristan, stretched motionless under a linden
tree, and Kurwenal, watching over him with the intensity of a faithful
dog, look like painted figures on a tapestry. Then there floats to us the
thin, tenuous note of a shepherd's pipe—

—A bleak, forlorn little melody that seems the very soul of silence
and desolation made audible. The spell is snapped; Tristan wakes.
He remembers nothing since he was wounded; but Kurwenal, frantic
with joy at his return to life, tells him that he brought him here to
his castle and has sent for Isolde to come to him and heal him. She
will come; even now the shepherd is watching for her ship. *Tristan and
Isolde* is the intensest expression, not only of the love of man and
woman, but also of the love of man and man, and it is impossible in
this act to look on Kurwenal's devotion, with its rough, jogging,
homespun theme—

—without a trembling of the lips. Tristan grows more and more disordered and feverish, and in his delirium he curses the love-draught that has so shattered their lives. "The ship, Kurwenal," he wails, "the ship! Is she in sight?" For answer comes the shepherd's mournful little tune, like the wind whispering through a shell. The dying man sinks back, but in a few moments strength comes back to him. Passionately he lives again the tempestuous life of their love, alternately comforting and scourging himself with memories, and every now and then: "The ship, Kurwenal, the ship! Is she in sight?" Suddenly the music suffers a dramatic change: the shepherd breaks into a merry tune and Kurwenal rushes to the edge of the cliff. Yes! The ship is in sight. Swiftly she cuts through the blue sea and at last Isolde springs ashore. Kurwenal, fairly babbling with delight, dashes down to welcome her, and Tristan, left alone, staggers to his feet and madly tears away his bandages. It is her voice—her voice! And as she comes into sight he stumbles forward and falls into her arms. "Tristan!" "Isolde!" And he sinks back into death. Then there is a wild alarm: another ship has cast anchor. King Mark and his men are leaping up the cliff. Kurwenal makes a desperate stand, slays Melot, but at last receives his own death-wound. Painfully he drags himself towards Tristan's body. His last words are: "Tristan, blame me not that I follow thee!" and once again our hearts go out to that great spirit in pity and love. But Mark has come to forgive, and he gazes grief-stricken at the ruin around him. And Isolde? Yes—she will follow Tristan into the land where there is no sunlight. Her life is his. As in a dream, she begins her great paean of love, and at the close, death releases her and makes her passion immortal.

And so these twain pass 'to the lifeless life of night'. There is apparently no physical reason why Isolde should die, but no imagination could accept the idea of her living on when her sole reason for living was taken from her. Nothing but death could bring a sufficiently august conclusion to the love that made life too strong for life.

The Mastersingers

Libretto by the Composer.
Time: Sixteenth Century.

First Production,
Munich, 1868.

> 'Of the singers there were three or foure so excellent that I thinke few or none in Christendome do excell them, especially, one, who had such a purnesse and (as I may in a manner say) such a supernaturall voice for sweetnesse, that I think there was never a better singer in all the world, insomuch that he did not onely give the most pleasant contentment that could be imagined, to all the hearers but also did as it were astonish and amaze them. I alwaies thought he was an eunuch, which if he had beene, it had taken away some part of my admiration.'
>
> THOMAS CORYATE: *Coryate's Crudities.*

The Mastersingers is, in the opinion of one man at least, the greatest comedy-opera in the world. I may find it hard to speak in temperate and reasonable terms of this noble compliment to human nature, so if you dislike or disapprove of Wagner you had better skip the chapter: it will only annoy you. Like Shakespeare in *The Tempest*, like Verdi in *Falstaff*, Wagner has won through here to 'a peace after pain', when his spirit expands and overflows in an all-embracing love of humanity. Prospero-like, he fills the isle with music, raises and quells storms, forgives enemies and creates lovers. What formerly roused his hate now rouses only his laughter or his pity. Even Beckmesser, dolt and pedant that he is, becomes a figure of fun. We laugh at him and love him: at his silly serenade, when he is so childishly unaware that he is making an ass of himself, at his credulous cunning when he steals the song—as if he had the slightest chance of doing it justice! As for Hans Sachs himself, where else in all opera shall we find such a blend of kindly wisdom and homespun dignity? Even the real Sachs of sixteenth-century Nuremberg strikes us, when we read of him, as a worthy and lovable character; but Wagner makes of him a man who can talk with kings nor lose the common touch. And that common touch is one of Sachs' most significant qualities. He is a working man, whose pride in the work of his hands makes him respected and whose brusque sincerity, born of a mature sense of values, makes him almost feared. Only the desperate courage of love, we feel, could have emboldened Eva to tell such a man that her shoe was wrongly made!

The Mastersingers is the story not only of a contest of song, but of the eternal contest between the old music and the new. Consequently, it is, more than any other of Wagner's later works, a *singers'* opera, with *arias* and concerted numbers, which are, however, skilfully woven into a continuous musical pattern. It is also a tribute to the soul of a great and good man; and although it is Walther who wins the bride, it is Sachs who wins our undying love and veneration.

However often we may hear it, the Overture never ceases to astonish and delight us with its brilliant counterpoint. There are roughly three sections: the old Mastersingers with their pomp and circumstance, the apprentices (a disrespectful parody of their elders), and the love of Walther and Eva, which finally comes to full flower in the 'Prize Song'. You will notice towards the end that the 'Prize Song' melody is played with the Mastersingers' theme humming below it, as if to denote the triumph of the new art over the old.

ACT I

Walther (tenor), a young Franconian knight, stands in the choir of the church of St. Katharine in Nuremberg, watching Eva (soprano), who is seated near the door with Magdalena (soprano), her nurse. Fragments of the 'Prize Song' that is to be express his dawning love for her. When the service is over he approaches them and asks Eva if she is betrothed. They tell him that her father, Pogner the goldsmith, has decreed that she shall marry the winner of the song-tournament tomorrow—Eva adding impulsively that she wishes it could be Walther. Upon which Walther resolves that he will try his skill. Surely love will inspire him! The apprentices come in and set up a marker's box for the meeting of the Masters. The Masters then stroll into the choir in twos and threes. They are the burghers of Nuremberg: plain, honest craftsmen, to whom music is one of the sternest of crafts. Pogner (bass) enters first, listening to the insidious chatter of Beckmesser (baritone), the town clerk. Beckmesser, a preposterous pedant, is in love with Eva (or more likely with her father's money), and determined to win the contest and the bride by fair means or foul. Last comes Sachs (high bass), the shoemaker, and when the meeting is assembled Walther comes forward and asks if he may join their guild. Pogner greets him courteously (Beckmesser fuming at the prospect of a new rival), but first opens the meeting by setting forth with great earnestness the details of the song-tournament. "To him who wins this contest, I freely give, with all my wealth and lands, Eva, my only child, as bride":

Das schö-ne Fest, Jo-han-nis-tag, ihr wisst, bege-h'n wir mor-gen:
The feast of   John, Mid-sum-mer day, Ye know we keep to - mor-row:

But he adds, humanely enough, that if Eva does not like the victor she may still refuse him. They now ask Walther what master taught him his singing. In music that murmurs like the green forest he tells them that he learned from Walther von der Vogelweide and from the songs of birds and the wind in the reeds:

Am   stil-len Herd— in Win-ters- zeit,—
In   snow-bound hall—— by fire - side,—

Very well, they say, he must sing a trial song; and Beckmesser goes into the marker's box to mark his faults. Walther launches into a soaring passionate lyric of spring and love:

So rief der Lenz in den Wald, dass laut es ihn durch-hallt—
So cried the   spring through the land: loud e-choed her com - mand—

But they do not understand it; it is not 'according to the rules'. And Beckmesser bursts out of the box with the blackboard literally covered with chalk-marks. Walther loses his temper, the Masters fall to wrangling and the meeting eventually breaks up in disorder. Only Sachs lingers for a moment in deep thought, and the orchestra tells us that at least a fragment of this strange new music has stuck in his memory.

Act II

On the evening of the same day twilight is closing in on the Nuremberg street where the houses of Pogner and Sachs face each other. David (tenor), Sachs's apprentice, and his companions are closing the shutters of the shops, the orchestra taking the first theme of Pogner's Address in the first act and whipping it up into a joyful, jingling measure. David tells Magdalena of Walther's discomfiture at the morning trial; then Sachs comes home and scolds him for roystering with the other apprentices. By and by, after Pogner and Eva have gone into their house, Sachs sits at his open door. He has work to do, but gradually he is overcome by the spell of Midsummer Eve, the scent of the elder tree in front of his house, and—why, yes, of course: the song he heard that morning:

Was duf-tet doch der Flie - der So mild, so stark und voll!
The   el-der's scent floats round me,   So mild, so rich   it falls!

And here Wagner faithfully follows Sachs's train of thought in the music. Snatches of melody from Walther's songs flicker up in his mind, burn into a clear flame and fade out again. No, he cannot piece them together. There are no rules to fit this music, he says; perhaps it is above rules. There is a light step, and turning round he sees Eva. From the tender and charming dialogue that follows between them we learn that Sachs is a widower, and we begin to guess that he loves Eva; but it is an unselfish love, a love that desires her happiness above his own. She then presses him for details of the morning trial. Sachs tells her about it, and watches with amusement her indignation when he abuses the young knight. So that's how it is? She's in love with the fellow! Eva flounces away, and Sachs, watching, sees Walther join her in the shadows. The young man tries to drag her away to elope with him, but they are interrupted—first by a beam of light which the cobbler cunningly shines on them, next by the Night Watchman (bass). Then a lute is heard, and Beckmesser comes sidling down the street to serenade Eva. Immediately Sachs starts hammering very loudly, and singing at his work. Beckmesser is furious at being shouted down. But Sachs explains that he must work at his shoes. If the town clerk likes to sing his serenade the cobbler will act as marker with his hammer. The town clerk sees no remedy, and dives desperately into his song. It is just the kind of nonsense one would expect from him, and Sachs goes on hammering until he practically drowns it. By now the whole town is awake. People open their windows and shout to them to be quiet; then they stream into the street in their night-clothes, jostling each other in the darkness. David sees Magdalena at a window, and thinking Beckmesser is serenading her, springs upon him and begins to beat him. The tumult grows until the whole stage is in an uproar, all the townsfolk quarrelling among themselves and clawing and buffeting one another. Women empty jugs of water on them from the windows, and eventually, as the Night Watchman approaches again, the mob disperses. Pogner pulls Eva through his front door, and

Sachs, finding Walther alone and bewildered, drags him into his own house. When it is safe for him to do so, the Night Watchman steps along the street again, singing his verse—with rather less confidence than before. As he slowly passes out of sight, the full moon shines out, and her radiance is reflected in a delicious little twinkling aftermath in the orchestra.

Act III: *Scene* i

The orchestral Prelude opens with a striking phrase—

—which represents Sachs brooding on the folly of mankind. It grow into a full portrait of the man, and when the curtain rises, there he sits in his workshop on Midsummer morning, a large folio open in front of him. David enters from the street. He rouses his master, and an exquisitely playful scene follows, in which David sings his ingenuous little song about St. John. But when the boy has gone Sachs sinks again into reverie:

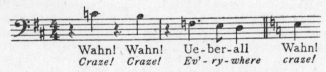

Wahn! Wahn! Ue-ber-all Wahn!
Craze! Craze! Ev'-ry-where craze!

He recalls last night's tumult. The whole town went mad! Were the sprites of Midsummer Eve at their mischief? "Well, it's Midsummer Day now," he says; "let's see if we can turn this madness to profit." Walther comes in from the inner room. He has slept well and dreamed a wondrous dream. "Sing to me about your dream," says Sachs, and, as Walther sings a kind of sketch for the Prize Song, his host sits at the table and notes it down. It shall be the Master-song! In high spirits they go in to dress for the festival. There is a pause, and then to creaking, limping figures in the orchestra Beckmesser crawls in from the street. As with Sachs's meditation in Act II, the orchestra follows and translates all the workings of his brain as he limps round the room, occasionally remembering last night and rubbing his bruises. Suddenly he sees the song on the table. "A trial song—by Sachs!" he shouts, and, hearing the cobbler's step, slips it into his pocket. Sachs soon guesses what he has done. "I am not competing today," he tells him contemptuously; "you may have the song if it'll do you any good." Beckmesser is overjoyed. A song by the great Sachs himself! It can't possibly fail. And he forgets his bruises and dances in triumph out of the workshop.

The next visitor is Eva, dressed in white for the tournament. Sachs greets her, and rather hesitantly she says that her shoe does not fit. He smiles shrewdly to himself, and, while he is bending down over it, Walther appears at the door of the inner room. The two lovers stand transfixed, gazing into one another's eyes. Sachs seems to notice nothing. He takes the shoe to the table, muttering and grumbling over it, and by and by says, as if to himself: "I heard a beautiful song lately. I wish someone would sing me the third verse." And softly and tenderly, without moving, Walther sings the verse to Eva, every word born of his love for her, every note dedicated to her beauty. "Hark, child!" says Sachs, still intent on his work, "that is a Master-song!" And as it comes to an end he asks her—perhaps a trifle slyly, "Now let us see: does the shoe fit?" Eva is overcome with emotion, and in a passionate outburst she embraces the noble friend who is thus helping them to their hearts' desire. Impetuously, she tells him that if she were not in love with Walther, Sachs above all men would be her choice. But Sachs smiles gently. "My child, I remember the tale of Tristan and Isolde; and I would not be King Mark!" And the orchestra steals in with a few bars from *Tristan and Isolde*. Sachs quickly recovers himself, and as David and Magdalena enter he summons them to the 'baptism' of the new song. The voices blend in the immortal, unforgettable quintet:

Se - lig, wie die Son - ne mei-nes Glü-ckes lacht,
Bright-ly as the sun — up-on my for-tune breaks,

Walther and Eva and David and Magdalena (who have just become betrothed) sing of their mutual love, while Sachs reflects that love has passed him by, but art endures for ever.

ACT III: *Scene 2*

The quintet slowly dies away and the festival music begins. The scene has changed to an open meadow outside the town. All Nuremberg is here in holiday attire. The various guilds march in with their banners and the apprentices dance on the green:

At last it is time for the song-tournament. Beckmesser stumbles on to the little mound and, almost paralysed with nervousness, begins on the stolen song. It is a complete fiasco, and he eventually gives it up in despair, amid the jeers of the crowd. (Wagner makes him distort the words so that they sound like the original, but mean something ludicrously different.) Sachs says the song is a good one if only it is properly sung. Now is Walther's great moment. He steps on to the mound and begins:

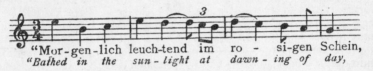

"Mor-gen-lich leuch-tend im ro - si-gen Schein,
"Bathed in the sun-light at dawn-ing of day,

After the first few bars there is no possible doubt: this is indeed the Master-song! The alliance of love and music has won the day, and Walther proudly claims his bride. Pogner offers him the golden chain that will make him a Mastersinger. At first, recalling the humiliation of yesterday, Walther refuses; but Sachs reads him a grave homily on the respect due to art. "Disaster overtakes the land that forgets its songs and its singers," he says. Then Nuremberg once more acclaims its shoemaker-poet, and the opera ends, as it began, in the broad, good-hearted, reassuring key of C major.

Parsifal

Libretto by the Composer.   First Production,
Time: Mediaeval.   Bayreuth, 1882.

> '. . . First they heard a crackling and crying of thunder . . . and in the midst of the blast entered a sunbeam more clear by seven times than ever they saw day, and all were lighted of the grace of the Holy Ghost . . . then there entered the hall the Holy Grail.'
>
> SIR THOMAS MALORY.

Parsifal is Wagner's last testament. In substance it is a mystic legend of the Middle Ages; in essence it is an ecstasy of the spirit, a hymn in praise of asceticism. It is not at all fanciful, indeed, to see in it Wagner's reproof to himself for the apotheosis of earthly love which flamed up like a pillar of fire from the passion of Tristan and Isolde; as we have seen, Wagner was even more of an egoist than most great creative artists and saw the world as a reflection of his own personality. Thus, the Flying Dutchman is Wagner seeking the woman who shall understand and redeem him, Tristan is Wagner in the throes of human love, Parsifal—or, possibly, Amfortas—is Wagner in violent revulsion from human love and reaching for the love that is divine. We cannot be surprised that many people dislike *Parsifal*. Nietzsche condemned it as an outrage on morals, and although few of us would go as far as that, it is difficult nowadays to accept this theory of an inflexible division between soul and body, or to feel much sympathy with those ascetics who used to starve, torture and deface God's image in their zeal to mortify the flesh. There is something of this attitude in *Parsifal*, this negation of life and of the forces that intensify and re-create life, which many people find unnatural, even unwholesome.

Nevertheless we are concerned with *Parsifal* not as a work of philosophy but as a work of art. We may reject the theology of *Paradise Lost*, but only a theologian or a fool would deny that it is a great poem. Similarly, with *Parsifal* we must ask ourselves does it succeed as a work of art? Whether we agree or not with the case Wagner is stating, does he state it eloquently? The answer is, of course, that he states it magnificently and unforgettably. As always, the music redeems (to use a favourite word with Wagner) anything that might otherwise be distasteful; individual, utterly characteristic music, not a single page of which could be transferred to any other opera. Here once again we feel Wagner's uncanny genius for translating light, heat and colour into unmistakable sound. We don't need to see the light of the Grail; we can hear it, we can feel it flowing through our veins, blessing us with an ineffable peace.

The one weakness of this score—if weakness is not too 'strong' a word—is one that grew as Wagner grew in artistic stature, and was perhaps inseparable from his conception and practice of music drama as an art form: the difficuty he found in fitting the voices into the musical texture. *Parsifal* is emphatically *not* a 'singers' opera'. It is conceived orchestrally throughout; the voices have the quality of an afterthought and at times sound even intrusive.

ACT I

It is daybreak, and by a lake on the edge of a forest in Spain, within sight of the castle of Montsalvat, Gurnemanz (bass), an old but vigorous man, and two esquires (soprano and tenor) are sleeping under a tree. They rouse themselves to prepare the morning bath for Amfortas. A moment later a wild horse gallops furiously up to them and Kundry (soprano) dismounts. She is a strange, swarthy, beastlike creature, with staring eyes and smoky, dishevelled hair, and her black dress is fastened with a girdle of snakeskins. She has brought a balsam for Amfortas's wound. Amfortas himself (baritone) is now carried on in a litter. He accepts the balsam, and is borne away towards the lake. Kundry falls exhausted into a stupor, and Gurnemanz then tells the esquires (and, incidentally, the audience) the history of Amfortas's wound. The Holy Grail, the chalice from which Christ drank at the Last Supper, and the spear with which he was wounded, passed into the keeping of the aged Titurel and his band of Christian knights at Montsalvat. Amfortas, however, Titurel's son, sinned with Kundry, who was at that time being used as a decoy by the pagan magician, Klingsor. Klingsor wounded Amfortas with the sacred spear, which Klingsor now holds. It is fated that one alone can heal Amfortas —'The Guileless Fool by pity enlightened'—who will touch him once more with the spear. As if in answer to the prophecy there is a commotion near the lake, and a wild swan flutters to the ground, transfixed by an arrow. Here the orchestra recalls the Swan theme in *Lohengrin*. The archer is Parsifal (tenor), a raw youth with an air of awkwardness and simplicity about him. Gurnemanz angrily rebukes him for his deed: these beautiful wild creatures are their friends; only a stupid callow boy would go about destroying God's handiwork. Parsifal is ashamed, and breaks his bow and arrows. The old man questions him, but he does not know who he is or whence he came. Then Kundry looks up from the ground and says that the boy's father perished in battle and his mother brought him up in the desert. She has since died. Gurnemanz ponders: 'The Guileless Fool . . .'; . . . can this be he? He decides to take him to the castle. The landscape now begins to move past them so that they appear to be walking. The nature and colours of the music, too, gradually change, and at last we are in the Hall of the Grail. Bells ring to summon the knights to the Love Feast, and as they enter the orchestra gives out a solemn march theme:

—one of the basic melodies of the scene. It swells at last into the Grail theme:

—which is heard frequently during the whole work. Amfortas is carried in on the litter and the voice of the aged Titurel (bass) is heard: "Reveal ye the Grail." But Amfortas starts up in agony . . .

. . . and tells of the anguish and remorse he feels when the Grail shines on him and his defiled blood gushes out through the spear wound; he, the only sinner of his people! Amfortas's agony drew from Wagner like the blood from the spear wound—what is surely the most lacerating expression of human pain in all music. Elgar surely remembered this scene when he expressed a like agony in *Gerontius*. Amfortas fights down his anguish, and consecrates the bread and wine. The Grail shines, and the Holy Supper is eaten. At the end, as they carry Amfortas away, his wound breaks out afresh, and Parsifal clutches his own heart in tortured sympathy. 'The Guileless Fool by pity enlightened.' When Gurnemanz addresses him he simply stares, as in a stupor, and the old man impatiently calls him a fool and turns him out.

ACT II

Klingsor the Magician (bass-baritone) sits in the tower of his magic castle. He represents the spirit of evil and uses his beautiful flower maidens to tempt the knights from their vows of chastity. Parsifal is approaching and has already struck down Klingsor's guards. Klingsor summons Kundry: she must tempt him, as she tempted Amfortas. We now perceive that Kundry is a kind of dual personality: in her intervals of freedom she serves the knights, but Klingsor has a Svengali-like power over her, and when his call comes she must obey. The scene changes to the castle garden, and the Flower Maidens surround Parsifal, singing and dancing to a measure of languorous grace:

Komm'! Komm'! Hol-der Kna - be!
Come! *Come!* *Gen-tle* *lov - er!*

Parsifal looks upon them in perfect innocence. Kundry now appears, transformed into a young and beautiful woman, and the maidens dance away laughing. She speaks gently to Parsifal of his dead mother; but later her voice gradually grows more voluptuous. Slowly she takes him in her arms, and at last presses her mouth on his in a long and sensual kiss. In an instant the youth springs up in terror: all is revealed to him in a blinding flash—Amfortas's sin, the sting of remorse, the spear, which he feels tearing through his own flesh. And, as in a trance, he hears the Saviour's voice summoning him to his divine mission. He casts Kundry from him. She curses him, and Klingsor, appearing on the battlements, hurls the sacred spear at Parsifal. It stops in mid-flight and remains suspended over Parsifal's head. Parsifal seizes it and swings it round in the sign of the cross. The castle crashes into ruins, and the garden withers to a desert. As he hurries away Parsifal turns to Kundry, who is now crouching on the ground in terror: "Thou knowest where thou canst meet with me again!"

Act III

Some years later we find Gurnemanz, grown very old and white and dressed as a hermit, standing beside his hut near the forest on Good Friday morning. He hears moaning sounds, and in a thicket he finds Kundry. At first he fears that those moans were her last, but she slowly revives, and in a few moments a knight in black armour comes forward. In his hand he holds the sacred spear, and Gurnemanz eventually recognizes him as Parsifal. He realizes also that he and he alone is the 'Guileless Fool', divinely chosen to heal Amfortas and restore the brotherhood to a state of grace; and that his guilelessness is that simplicity which, they say, places fools and children nearest to God. Kundry bathes Parsifal's feet and dries them with her hair, and Gurnemanz anoints him King. Parsifal then baptises Kundry. And now the orchestra begins very softly—like the whisper of a spring breeze—a rapturous piece of tone-painting, in which one can positively *see* the blue sky, the feathery white clouds, and the meadows golden with daffodils:

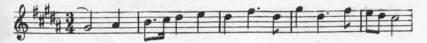

Gurnemanz tells Parsifal that nature has performed the recurring miracle of Spring in joyous memory of the Saviour's redemption of mankind. They now walk slowly towards the castle, the scene moving past them as in the first act. There the knights stand in mourning round the coffin of Titurel, who has died because Amfortas has refused to reveal the Grail or administer the sacred bread and wine. Amfortas breaks into an impassioned lament:

Mein   Va - ter!   Hoch - ge - seg -   - ne - ter   der Hel - den!
My   fa - ther!   High - ly bless -   - ed thou of   he - roes!

Then in a frenzy of despair he calls on the knights to take away his accursed life. "Plunge your sword-blades into my wound! Deep, deep, to the hilt!" But Parsifal now comes forward. "Only one weapon serves," he says; "the spear that smote thee must heal thee." And he touches Amfortas with the sacred spear. Amfortas's face is lighted up with a holy ecstasy. The Grail shines, and a white dove descends from the dome and hovers over Parsifal's head. Kundry sinks slowly to the ground and her spirit finds blessed release in death.

CARL MARIA VON WEBER
(1786-1826)

Der Freischütz

Libretto by Friedrich Kind.
Time: Eighteenth Century

First Production,
Berlin, 1821.

> 'Where throngs of knights and barons bold,
> In weeds of peace, high triumphs hold,
> With store of ladies, whose bright eyes
> Rain influence, and judge the prize
> Of wit or arms, while both contend
> To win her grace whom all commend.'
>
> MILTON: *L'Allegro.*

Der Freischütz means literally 'The Free Shot'; but as all attempts at an acceptable English title have failed, the work is generally known to us by its original one; and it would be as foolish to depart from it now as to announce *I Pagliacci* as *The Strolling Players* or *Il Trovatore* as *The Troubadour.* Most competent judges (including Wagner, who was strongly influenced by Weber's style) agree that *Der Freischütz* is Weber's best opera. It is chiefly on this work that his reputation rests as the founder of German national opera and pioneer of romantic music in the theatre.

There is nothing profound or subtle about *Der Freischütz*: it is a jolly, romantic story of green-clad foresters, huntsmen's flaxen-haired daughters, magic bullets, midnight witchcraft, and the triumph of youth and love over the powers of evil. We don't need to rack our brains in search of any inner symbolism; we can just lean back in our seats and surrender ourselves to Weber's charming melodies and the naïve, fairy-tale folklore of German romanticism. And German romanticism, as one eminent critic remarked, is like German beer: "the more you have the better you feel".

The Overture, familiar to anyone who has ever stepped inside a concert-hall, even by mistake, is of the *pot-pourri* type and uses several melodies from the score, culminating in the jocund, glittering figure from Agatha's *aria* in Act II:

ACT I

An open space by a forest in Bohemia. A shooting-match has just finished in which Max (tenor), a forester, has been defeated by (supreme humiliation!) a mere farmer, one Kilian (baritone). Surprising indeed that Max, the leading tenor and obviously the hero of the story, should be defeated in anything, particularly by a baritone! But we console ourselves with the reflection that if he had won there would have been no opera. The rustics congratulate Kilian in an appropriate chorus, and commiserate humorously with the forester whose marksmanship has fallen so much lower than his vocal compass. But Max himself is nearly broken-hearted. There is to be a 'shoot' next day before Prince Ottokar, and if he wins he will win the hand of his beloved Agatha, daughter of Cuno, chief huntsman. Incidentally, it is a curious custom in German opera by which fathers, otherwise of sound mind, offer their daughters as prizes in song contests, shooting-matches, and similar tests of skill, on the intelligent assumption that the man who can sing a ballad or shoot a pheasant on the wing has, *ipso facto*, the makings of a good husband.

Left alone, Max sums up the melancholy situation in an expressive *aria*:

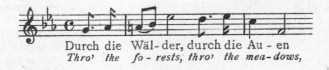

Durch die Wäl-der, durch die Au - en
Thro' the fo - rests, thro' the mea-dows,

Villainy now rears its ugly head. Kaspar (bass), another forester, whose character is as dark as his voice, invites Max to join him in a drink. He then hands him a rifle and bids him shoot at an eagle circling overhead. Max fires, and the bird falls dead. Kaspar then explains that the bullet was a magic one which cannot fail. If Max will meet him in the Wolf's Glen at midnight they will make more of these bullets. Max, whom love has apparently blinded to the finer points of sportsmanship, agrees to this very doubtful proposal. Then follows Kaspar's 'Vengeance' *aria*, which always seems to me to have more force than strength. It is not made quite clear yet why it is 'vengeance' that Kaspar desires; and we are left to conclude that his grudge against Max is the traditional grudge of the operatic bass against the tenor, to whom the composer has, of course, given much more attractive music.

ACT II: *Scene* 1

Perhaps on the principle that we often have a premonition when
our loved ones are in danger, Weber now shows us Agatha (soprano)
troubled by uneasy forebodings. Her sprightly cousin, Aennchen
(soprano), tries in vain to cheer her. By and by Agatha leans out of
her window and invokes the spirit of the soft, scented, summer night,
in perhaps the most sheerly beautiful air Weber ever wrote:

Lei - se, lei - se, from - me Wei - se,
Soft - ly sigh - ing, day is_ dy - ing,

Suddenly she sees Max approaching and her voice leaps into the
joyous melody we have already heard in the Overture. Max announces
that this is only a brief visit, as he is on his way to the Wolf's Glen
to recover the carcase of a stag he has shot there. This seems to the girls
a very thin story, and they solemnly warn him against the Wolf's
Glen, which is reputed to be haunted. But Max explains, by implica-
tion, that, being an operatic hero, he is incapable of fear, and departs.

ACT II: *Scene* 2

In the Wolf's Glen scene Weber, like the Fat Boy in 'Pickwick',
wants to make our flesh creep, and to a certain extent he succeeds.
He succeeded completely, no doubt, in 1821, when such 'bogy-bogy'
apparatus had a keener thrill of novelty than it has today. To us these
midnight incantations amid hooting owls, gibbering spectres and
phosphorescent death's-heads are rather reminiscent of those grottoes
on seaside fairgrounds in which all manner of pantomime 'spooks'
evoke delighted squeals from trippers enjoying their 'sixpenn'orths'.
Nevertheless, the music has a certain grisly suggestiveness that saves
the scene from toppling over into mere farce. Here Kaspar invokes
Zamiel, a kind of Bohemian Herne the Hunter, to whom he has sold
his soul. His time is nearly up; he offers Max as a substitute and Zamiel
(speaking part) at last agrees to this obviously superior bargain. In
spite of a warning from the ghost of his mother, Max joins Kaspar in
the unhallowed spot and, amid typical Maskelyne-and-Devant effects,
they cast seven bullets, six to go true to the mark, the seventh whither
Zamiel wills.

ACT III: *Scene* 1

On the morning of the great 'shoot' Agatha is still dejected—rather fortunately for us, since her dejection expresses itself in another of Weber's most enchanting airs:

Und ob die Wol - ke sie— ver-hül - le,
Al - tho' a cloud o'er - spread the hea - ven,

The bridesmaids enter and sing a bridal chorus, while Aennchen brings in the bridal wreath. All start back in consternation: it is a funeral wreath! Some ominous mistake has been made, and instead of the wreath Agatha decks herself with some consecrated white roses given her by an aged hermit.

ACT III: *Scene* 2

The final scene has an air of festival. Prince Ottokar (baritone) is here with the nobles of his court, tents have been erected and all is ready for the trial of skill. The scene opens with a rollicking chorus in praise of the chase, a commonplace tune, but quite in the picture, with its hunting-horn cadences and flavour of rustic heartiness. Then comes the fatal test to decide Max's future. He has one bullet left— the one that shall go whither Zamiel wills. Kaspar has hidden in a tree. Max takes aim at a white dove, but as he is pressing the trigger Agatha appears among the trees. The Hermit (bass), with great presence of mind, directs the dove to the tree in which Kaspar is hidden. Max fires, and both Agatha and Kaspar fall, the one in a faint, the other in his death agony. The Devil has claimed his own.

Max confesses dabbling with the powers of evil, and the Prince places him on probation for a year. We are confident that at the end of that time he will have proved himself a worthy bridegroom, and that Agatha will no longer have time or inclination to sigh in solitude to the evening breezes.

WHO'S WHO

(The characters are listed here under the names by which they are most familiar and recognisable. This may result in occasional inconsistencies, but inconsistencies in opera are not exactly unknown; and it would obviously be as misleading to index, for instance, Tchaikovsky's Tatiana under her surname of Larin as it would to index Verdi's Mistress Ford under her christian name of Alice.)

ABBESS	... ...	*Sister Angelica*
ABIMELECH	... ...	*Samson and Delilah*
ADALGISA	... ...	*Norma*
ADELIA	... ...	*A Masked Ball*
AFON, PRINCE	... ...	*The Golden Cockerel*
AGATHA	... ...	*Der Freischütz*
AGED HEBREW	... ...	*Samson and Delilah*
AÏDA ...	... ...	*Aïda*
ALBERICH	... ...	*The Ring*
ALCINDORO	... ...	*La Bohème*
ALFIO ...	... ...	*Cavalleria Rusticana*
ALFONSO, DON	...	*Così Fan Tutte*
ALMAVIVA, COUNT	... ...	⎰ *The Barber of Seville* ⎱ *The Marriage of Figaro*
,, COUNTESS	...	*The Marriage of Figaro*
ALVARO, DON	... ...	*The Force of Destiny*
AMFORTAS	... ...	*Parsifal*
AMNERIS	... ...	*Aïda*
AMONASRO	... ...	,,
ANGELICA	... ...	*Sister Angelica*
ANGELOTTI	... ...	*Tosca*
ANNA, DONNA	... ...	*Don Giovanni*
ANNETTE	... ...	*Der Freischütz*
ANNINA	... ...	*La Traviata*
ARKEL	... ...	*Pelléas and Mélisande*
ASHBY ...	... ...	*The Girl of the Golden West*

COMMENDATORE	... ...	*Don Giovanni*
CONSTANCE	... ...	*Il Seraglio*
COPPELIUS	... ...	*The Tales of Hoffmann*
COUPAVA	... ...	*The Snow Maiden*
CRESPEL	... ...	*The Tales of Hoffman*
DALAND	... ...	*The Flying Dutchman*
DANCAIRO	... ...	*Carmen*
DAPPERTUTTO	... ...	*The Tales of Hoffmann*
DAVID ...	... ...	*The Mastersingers*
DE BRÉTIGNY	... ...	*Manon*
DE MORTFORTAINE, GUILLOT		,,
DE NANGIS, RAOUL ...	...	*The Huguenots*
DE NEVERS, COUNT ...	...	,, ,,
DE RAVOIR, GERONTE	...	*Manon Lescaut*
DE SAINT BRIS, COUNT	...	*The Huguenots*
,, ,, ,, VALENTINE	...	,, ,,
DES GRIEUX, SENIOR	...	*Manon*
,, ,, CHEVALIER	... {	*Manon*
		Manon Lescaut
DELILAH	... ...	*Samson and Delilah*
DESDEMONA	... ...	*Othello*
DESPINA	... ...	*Così Fan Tutte*
DEW FAIRY	... ...	*Hänsel and Gretel*
DI COIGNY, COUNTESS	...	*Andrea Chènier*
,, ,, MADELEINE	...	,, ,,
DI LUNA, COUNT	... ...	*Il Trovatore*
DOCTOR	... ...	*La Traviata*
DODON, KING	... ...	*The Golden Cockerel*
DONNER	... ...	*The Ring*
DORABELLA	... ...	*Così Fan Tutte*
DOUPHOL, BARON	... ...	*La Traviata*
DUTCHMAN (VANDERDECKEN)		*The Flying Dutchman*
EDGAR	... ...	*Lucia di Lammermoor*
,, ...	... ...	*A Masked Ball*
ELISABETH	... ...	*Tannhäuser*

ELSA	*Lohengrin*
ELVIRA, DONNA	*Don Giovanni*
EMILIA	*Othello*
EMPEROR OF CHINA	*Turandot*
ERDA	*The Ring*
ERIC	*The Flying Dutchman*
ERNESTO	*Don Pasquale*
EROSHKA	*Prince Igor*
ESCAMILLO	*Carmen*
EVA	*The Mastersingers*
FAFNER	*The Ring*
FALSTAFF, SIR JOHN	*Falstaff*
FANINAL	*Der Rosenkavalier*
FASOLT...	*The Ring*
FATHER	*Hänsel and Gretel*
„	*Louise*
FATHER SUPERIOR	*The Force of Destiny*
FAUST	*Faust*
FENTON	*Falstaff*
FEODOR	*Boris Godounov*
FERRANDO	*Così Fan Tutte*
„	*Il Trovatore*
FIGARO ... ... {	*The Barber of Seville* / *The Marriage of Figaro*
FIORDILIGI	*Così Fan Tutte*
FLAVIO...	*Norma*
FLORESTANO	*Fidelio*
FOOL	*The Perfect Fool*
FORD	*Falstaff*
„ MISTRESS	„
FRASQUITA	*Carmen*
FREDERICK (OF TELRAMUND)	*Lohengrin*
FREIA	*The Ring*
FRICKA...	„ „
FROH	„ „
FROST, KING	*The Snow Maiden*

FRUGOLA	... ...	...	*Il Tabarro*
GALITSKY, PRINCE	...	...	*Prince Igor*
GENEVIÈVE	... ...	...	*Pelléas and Mélisande*
GENEVIÈVE, SISTER	...	...	*Sister Angelica*
GÉRARD	...	...	*Andrea Chénier*
GERMONT, SENIOR	...	...	*La Traviata*
,, ALFRED	...	...	,, ,,
GIACCHINO	...	...	*Fidelio*
GILDA ...	...	...	*Rigoletto*
GIORGIETTA	...	...	*Il Tabarro*
GIOVANNI, DON	...	...	*Don Giovanni*
GIULIETTA	...	...	*The Tales of Hoffmann*
GODOUNOV, BORIS	...	...	*Boris Godounov*
GOLAUD	... ...	...	*Pélleas and Mélisande*
GORO ...	...	...	*Madam Butterfly*
GREMIN, PRINCE	...	...	*Eugene Onegin*
GRETEL	... ...	...	*Hänsel and Gretel*
GRIGORI	... ...	...	*Boris Godounov*
GRIMES, PETER	...	...	*Peter Grimes*
GUGLIELMO	...	...	*Così Fan Tutte*
GUIDON, PRINCE	...	...	*The Golden Cockerel*
GUNTHER	... ...	...	*The Ring*
GURNEMANZ	...	...	*Parsifal*
GUTRUNE	... ...	...	*The Ring*
HAGEN...	... ...	...	*The Ring*
HÄNSEL	... ...	...	*Hänsel and Gretel*
HENRY, KING...	...	...	*Lohengrin*
HERALD	... ...	...	,,
HERMIT	... ...	...	*Der Freischütz*
HIGH PRIEST ...	...	...	*Samson and Delilah*
HOFFMANN	... ...	...	*The Tales of Hoffmann*
HOSTESS	... ...	...	*Boris Godounov*
HUNDING	... ...	...	*The Ring*
IAGO ...	... ...	...	*Othello*
IDIOT ...	... ...	...	*Boris Godounov*
IGOR, PRINCE	...	...	*Prince Igor*

LINDORF	...	...	...	*The Tales of Hoffmann*
LIU ...	...	...	...	*Turandot*
LODOVICO	...	...	...	*Othello*
LOGE ...	...	...	...	*The Ring*
LOHENGRIN	...	...	...	*Lohengrin*
LOLA ...	...	...	...	*Cavalleria Rusticana*
LOUISE	...	...	...	*Louise*
LUCIA, MOTHER	...	...	*Cavalleria Rusticana*
LUDMILLA	...	...	...	*The Bartered Bride*
LUIGI ...	...	...	...	*Il Tabarro*
MADDALENA ...	...	...	*Rigoletto*
MAGDALENA ...	...	...	*The Mastersingers*
MALATESTA, DR.	...	...	*Don Pasquale*
MANDARIN	...	...	...	*Turandot*
MANRICO	...	...	...	*Il Trovatore*
MANTUA, DUKE OF ...	...	*Rigoletto*
MARCEL	...	...	...	*The Huguenots*
,,	...	...	...	*La Bohème*
MARCELLINA ...	...	...	*Fidelio*
,,	...	...	...	*The Marriage of Figaro*
MARENKA	...	...	...	*The Bartered Bride*
MARGUÉRITE ...	...	...	*Faust*
MARIANNE	...	...	...	*Der Rosenkavalier*
MARINA	...	...	...	*Boris Godounov*
MARK, KING ...	...	...	*Tristan and Isolde*
MARSCHALLIN	...	...	*Der Rosenkavalier*
MARTHA	...	...	...	*Faust*
MASETTO	...	...	...	*Don Giovanni*
MAUREVERT ...	...	...	*The Huguenots*
MAX ...	...	...	...	*Der Freischütz*
MÉLISANDE	...	...	...	*Pelléas and Mélisande*
MELITONE, BROTHER...	...	*The Force of Destiny*
MELOT...	...	...	...	*Tristan and Isolde*
MEPHISTOPHELES	...	...	*Faust*
MERCEDES	...	...	...	*Carmen*
MERCUTIO	...	...	...	*Romeo and Juliet*

MICAELA ... ... *Carmen*
MICHELE ... ... *Il Tabarro*
MIME ... ... *The Ring*
MIMI ... ... *La Bohème*
MINISTER OF STATE ... ... *Fidelio*
MINNIE ... ... *The Girl of the Golden West*
MIRACLE, DR. ... ... *The Tales of Hoffmann*
MISGIR ... ... *The Snow Maiden*
MISSAIL ... ... *Boris Godounov*
MONITOR ... ... *Sister Angelica*
MONOSTATOS ... ... *The Magic Flute*
MONTANO ... ... *Othello*
MONTERONE ... ... *Rigoletto*
MOTHER ... ... *Hänsel and Gretel*
    ,, ... *The Perfect Fool*
    ,, ... *Louise*
MUSETTA ... ... *La Bohème*

NANETTA ... ... *Falstaff*
NEDDA ... ... *Pagliacci*
NICK ... ... *The Girl of the Golden West*
NICKLAUS ... ... *The Tales of Hoffmann*
NIGHT WATCHMAN ... ... *The Mastersingers*
NOCTAMBULIST ... ... *Louise*
NORINA ... ... *Don Pasquale*
NORMA ... ... *Norma*
NORNS ... ... *The Ring*
NURSE ... ... *Boris Godounov*

OCHS, BARON ... ... *Der Rosenkavalier*
OCTAVIAN ... ... ,,   ,,
OLGA ... ... *Eugene Onegin* ...
OLYMPIA ... ... *The Tales of Hoffmann*
ONEGIN, EUGENE ... ... *Eugene Onegin*
ORFORD, ELLEN ... ... *Peter Grimes*
OROVESO ... ... *Norma*

ORTRUD	...	...	*Lohengrin*
OSMIN	...	...	*Il Seraglio*
OTHELLO	...	...	*Othello*
OTTAKAR, PRINCE	...	...	*Der Freischütz*
OTTAVIO, DON	...	...	*Don Giovanni*
OVLOUR	...	...	*Prince Igor*
PAGE, MISTRESS	...	...	*Falstaff*
PAMINA	...	...	*The Magic Flute*
PANG ...	...	...	*Turandot*
PAPAGENA	...	...	*The Magic Flute*
PAPAGENO	...	...	" " "
PARSIFAL	...	...	*Parsifal*
PASQUALE, DON	...	...	*Don Pasquale*
PEDRILLO	...	...	*Il Seraglio*
PELLÉAS	...	...	*Pelléas and Mélisande*
PEPPE...	...	...	*Pagliacci*
PIMEN ...	...	...	*Boris Godounov*
PING ...	...	...	*Turandot*
PINKERTON, LIEUT.	...	...	*Madam Butterfly*
" KATE	...	...	" "
PISTOL ...	...	...	*Falstaff*
PIZARRO	...	...	*Fidelio*
POGNER	...	...	*The Mastersingers*
POLKAN, GENERAL	...	...	*The Golden Cockerel*
POLLIO...	...	...	*Norma*
PONG ...	...	...	*Turandot*
PREZIOSILLA	...	...	*The Force of Destiny*
PRINCESS	...	...	*The Perfect Fool*
"	...	...	*Sister Angelica*
QUEEN OF FRANCE	...	...	*The Huguenots*
QUEEN OF SHEMAKA	...	...	*The Golden Cockerel*
QUEEN OF THE NIGHT	...	...	*The Magic Flute*
QUICKLY, DAME	...	...	*Falstaff*
RADAMES	...	...	*Aïda*
RAGMAN	...	...	*Louise*

RAMPHIS	...	...	*Aïda*
RANCE, JACK	...	...	*The Girl of the Golden West*
RANGONI	...	...	*Boris Godounov*
REMENDADO	...	...	*Carmen*
RENATO	...	...	*A Masked Ball*
RHINE-MAIDENS	...	...	*The Ring*
RICCARDO	...	...	*A Masked Ball*
RIGOLETTO	...	...	*Rigoletto*
RINUCCIO	...	...	*Gianni Schicchi*
ROCCO	...	...	*Fidelio*
RODERIGO	...	...	*Othello*
ROMEO	...	...	*Romeo and Juliet*
ROSINA	...	...	*The Barber of Seville*
RUDOLPH	...	...	*La Bohème*
SACHS, HANS	...	...	*The Mastersingers*
SACRISTAN	...	...	*Tosca*
SAINT-BRIS	...	...	*The Huguenots*
SAMSON	...	...	*Samson and Delilah*
SAMUEL	...	...	*A Masked Ball*
SANDMAN	...	...	*Hänsel and Gretel*
SANTUZZA	...	...	*Cavalleria Rusticana*
SARASTRO	...	...	*The Magic Flute*
SCARPIA, BARON	...	...	*Tosca*
SCHAUNARD	...	...	*La Bohème*
SCHICCHI, GIANNI	...	...	*Gianni Schicchi*
SCHLEMIL	...	...	*The Tales of Hoffmann*
SELIM, PASHA	...	...	*Il Seraglio*
SENTA	...	...	*The Flying Dutchman*
SHARPLESS	...	...	*Madam Butterfly*
SIEBEL	...	...	*Faust*
SIEGFRIED	...	...	*The Ring*
SIEGLINDE	...	...	*,, ,,*
SIEGMUND	...	...	*,, ,,*
SILVANO	...	...	*A Masked Ball*
SILVIO	...	...	*Pagliacci*

SIMONE...	...	...	...	*Gianni Schicchi*
SKOULA	...	...	...	*Prince Igor*
SNEGOUROCHKA		...	...	*The Snow Maiden*
SOPHIE...	...	...	...	*Der Rosenkavalier*
SPALLANZANI, DR.	...	...	...	*The Tales of Hoffmann*
SPARAFUCILE ...		...	...	*Rigoletto*
SPOLETTA	...	...	...	*Tosca*
SPRING, FAIRY		...	...	*The Snow Maiden*
STCHELKALOV ...		...	...	*Boris Godounov*
STEPHANO	...	...	...	*Romeo and Juliet*
SUSANNA	...	...	...	*The Marriage of Figaro*
SUZUKI...	...	...	...	*Madam Butterfly*
TALPA	...	...	...	*Il Tabarro*
TAMINO	...	...	...	*The Magic Flute*
TANNHÄUSER ...		...	...	*Tannhäuser*
TATIANA	...	...	...	*Eugene Onegin*
TIMUR ...	...	...	...	*Turandot*
TINCA ...	...	...	...	*Il Tabarro*
TITUREL	...	...	...	*Parsifal*
TOM ...	...	...	...	*A Masked Ball*
TONIO ...	...	...	...	*Pagliacci*
TOSCA, FLORIA		...	...	*Tosca*
TRAVELLER	...	...	...	*The Perfect Fool*
TRISTAN	...	...	...	*Tristan and Isolde*
TROUBADOUR ...		...	...	*The Perfect Fool*
TURANDOT	...	...	...	*Turandot*
TURIDDU	...	...	...	*Cavalleria Rusticana*
TYBALT	...	...	...	*Romeo and Juliet*
ULRICA	...	...	...	*A Masked Ball*
VALENTINE	...	...	...	*The Huguenots*
VALENTINE	...	...	...	*Faust*
VARLAAM	...	...	...	*Boris Godounov*
VASEK	...	...	...	*The Bartered Bride*
VENUS ...	...	...	...	*Tannhäuser*

VERONA, DUKE OF	... ...	*Romeo and Juliet*
VIOLETTA ...	... ...	*La Traviata*
VLADIMIR ...	... ...	*Prince Igor*
WALLACE, JAKE	... ...	*The Girl of the Golden West*
WALTHER ...	... ...	*The Mastersingers*
WALTRAUTE ...	... ...	*The Ring*
WITCH	... ...	*Hänsel and Gretel*
WIZARD ...	... ...	*The Perfect Fool*
WOLFRAM ...	... ...	*Tannhäuser*
WOOD-BIRD ...	... ...	*The Ring*
WOTAN ...	... ...	*„ „*
WOWKLE ...	... ...	*The Girl of the Golden West*
XENIA	... ...	*Boris Godounov*
YAMADORI, PRINCE ...	...	*Madam Butterfly*
YNSOLD ...	... ...	*Pelléas and Mélisande*
ZAMIEL ...	... ...	*Der Freischütz*
ZERLINA ...	... ...	*Don Giovanni*
ZUNIGA ...	... ...	*Carmen*